The Life Of Cesare Borgia
A History And Some Criticisms

by

Rafael Sabatini

Double9
BOOKS

The Life Of Cesare Borgia
A History And Some Criticisms
by Rafael Sabatini

ISBN: 978-93-65787-80-1

Published by

DOUBLE 9 BOOKS
2/13-B, Ansari Road
Daryaganj, New Delhi – 110002
info@double9books.com
www.double9books.com
Tel. 011-40042856

ABOUT THE AUTHOR

Rafael Sabatini (1875–1950) was an Italian-English author best known for his swashbuckling historical novels filled with adventure, romance, and intrigue. Born in Jesi, Italy, to an Italian father and an English mother—both opera singers—Sabatini was raised in a multilingual environment, becoming fluent in several languages. This diverse cultural background influenced his literary style, marked by a blend of English wit and Italian passion. Sabatini began his writing career in the late 19th century, initially producing short stories before gaining widespread recognition with his novels. His most famous works include Scaramouche (1921), Captain Blood (1922), and The Sea-Hawk (1915), all of which were adapted into successful films. These novels are characterized by their vivid historical settings, complex characters, and fast-paced plots. Sabatini's works often explore themes of honor, loyalty, and the conflict between personal desires and larger societal forces. His protagonists are typically dashing, morally complex heroes who navigate turbulent political landscapes with a blend of cunning and courage. Despite his success, Sabatini lived a relatively private life, dedicating himself to writing until his death in 1950. His legacy endures as one of the great storytellers of historical fiction.

CONTENTS

PREFACE...9

BOOK I
THE HOUSE OF THE BULL

CHAPTER I
THE RISE OF THE HOUSE OF BORGIA 20

CHAPTER II
THE REIGNS OF SIXTUS IV AND INNOCENT VIII...........................29

CHAPTER III
ALEXANDER VI...43

CHAPTER IV
BORGIA ALLIANCES 56

BOOK II
THE BULL PASCANT

CHAPTER I
THE FRENCH INVASION..69

CHAPTER II
THE POPE AND THE SUPERNATURAL 81

CHAPTER III
THE ROMAN BARONS 88

CHAPTER IV
THE MURDER OF THE DUKE OF GANDIA 94

CHAPTER V
THE RENUNCIATION OF THE PURPLE..108

BOOK III
THE BULL RAMPANT

CHAPTER I
THE DUCHESS OF VALENTINOIS 117

CHAPTER II
THE KNELL OF THE TYRANTS 126

CHAPTER III
IMOLA AND FORLI 133

CHAPTER IV
GONFALONIER OF THE CHURCH 145

CHAPTER V
THE MURDER OF ALFONSO OF ARAGON 153

CHAPTER VI
RIMINI AND PESARO 161

CHAPTER VII
THE SIEGE OF FAENZA 172

CHAPTER VIII
ASTORRE MANFREDI 182

CHAPTER IX
CASTEL BOLOGNESE AND PIOMBINO 187

CHAPTER X
THE END OF THE HOUSE OF ARAGON 193

CHAPTER XI
THE LETTER TO SILVIO SAVELLI 199

CHAPTER XII
LUCREZIA'S THIRD MARRIAGE 207

CHAPTER XIII
URBINO AND CAMERINO 212

CHAPTER XIV
THE REVOLT OF THE CONDOTTIERI 222

CHAPTER XV
MACCHIAVELLI'S LEGATION 230

CHAPTER XVI
RAMIRO DE LORQUA 240

CHAPTER XVII
"THE BEAUTIFUL STRATAGEM" 246

CHAPTER XVIII
THE ZENITH 254

BOOK IV
THE BULL CADENT

CHAPTER I
THE DEATH OF ALEXANDER VI 266

CHAPTER II
PIUS III 275

CHAPTER III
JULIUS II 282

CHAPTER IV
ATROPOS 292

PREFACE

This is no Chronicle of Saints. Nor yet is it a History of Devils. It is a record of certain very human, strenuous men in a very human, strenuous age; a lustful, flamboyant age; an age red with blood and pale with passion at white-heat; an age of steel and velvet, of vivid colour, dazzling light and impenetrable shadow; an age of swift movement, pitiless violence and high endeavour, of sharp antitheses and amazing contrasts.

To judge it from the standpoint of this calm, deliberate, and correct century—as we conceive our own to be—is for sedate middle-age to judge from its own standpoint the reckless, hot, passionate, lustful humours of youth, of youth that errs grievously and achieves greatly.

So to judge that epoch collectively is manifestly wrong, a hopeless procedure if it be our aim to understand it and to be in sympathy with it, as it becomes broad-minded age to be tolerantly in sympathy with the youth whose follies it perceives. Life is an ephemeral business, and we waste too much of it in judging where it would beseem us better to accept, that we ourselves may come to be accepted by such future ages as may pursue the study of us.

But if it be wrong to judge a past epoch collectively by the standards of our own time, how much more is it not wrong to single out individuals for judgement by those same standards, after detaching them for the purpose from the environment in which they had their being? How false must be the conception of them thus obtained! We view the individuals so selected through a microscope of modern focus. They appear monstrous and abnormal, and we straight-way assume them to be monsters and abnormalities, never considering that the fault is in the adjustment of the instrument through which we inspect them, and that until that is corrected others of that same past age, if similarly viewed, must appear similarly distorted.

Hence it follows that some study of an age must ever prelude and accompany the study of its individuals, if comprehension is to wait upon our labours. To proceed otherwise is to judge an individual Hottentot or South Sea Islander by the code of manners that obtains in Belgravia or Mayfair.

Mind being the seat of the soul, and literature being the expression of the mind, literature, it follows, is the soul of an age, the surviving and immortal part of it; and in the literature of the Cinquecento you shall behold for the looking the ardent, unmoral, naïve soul of this Renaissance that was sprawling in its lusty, naked infancy and bellowing hungrily for the pap of knowledge, and for other things. You shall infer something of the passionate mettle of this infant: his tempestuous mirth, his fierce rages, his simplicity, his naïveté, his inquisitiveness, his cunning, his deceit, his cruelty, his love of sunshine and bright gewgaws.

To realize him as he was, you need but to bethink you that this was the age in which the Decamerone of Giovanni Boccaccio, the Facetiae of Poggio, the Satires of Filelfo, and the Hermaphroditus of Panormitano afforded reading-matter to both sexes. This was the age in which the learned and erudite Lorenzo Valla—of whom more anon—wrote his famous indictment of virginity, condemning it as against nature with arguments of a most insidious logic. This was the age in which Casa, Archbishop of Benevento, wrote a most singular work of erotic philosophy, which, coming from a churchman's pen, will leave you cold with horror should you chance to turn its pages. This was the age of the Discovery of Man; the pagan age which stripped Christ of His divinity to bestow it upon Plato, so that Marsilio Ficino actually burnt an altar-lamp before an image of the Greek by whose teachings—in common with so many scholars of his day—he sought to inform himself.

It was an age that had become unable to discriminate between the merits of the Saints of the Church and the Harlots of the Town. Therefore it honoured both alike, extolled the carnal merits of the one in much the same terms as were employed to extol the spiritual merits of the other. Thus when a famous Roman courtesan departed this life in the year 1511, at the early age of twenty-six, she was accorded a splendid funeral and an imposing tomb in the Chapel Santa Gregoria with a tablet bearing the following inscription:

"IMPERIA CORTISANA ROMANA QUAE DIGNA TANTO NOMINE, RARAE INTER MORTALES FORMAE SPECIMEN DEDIT."

It was, in short, an age so universally immoral as scarcely to be termed immoral, since immorality may be defined as a departure from the morals that obtain a given time and in a given place. So that whilst from our own standpoint the Cinquecento, taken collectively, is an age of grossest licence and immorality, from the standpoint of the Cinquecento itself few of its individuals might with justice be branded immoral.

For the rest, it was an epoch of reaction from the Age of Chivalry: an epoch of unbounded luxury, of the cult and worship of the beautiful externally; an epoch that set no store by any inward virtue, by truth or honour; an epoch that laid it down as a maxim that no inconvenient engagement should be kept if opportunity offered to evade it.

The history of the Cinquecento is a history developed in broken pledges, trusts dishonoured and basest treacheries, as you shall come to conclude before you have read far in the story that is here to be set down.

In a profligate age what can you look for but profligates? Is it just, is it reasonable, or is it even honest to take a man or a family from such an environment, for judgement by the canons of a later epoch? Yet is it not the method that has been most frequently adopted in dealing with the vast subject of the Borgias?

To avoid the dangers that must wait upon that error, the history of that House shall here be taken up with the elevation of Calixtus III to the Papal Throne; and the reign of the four Popes immediately preceding Roderigo Borgia—who reigned as Alexander VI—shall briefly be surveyed that a standard may be set by which to judge the man and the family that form the real subject of this work.

The history of this amazing Pope Alexander is yet to be written. No attempt has been made to exhaust it here. Yet of necessity he bulks large in these pages; for the history of his dazzling, meteoric son is so closely interwoven with his own that it is impossible to present the one without dealing at considerable length with the other.

The sources from which the history of the House of Borgia has been culled are not to be examined in a preface. They are too numerous, and they require too minute and individual a consideration that their precise value and degree of credibility may be ascertained. Abundantly shall such examination be made in the course of this history, and in a measure as the need arises to cite evidence for one side or for the other shall that evidence be sifted.

Never, perhaps, has anything more true been written of the Borgias and their history than the matter contained in the following lines of Rawdon Brown in his Ragguagli sulla Vita e sulle Opere di Marino Sanuto: "It seems to me that history has made use of the House of Borgia as of a canvas upon which to depict the turpitudes of the fifteenth and sixteenth centuries."

Materials for the work were very ready to the hand; and although they do not signally differ from the materials out of which the histories of half a dozen Popes of the same epoch might be compiled, they are far more abundant in the case of the Borgia Pope, for the excellent reason that the

Borgia Pope detaches from the background of the Renaissance far more than any of his compeers by virtue of his importance as a political force.

In this was reason to spare for his being libelled and lampooned even beyond the usual extravagant wont. Slanders concerning him and his son Cesare were readily circulated, and they will generally be found to spring from those States which had most cause for jealousy and resentment of the Borgia might—Venice, Florence, and Milan, amongst others.

No rancour is so bitter as political rancour—save, perhaps, religious rancour, which we shall also trace; no warfare more unscrupulous or more prone to use the insidious weapons of slander than political warfare. Of this such striking instances abound in our own time that there can scarce be the need to labour the point. And from the form taken by such slanders as are circulated in our own sedate and moderate epoch may be conceived what might be said by political opponents in a fierce age that knew no pudency and no restraint. All this in its proper place shall be more closely examined.

For many of the charges brought against the House of Borgia some testimony exists; for many others—and these are the more lurid, sensational, and appalling covering as they do rape and murder, adultery, incest, and the sin of the Cities of the Plain—no single grain of real evidence is forthcoming. Indeed, at this time of day evidence is no longer called for where the sins of the Borgias are concerned. Oft-reiterated assertion has usurped the place of evidence—for a lie sufficiently repeated comes to be credited by its very utterer. And meanwhile the calumny has sped from tongue to tongue, from pen to pen, gathering matter as it goes. The world absorbs the stories; it devours them greedily so they be sensational, and writers well aware of this have been pandering to that morbid appetite for some centuries now with this subject of the Borgias. A salted, piquant tale of vice, a ghastly story of moral turpitude and physical corruption, a hair-raising narrative of horrors and abominations—these are the stock-in-trade of the sensation-monger. With the authenticity of the matters he retails such a one has no concern. "Se non é vero é ben trovato," is his motto, and in his heart the sensation-monger—of whatsoever age—rather hopes the thing be true. He will certainly make his public so believe it; for to discredit it would be to lose nine-tenths of its sensational value. So he trims and adjusts his wares, adds a touch or two of colour and what else he accounts necessary to heighten their air of authenticity, to dissemble any peeping spuriousness.

A form of hypnosis accompanies your study of the subject—a suggestion that what is so positively and repeatedly stated must of necessity be true, must of necessity have been proved by irrefutable evidence at some time or other. So much you take for granted—for matters which began their existence perhaps as tentative hypotheses have imperceptibly developed into established facts.

Occasionally it happens that we find some such sentence as the following summing up this deed or that one in the Borgia histories: "A deal of mystery remains to be cleared up, but the Verdict of History assigns the guilt to Cesare Borgia."

Behold how easy it is to dispense with evidence. So that your tale be well-salted and well-spiced, a fico for evidence! If it hangs not overwell together in places, if there be contradictions, lacunae, or openings for doubt, fling the Verdict of History into the gap, and so strike any questioner into silence.

So far have matters gone in this connection that who undertakes to set down to-day the history of Cesare Borgia, with intent to do just and honest work, must find it impossible to tell a plain and straightforward tale—to present him not as a villain of melodrama, not a monster, ludicrous, grotesque, impossible, but as human being, a cold, relentless egotist, it is true, using men for his own ends, terrible and even treacherous in his reprisals, swift as a panther and as cruel where his anger was aroused, yet with certain elements of greatness: a splendid soldier, an unrivalled administrator, a man pre-eminently just, if merciless in that same justice.

To present Cesare Borgia thus in a plain straightforward tale at this time of day, would be to provoke the scorn and derision of those who have made his acquaintance in the pages of that eminent German scholar, Ferdinand Gregorovius, and of some other writers not quite so eminent yet eminent enough to serve serious consideration. Hence has it been necessary to examine at close quarters the findings of these great ones, and to present certain criticisms of those same findings. The author is overwhelmingly conscious of the invidious quality of that task; but he is no less conscious of its inevitability if this tale is to be told at all.

Whilst the actual sources of historical evidence shall be examined in the course of this narrative, it may be well to examine at this stage the sources of the popular conceptions of the Borgias, since there will be no occasion later to allude to them.

Without entering here into a dissertation upon the historical romance, it may be said that in proper hands it has been and should continue to be one of the most valued and valuable expressions of the literary art. To render and maintain it so, however, it is necessary that certain well-defined limits should be set upon the licence which its writers are to enjoy; it is necessary that the work should be honest work; that preparation for it should be made by a sound, painstaking study of the period to be represented, to the end that a true impression may first be formed and then conveyed. Thus, considering how much more far-reaching is the novel than any other form of literature, the good results that must wait upon such endeavours are beyond question. The neglect of them—the distortion of character to suit the romancer's ends, the like distortion of historical facts, the gross anachronisms arising out of a lack of study, have done much to bring the historical romance into disrepute. Many writers frankly make no pretence—leastways none that can be discerned—of aiming at historical precision; others, however, invest their work with a spurious scholarliness, go the length of citing authorities to support the point of view which they have taken, and which they lay before you as the fruit of strenuous lucubrations.

These are the dangerous ones, and of this type is Victor Hugo's famous tragedy Lucrezia Borgia, a work to which perhaps more than to any other (not excepting Les Borgias in Crimes Célèbres of Alexandre Dumas) is due the popular conception that prevails to-day of Cesare Borgia's sister.

It is questionable whether anything has ever flowed from a distinguished pen in which so many licences have been taken with the history of individuals and of an epoch; in which there is so rich a crop of crude, transpontine absurdities and flagrant, impossible anachronisms. Victor Hugo was a writer of rare gifts, a fertile romancer and a great poet, and it may be unjust to censure him for having taken the fullest advantages of the licences conceded to both. But it would be difficult to censure him too harshly for having—in his Lucrezia Borgia—struck a pose of scholarliness, for having pretended and maintained that his work was honest work founded upon the study of historical evidences. With that piece of charlatanism he deceived the great mass of the unlettered of France and of all Europe into believing that in his tragedy he presented the true Lucrezia Borgia.

"If you do not believe me," he declared, "read Tommaso Tommasi, read the Diary of Burchard."

Read, then, that Diary, extending over a period of twenty-three years, from 1483 to 1506, of the Master of Ceremonies of the Vatican (which largely contributes the groundwork of the present history), and the one conclusion to which you will be forced is that Victor Hugo himself had never read it, else he would have hesitated to bid you refer to a work which does not support a single line that he has written.

As for Tommaso Tommasi—oh, the danger of a little learning! Into what quagmires does it not lead those who flaunt it to impress you!

Tommasi's place among historians is on precisely the same plane as Alexandre Dumas's. His Vita di Cesare Borgia is on the same historical level as Les Borgias, much of which it supplied. Like Crimes Célèbres, Tommasi's book is invested with a certain air of being a narrative of sober fact; but like Crimes Célèbres, it is none the less a work of fiction.

This Tommaso Tommasi, whose real name was Gregorio Leti—and it is under this that such works of his as are reprinted are published nowadays— was a most prolific author of the seventeenth century, who, having turned Calvinist, vented in his writings a mordacious hatred of the Papacy and of the religion from which he had seceded. His Life of Cesare Borgia was published in 1670. It enjoyed a considerable vogue, was translated into French, and has been the chief source from which many writers of fiction and some writers of "fact" have drawn for subsequent work to carry forward the ceaseless defamation of the Borgias.

History should be as inexorable as Divine Justice. Before we admit facts, not only should we call for evidence and analyse it when it is forthcoming, but the very sources of such evidence should be examined, that, as far as possible, we may ascertain what degree of credit they deserve. In the study of the history of the Borgias, we repeat, there has been too much acceptance without question, too much taking for granted of matters whose incredibility frequently touches and occasionally oversteps the confines of the impossible.

One man knew Cesare Borgia better, perhaps, than did any other contemporary, of the many who have left more or less valuable records; for the mind of that man was the acutest of its age, one of the acutest Italy and the world have ever known. That man was Niccolô Macchiavelli, Secretary of State to the Signory of Florence. He owed no benefits to Cesare; he was the ambassador of a power that was ever inimical to the Borgias; so that it is not to be dreamt that his judgement suffered from any bias in Cesare's favour. Yet he accounted Cesare Borgia—as we shall see—the incarnation of an ideal conqueror and ruler; he took Cesare Borgia as the model for his famous work The Prince, written as a grammar of statecraft for the instruction in the art of government of that weakling Giuliano de'Medici.

Macchiavelli pronounces upon Cesare Borgia the following verdict:

"If all the actions of the duke are taken into consideration, it will be seen how great were the foundations he had laid to future power. Upon these I do not think it superfluous to discourse, because I should not know what better precept to lay before a new prince than the example of his actions; and if success did not wait upon what dispositions he had made, that was through no fault of his own, but the result of an extraordinary and extreme malignity of fortune."

In its proper place shall be considered what else Macchiavelli had to say of Cesare Borgia and what to report of events that he witnessed connected with Cesare Borgia's career.

Meanwhile, the above summary of Macchiavelli's judgement is put forward as a justification for the writing of this book, which has for scope to present to you the Cesare Borgia who served as the model for The Prince.

Before doing so, however, there is the rise of the House of Borgia to be traced, and in the first two of the four books into which this history will be divided it is Alexander VI, rather than his son, who will hold the centre of the stage.

If the author has a mercy to crave of his critics, it is that they will not impute it to him that he has set out with the express aim of "whitewashing"— as the term goes—the family of Borgia. To whitewash is to overlay, to mask the original fabric under a superadded surface. Too much superadding has there been here already. By your leave, all shall be stripped away. The grime shall be removed and the foulness of inference, of surmise, of deliberate and cold-blooded malice, with which centuries of scribblers, idle, fantastic, sensational, or venal, have coated the substance of known facts.

But the grime shall be preserved and analysed side by side with the actual substance, that you may judge if out of zeal to remove the former any of the latter shall have been included in the scraping.

The author expresses his indebtedness to the following works which, amongst others, have been studied for the purposes of the present history:

Alvisi, Odoardo, Cesare Borgia, Duca di Romagna. Imola, 1878.

Auton, Jean d', Chroniques de Louis XII (Soc. de l'Hist. de France).

Paris, 1889.

Baldi, Bernardino, Della Vita e Fatti di Guidobaldo. Milano, 1821.

Barthélemy, Charles, Erreurs et Mensonges Historiques. Paris, 1873.

Bernardi, Andrea, Cronache Forlivese, 1476-1517. Bologna, 1897.

Bonnaffé, Edmond, Inventaire de la Duchesse de
Valentinois, Paris, 1878.

Bonoli, Paolo, Istorie della Città di Forli. Forli, 1661.

Bourdeilles, Pierre, Vie des Hommes Illustres. Leyde, 1666.

Brown, Rawdon, Ragguagli Sulla Vita e sulle Opere di Marino
Sanuto. Venezia, 1837.

Buonaccorsi, Biagio, Diario. Firenze, 1568.

Burchard, Joannes, Diarium, sive Rerum Urbanarum Commentarii.

(Edited by L. Thuasne.) Paris, 1885.

Burckhardt, Jacob, Der Cultur der Renaissance in Italien. Basel, 1860.

Castiglione, Baldassare, Il Cortigiano. Firenze, 1885.

Chapelles, Grillon des, Esquisses Biographiques. Paris, 1862.

Cerri, Domenico, Borgia. Tonino, 1857.

Clementini, Cesare, Raccolto Istorico delle Fondatione di Rimino.

Rimini, 1617.

Corio, Bernardino, Storia di Milano. Milano, 1885.

Corvo, Baron, Chronicles of the House of Borgia. London, 1901.

Espinois, Henri de l', Le Pape Alexandre VI (in the Revue des Questions

Historiques, Vol. XXIX). Paris, 1881.

Giovio, Paolo, La Vita di Dicenove Uomini Illustri. Venetia, 1561.

Giovio, Paolo, Delle Istorie del Suo Tempo. Venetia, 1608.

Giustiniani, Antonio, Dispacci, 1502-1505. (Edited by Pasquale Villari.) Firenze, 1876.

Granata, F., Storia Civile di Capua. 1752.

Gregorovius, Ferdinand, Geschichte der Stadt Rom im Mittelalter. Stuttgart, 1889.

Gregorovius, Ferdinand, Lacrezia Borgia (Italian translation). Firenze, 1855.

Guicciardini, Francesco, Istoria d'Italia. Milan, 1803.

Guingené, P. L., Histoire Littéraire d'Italie. Milano, 1820.

Infessura, Stefano, Diarum Rerum Romanum. (Edited by 0. Tommassini.) Roma, 1887.

Leonetti, A., Papa Alessandro VI. Bologna, 1880.

Leti, Gregorio ("Tommaso Tommasi"), Vita di Cesare Borgia, Milano, 1851.

Lucaire, Achille, Alain le Grand, Sire d'Albret. Paris, 1877.

Macchiavelli, Niccolô, Il Principe. Torino, 1853.

Macchiavelli, Niccolô, Le Istorie Fiorentine. Firenze, 1848.

Macchiavelli, Niccolô, Opere Minori. Firenze, 1852.

Matarazzo, Francesco, Cronaca della Città di Perugia, 1492-1503.

(Edited by F. Bonaini and F. Polidori.) In Archivio Storico

Italiano, Firenze, 1851.

Panvinio, Onofrio, Le Vite dei Pontefici. Venezia, 1730.

Pascale, Aq., Racconto del Sacco di Capova. Napoli, 1632.

Righi, B., Annali di Faenza. Faenza, 1841.

Sanazzaro, Opere. Padua, 1723.

Sanuto Marino, Diarii, Vols. I to V. (Edited by F. Stefani.) Venice, 1879.

Tartt, W. M., Pandolfo Collenuccio, Memoirs connected with his life. 1868.

"Tommaso Tommasi" (Gregorio Leti), Vita di Cesare Borgia. 1789.

Varchi, Benedetto, Storia Fiorentina. Florence, 1858.

Visari, Gustavo, Vita degli Artefici.

Villari, Pasquale, La Storia di Girolamo Savonarola, etc. Florence, 1861.

Villari, Pasquale, Niccolò Machiavelli e I suoi Tempi. Milano, 1895.

Yriarte, Charles, La Vie de César Borgia. Paris, 1889.

Yriarte, Charles, Autour des Borgia. Paris, 1891.

Zurita, Geronimo, Historia del Rey Don Hernando el Catolico (in Anales). Çaragoça, 1610.

BOOK I
THE HOUSE OF THE BULL

"Borgia stirps: BOS: atque Ceres transcendit
Olympo, Cantabat nomen saecula cuncta suum."

Michele Ferno

CHAPTER I
THE RISE OF THE HOUSE OF BORGIA

Although the House of Borgia, which gave to the Church of Rome two popes and at least one saint,(1) is to be traced back to the eleventh century, claiming as it does to have its source in the Kings of Aragon, we shall take up its history for our purposes with the birth at the city of Xativa, in the kingdom of Valencia, on December 30, 1378, of Alonso de Borja, the son of Don Juan Domingo de Borja and his wife Doña Francisca.

1 St. Francisco Borgia, S.J.—great-grandson of Pope

Alexander VI, born at Gandia, in Spain, in 1510.

To this Don Alonso de Borja is due the rise of his family to its stupendous eminence. An able, upright, vigorous-minded man, he became a Professor and Doctor of Jurisprudence at the University of Lerida, and afterwards served Alfonso I of Aragon, King of Naples and the Two Sicilies, in the capacity of secretary. This office he filled with the distinction that was to be expected from one so peculiarly fitted for it by the character of the studies he had pursued.

He was made Bishop of Valencia, created Cardinal in 1444, and finally—in 1455—ascended the throne of St. Peter as Calixtus III, an old man, enfeebled in body, but with his extraordinary vigour of mind all unimpaired.

Calixtus proved himself as much a nepotist as many another Pope before and since. This needs not to be dilated upon here; suffice it that in February of 1456 he gave the scarlet hat of Cardinal-Deacon of San Niccoló, in Carcere Tulliano, to his nephew Don Roderigo de Lanzol y Borja.

Born in 1431 at Xativa, the son of Juana de Borja (sister of Calixtus) and her husband Don Jofrè de Lanzol, Roderigo was in his twenty-fifth year at the time of his being raised to the purple, and in the following year he was further created Vice-Chancellor of Holy Church with an annual stipend of eight thousand florins. Like his uncle he had studied jurisprudence—at the University of Bologna—and mentally and physically he was extraordinarily endowed.

From the pen-portraits left of him by Gasparino of Verona, and Girolamo Porzio, we know him for a tall, handsome man with black eyes and full lips, elegant, courtly, joyous, and choicely eloquent, of such health and vigour and endurance that he was insensible to any fatigue. Giasone Maino of Milan refers to his "elegant appearance, serene brow, royal glance, a countenance that at once expresses generosity and majesty, and the genial and heroic air with which his whole personality is invested." To a similar description of him Gasparino adds that "all women upon whom he so much as casts his eyes he moves to love him; attracting them as the lodestone attracts iron;" which is, it must be admitted, a most undesirable reputation in a churchman.

A modern historian[1] who uses little restraint when writing of Roderigo Borgia says of him that "he was a man of neither much energy nor determined will," and further that "the firmness and energy wanting to his character were, however, often replaced by the constancy of his evil passions, by which he was almost blinded." How the constancy of evil passions can replace firmness and energy as factors of worldly success is not readily discernible, particularly if their possessor is blinded by them. The historical worth of the stricture may safely be left to be measured by its logical value. For the rest, to say that Roderigo Borgia was wanting in energy and in will is to say something to which his whole career gives the loud and derisive lie, as will—to some extent at least—be seen in the course of this work.

1 *Pasquale Villari in his Machiavelli i suoi Tempi*

His honours as Cardinal-Deacon and Vice-Chancellor of the Holy See he owed to his uncle; but that he maintained and constantly improved his position—and he a foreigner, be it remembered—under the reigns of the four succeeding Popes—Pius II, Paul II, Sixtus IV, and Innocent VIII—until finally, six-and-twenty years after the death of Calixtus III, he ascended, himself, the Papal Throne, can be due only to the unconquerable energy and stupendous talents which have placed him where he stands in history—one of the greatest forces, for good or ill, that ever occupied St. Peter's Chair.

Say of him that he was ambitious, worldly, greedy of power, and a prey to carnal lusts. All these he was. But for very sanity's sake do not let it be said that he was wanting either in energy or in will, for he was energy and will incarnate.

Consider that with Calixtus III's assumption of the Tiara Rome became the Spaniard's happy hunting-ground, and that into the Eternal City streamed in their hundreds the Catalan adventurers—priests, clerks, captains of fortune, and others—who came to seek advancement at the hands of a Catalan Pope. This Spanish invasion Rome resented. She grew restive under it.

Roderigo's elder brother, Don Pedro Luis de Lanzol y Borja, was made Gonfalonier of the Church, Castellan of all pontifical fortresses and Governor of the Patrimony of St. Peter, with the title of Duke of Spoleto and, later, Prefect of Rome, to the displacement of an Orsini from that office. Calixtus invested this nephew with all temporal power that it was in the Church's privilege to bestow, to the end that he might use it as a basis to overset the petty tyrannies of Romagna, and to establish a feudal claim on the Kingdom of Naples.

Here already we see more than a hint of that Borgia ambition which was to become a byword, and the first attempt of this family to found a dynasty for itself and a State that should endure beyond the transient tenure of the Pontificate, an aim that was later to be carried into actual—if ephemeral— fulfilment by Cesare Borgia.

The Italians watched this growth of Spanish power with jealous, angry eyes. The mighty House of Orsini, angered by the supplanting of one of its members in the Prefecture of Rome, kept its resentment warm, and waited. When in August of 1458 Calixtus III lay dying, the Orsini seized the chance: they incited the city to ready insurgence, and with fire and sword they drove the Spaniards out.

Don Pedro Luis made haste to depart, contrived to avoid the Orsini, who had made him their special quarry, and getting a boat slipped down the Tiber to Civita Vecchia, where he died suddenly some six weeks later, thereby considerably increasing the wealth of Roderigo, his brother and his heir.

Roderigo's cousin, Don Luis Juan, Cardinal-Presbyter of Santi Quattro Coronati, another member of the family who owed his advancement to his uncle Calixtus, thought it also expedient to withdraw from that zone of danger to men of his nationality and name.

Roderigo de Lanzol y Borja alone remained—leastways, the only prominent member of his house—boldly to face the enmity of the majority of the Sacred College, which had looked with grim disfavour upon his uncle's nepotism. Unintimidated, he entered the Conclave for the election of a successor to Calixtus, and there the chance which so often prefers to bestow its favours upon him who knows how to profit by them, gave him the opportunity to establish himself as firmly as ever at the Vatican, and further to advance his interests.

It fell out that when the scrutiny was taken, two cardinals stood well in votes—the brilliant, cultured Enea Silvio Bartolomeo de' Piccolomini, Cardinal of Siena, and the French Cardinal d'Estouteville—though neither had attained the minimum majority demanded. Of these two, the lead in number of votes lay with the Cardinal of Siena, and his election therefore might be completed by Accession—that is, by the voices of such cardinals as had not originally voted for him—until the minimum majority, which must exceed two-thirds, should be made up.

The Cardinal Vice-Chancellor Roderigo de Lanzol y Borja led this accession, with the result that the Cardinal of Siena became Pontiff—as Pius II—and was naturally enough disposed to advance the interests of the man who had been instrumental in helping him to that eminence. Thus, his position at the Vatican, in the very face of all hostility, became stronger and more prominent than ever.

A letter written two years later from the Baths at Petriolo by Pius II to Roderigo when the latter was in Siena—whither he had been sent by his Holiness to superintend the building of the Cathedral and the Episcopal and Piccolomini palaces—is frequently cited by way of establishing the young prelate's dissolute ways. It is a letter at once stern and affectionate, and it certainly leaves no doubt as to what manner of man was the Cardinal Vice-Chancellor in his private life, and to what manner of unecciesiastical pursuits he inclined. It is difficult to discover in it any grounds upon which an apologist may build.

"BELOVED SON,

"When four days ago, in the gardens of Giovanni de Bichis, were assembled several women of Siena addicted to worldly vanity, your worthiness, as we have learnt, little remembering the office which you fill, was entertained by them from the seventeenth to the twenty-second hour. For companion you had one of your colleagues, one whom his years if not the honour of the Holy See should have reminded of his duty. From what we have heard, dancing was unrestrainedly indulged, and not one of love's attractions was absent, whilst your behaviour was no different from that which might have been looked for in any worldly youth. Touching what happened there, modesty imposes silence. Not only the circumstance itself, but the very name of it is unworthy in one of your rank. The husbands, parents, brothers, and relations of these young women were excluded, in order that your amusements should be the more unbridled. You with a few servants undertook to direct and lead those dances. It is said that nothing is now talked of in Siena but your frivolity. Certain it is that here at the baths, where the concourse of ecclesiastics and laity is great, you are the topic of the day. Our displeasure is unutterable, since all this reflects dishonourably upon the sacerdotal estate and office. It will be said of us that we are enriched and promoted not to the end that we may lead blameless lives, but that we may procure the means to indulge our pleasures. Hence the contempt of us entertained by temporal princes and powers and the daily sarcasms of the laity. Hence also the reproof of our own mode of life when we attempt to reprove others. The very Vicar of Christ is involved in this contempt, since he appears to countenance such things. You, beloved son, have charge of the Bishopric of Valencia, the first of Spain; you are also Vice-Chancellor of the Church; and what renders your conduct still more blameworthy is that you are among the cardinals, with the Pope, one of the counsellors of the Holy See. We submit it to your own judgement whether it becomes your dignity to court young women, to send fruit and wine to her you love, and to have no thought for anything but pleasure. We are censured on your account; the blessed memory of your uncle Calixtus is vituperated, since in the judgement of many he was wrong to have conferred so many honours upon you. If you seek excuses in your youth, you are no longer so young that you cannot understand what duties are imposed upon you by your dignity. A cardinal should be irreproachable, a model of moral conduct to all. And what just cause have we for resentment when temporal princes bestow upon us titles that are little honourable, dispute with us our possessions, and attempt to bend us to their will? In truth it is we who inflict these wounds upon ourselves, and it is we who occasion ourselves these troubles, undermining more and more each day by our deeds the authority of the Church. Our guerdon is shame in this world and condign punishment in the next. May your prudence therefore set a restraint upon these vanities and keep you mindful of your dignity, and prevent that you be known for a gallant among married and unmarried women. But should similar facts recur, we shall be compelled to signify that they have happened against our will and to our sorrow, and our censure must be attended by your shame. We have always loved you, and we have held you worthy of our favour as a man of upright and honest nature. Act therefore in such a manner that we may maintain such an opinion of you, and nothing can better conduce to this than that you should lead a well-ordered life. Your age, which is such as still to promise improvement, admits that we should admonish you paternally."

"PETRIOLO, June 11, 1460."

Such a letter is calculated to shock us in our modern notions of a churchman. To us this conduct on the part of a prelate is scandalous beyond words; that it was scandalous even then is obvious from the Pontiff's letter; but that it was scandalous in an infinitely lesser degree is no less obvious from the very fact that the Pontiff wrote that letter (and in such terms) instead of incontinently unfrocking the offender.

In considering Roderigo's conduct, you are to consider—as has been urged already—the age in which he lived. You are to remember that it was an age in which the passions and the emotions wore no such masks as they wear to-day, but went naked and knew no shame of their nudity; an age in which personal modesty was as little studied as hypocrisy, and in which men, wore their vices as openly as their virtues.

No amount of simple statement can convey an adequate notion of the corrupt state of the clergy at the time. To form any just appreciation of this, it is necessary to take a peep at some of the documents that have survived—such a document, for instance, as that Bull of this Pope Pius II which forbade priests from plying the trades of keeping taverns, gaming-houses, and brothels.

Ponder also that under his successor, Sixtus IV, the tax levied upon the courtesans of Rome enriched the pontifical coffers to the extent of some 20,000 ducats yearly. Ponder further that when the vicar of the libidinous Innocent VIII published in 1490 an edict against the universal concubinage practised by the clergy, forbidding its continuation under pain of excommunication, all that it earned him was the severe censure of the Holy Father, who disagreed with the measure and who straightway repealed and cancelled the edict.(1)

1 See Burchard's Diarium, Thuasne Edition, Vol. II. p.442

et seq.

All this being considered, and man being admittedly a creature of his environment, can we still pretend to horror at this Roderigo and at the fact that being the man he was—prelate though he might be—handsome, brilliant, courted, in the full vigour of youth, and a voluptuary by nature, he should have succumbed to the temptations by which he was surrounded?

One factor only could have caused him to use more restraint—the good example of his peers. That example he most certainly had not.

Virtue is a comparative estate, when all is said; and before we can find that Roderigo was vile, that he deserves unqualified condemnation for his conduct, we must ascertain that he was more or less exceptional in his licence, that he was less scrupulous than his fellows. Do we find that? To find the contrary we do not need to go beyond the matter which provoked that letter from the Pontiff. For we see that he was not even alone, as an ecclesiastic, in the adventure; that he had for associate on that amorous frolic one Giacopo Ammanati, Cardinal-Presbyter of San Crisogno, Roderigo's senior and an ordained priest, which—without seeking to make undue capital out of the circumstance—we may mention that Roderigo was not. He was a Cardinal-Deacon, be it remembered.(1) We know that the very Pontiff who admonished these young prelates, though now admittedly a man of saintly ways, had been a very pretty fellow himself in his lusty young days in Siena; we know that Roderigo's uncle—the Calixtus to whom Pius II refers in that letter as of "blessed memory"—had at least one acknowledged son.(2) We know that Piero and Girolamo Riario, though styled by Pope Sixtus IV his "nephews," were generally recognized to be his sons.(3) And we know that the numerous bastards of Innocent VIII—Roderigo's immediate precursor on the Pontifical Throne—were openly acknowledged by their father. We know, in short, that it was the universal custom of the clergy to forget its vows of celibacy, and to circumvent them by dispensing with the outward form and sacrament of marriage; and we have it on the word of Pius II himself, that "if there are good reasons for enjoining the celibacy of the clergy, there are better and stronger for enjoining them to marry."

1 He was not ordained priest until 1471, after the election of Sixtus IV.

2 Don Francisco de Borja, born at Valencia in 1441.

3 Macchiavelli, Istorie Fiorentine.

What more is there to say? If we must be scandalized, let us be scandalized by the times rather than by the man. Upon what reasonable grounds can we demand that he should be different from his fellows; and if we find him no different, what right or reason have we for picking him out and rendering him the object of unparalleled obloquy?

If we are to deal justly with Roderigo Borgia, we must admit that, in so far as his concessions to his lusts are concerned, he was a typical churchman of his day; neither more nor less—as will presently grow abundantly clear.

It may be objected by some that had such been the case the Pope would not have written him such a letter as is here cited. But consider a moment the close relations existing between them. Roderigo was the nephew of the late Pope; in a great measure Pius II owed his election, as we have seen, to Roderigo's action in the Conclave. That his interest in him apart from that was paternal and affectionate is shown in every line of that letter. And consider further that Roderigo's companion is shown by that letter to be equally guilty in so far as the acts themselves are to be weighed, guilty in a greater degree when we remember his seniority and his actual priesthood. Yet to Cardinal Ammanati the Pope wrote no such admonition. Is not that sufficient proof that his admonition of Roderigo was dictated purely by his personal affection for him?

In this same year 1460 was born to Cardinal Roderigo a son—Don Pedro Luis de Borja—by a spinster (mulier soluta) unnamed. This son was publicly acknowledged and cared for by the cardinal.

Seven years later—in 1467—he became the father of a daughter— Girolama de Borja—by a spinster, whose name again does not transpire. Like Pedro Luis she too was openly acknowledged by Cardinal Roderigo. It was widely believed that this child's mother was Madonna Giovanna de' Catanei, who soon became quite openly the cardinal's mistress, and was maintained by him in such state as might have become a maîtresse en titre. But, as we shall see later, the fact of that maternity of Girolama is doubtful in the extreme. It was never established, and it is difficult to understand why not if it were the fact.

Meanwhile Paul II—Pietro Barbo, Cardinal of Venice—had succeeded Pius II in 1464, and in 1471 the latter was in his turn succeeded by the formidable Sixtus IV—Cardinal Francesco Maria della Rovere—a Franciscan of the lowest origin, who by his energy and talents had become general of his order and had afterwards been raised to the dignity of the purple.

It was Cardinal Roderigo de Lanzol y Borja who, in his official capacity of Archdeacon of Holy Church, performed the ceremony of coronation and placed the triple crown on the head of Pope Sixtus. It is probable that this was his last official act as Archdeacon, for in that same year 1471, at the age of forty, he was ordained priest and consecrated Bishop of Albano.

CHAPTER II
THE REIGNS OF SIXTUS IV AND INNOCENT VIII

The rule of Sixtus was as vigorous as it was scandalous. To say—as has been said—that with his succession to St. Peter's Chair came for the Church a still sadder time than that which had preceded it, is not altogether true. Politically, at least, Sixtus did much to strengthen the position of the Holy See and of the Pontificate. He was not long in giving the Roman factions a taste of his stern quality. If he employed unscrupulous means, he employed them against unscrupulous men—on the sound principle of similia similibus curantur—and to some extent they were justified by the ends in view.

He found the temporal throne of the Pontiffs tottering when he ascended it. Stefano Porcaro and his distinguished following already in 1453 had attempted the overthrow of the pontifical authority, inspired, no doubt, by the attacks that had been levelled against it by the erudite and daring Lorenzo Valla.

This Valla was the distinguished translator of Homer, Herodotus, and Thucydides, who more than any one of his epoch advanced the movement of Greek and Latin learning, which, whilst it had the effect of arresting the development of Italian literature, enriched Europe by opening up to it the sources of ancient erudition, of philosophy, poetry, and literary taste. Towards the year 1435 he drifted to the court of Alfonso of Aragon, whose secretary he ultimately became. Some years later he attacked the Temporal Power and urged the secularization of the States of the Church. "Ut Papa," he wrote, "tantum Vicarius Christi sit, et non etiam Coesari." In his De falso credita et ementita Constantini Donatione, he showed that the decretals of the Donation of Constantine, upon which rests the Pope's claim to the Pontifical States, was an impudent forgery, that Constantine had never had the power to give, nor had given, Rome to the Popes, and that they had no right to govern there. He backed up this terrible indictment by a round attack upon the clergy, its general corruption and its practices of simony; and as a result he fell into the hands of the Inquisition. There it might have gone very ill with him but that King Alfonso rescued him from the clutches of that dread priestly tribunal.

Meanwhile, he had fired his petard. If a pretext had been wanting to warrant the taking up of arms against the Papacy, that pretext Valla had afforded. Never was the temporal power of the Church in such danger, and ultimately it must inevitably have succumbed but for the coming of so strong and unscrupulous a man as Sixtus IV to stamp out the patrician factions that were heading the hostile movement.

His election, it is generally admitted, was simoniacal; and by simony he raised the funds necessary for his campaign to reestablish and support the papal authority. This simony of his, says Dr. Jacob Burckhardt, "grew to unheard-of proportions, and extended from the appointment of cardinals down to the sale of the smallest benefice."

Had he employed these means of raising funds for none but the purpose of putting down the assailants of the Pontificate, a measure of justification (political if not ecclesiastical) might be argued in his favour. Unfortunately, having discovered these ready sources of revenue, he continued to exploit them for purposes far less easy to condone.

As a nepotist Sixtus was almost unsurpassed in the history of the Papacy. Four of his nephews and their aggrandizement were the particular objects of his attentions, and two of these—as we have already said—Piero and Girolamo Riario, were universally recognized to be his sons.

Piero, who was a simple friar of twenty-six years of age at the time that his father became Pope, was given the Archbishopric of Florence, made Patriarch of Constantinople, and created Cardinal to the title of San Sisto, with a revenue of 60,000 crowns.

We have it on the word of Cardinal Ammanati(1)—the same gentleman who, with Roderigo de Lanzol y Borja made so scandalously merry in de Bichis' garden at Siena—that Cardinal Riario's luxury "exceeded all that had been displayed by our forefathers or that can even be imagined by our descendants"; and Macchiavelli tells us(2) that "although of very low origin and mean rearing, no sooner had he obtained the scarlet hat than he displayed a pride and ambition so vast that the Pontificate seemed too small for him, and he gave a feast in Rome which would have appeared extraordinary even for a king, the expense exceeding 20,000 florins."

1 *In a letter to Francesco Gonzaga.*

2 *Istorie Florentine.*

Knowing so much, it is not difficult to understand that in one year or less he should have dissipated 200,000 florins, and found himself in debt to the extent of a further 60,000.

In 1473, Sixtus being at the time all but at war with Florence, this Cardinal Riario visited Venice and Milan. In the latter State he was planning with Duke Galeazzo Maria that the latter should become King of Lombardy, and then assist him with money and troops to master Rome and ascend the Papal Throne—which, it appears, Sixtus was quite willing to yield to him—thus putting the Papacy on a hereditary basis like any other secular State.

It is as well, perhaps, that he should have died on his return to Rome in January of 1474—worn out by his excesses and debaucheries, say some; of poison administered by the Venetians, say others—leaving a mass of debts, contracted in his transactions with the World, the Flesh, and the Devil, to be cleared up by the Vicar of Christ.

His brother Girolamo, meanwhile, had married Caterina Sforza, a natural daughter of Duke Galeazzo Maria. She brought him as her dowry the City of Imola, and in addition to this he received from his Holiness the City of Forli, to which end the Ordelaffi were dispossessed of it. Here again we have a papal attempt to found a family dynasty, and an attempt that might have been carried further under circumstances more propitious and had not Death come to check their schemes.

The only one of the four "nephews" of Sixtus—and to this one was imputed no nearer kinship—who was destined to make any lasting mark in history was Giuliano della Rovere. He was raised by his uncle to the purple with the title of San Pietro in Vincoli, and thirty-two years later he was to become Pope (as Julius II). Of him we shall hear much in the course of this story.

Under the pontificate of Sixtus IV the position and influence of Cardinal Roderigo were greatly increased, for once again the Spanish Cardinal had made the most of his opportunities. As at the election of Pius II, so at the election of Sixtus IV it was Cardinal Roderigo who led the act of accession which gave the new Pope his tiara, and for this act Roderigo—in common with the Cardinals Orsini and Gonzaga who acceded with him—was richly rewarded and advanced, receiving as his immediate guerdon the wealthy Abbey of Subiaco.

At about this time, 1470, must have begun the relations between Cardinal Roderigo and Giovanna Catanei, or Vannozza Catanei, as she is styled in contemporary documents—Vannozza being a corruption or abbreviation of Giovannozza, an affectionate form of Giovanna.

Who she was, or whence she came, are facts that have never been ascertained. She is generally assumed to have been a Roman; but there are no obvious grounds for the assumption, her name, for instance, being common to many parts of Italy. And just as we have no sources of information upon her origin, neither have we any elements from which to paint her portrait. Gregorovius rests the probability that she was beautiful upon the known characteristics and fastidious tastes of the cardinal. Since it is unthinkable that such a man would have been captivated by an ugly woman or would have been held by a stupid one, it is fairly reasonable to conclude that she was beautiful and ready-witted.

All that we do know of her up to the time of her liaison with Cardinal Roderigo is that she was born on July 13, 1442, this fact being ascertainable by a simple calculation from the elements afforded by the inscription on her tomb in Santa Maria del Popolo:

Vix ann. LXXVI m. IV d. XII Objit anno MDXVIII XXVI, Nov.

And again, just as we know nothing of her family origin, neither have we any evidence of what her circumstances were when she caught the magnetic eye of Cardinal Roderigo de Lanzol y Borja—or Borgia as by now his name, which had undergone italianization, was more generally spelled.

Infessura states in his diaries that Roderigo desiring later—as Pope Alexander VI—to create cardinal his son by her, Cesare Borgia, he caused false witness to be borne to the fact that Cesare was the legitimate son of one Domenico d'Arignano, to whom he, the Pope, had in fact married her. Guicciardini(1) makes the same statement, without, however, mentioning name of this d'Arignano.

1 *Istoria d'Italia.*

Now, bastards were by canon law excluded from the purple, and it is probably upon this circumstance that both Infessura and Guicciardini have built the assumption that some such means as these had been adopted to circumvent the law, and—as so often happens in chronicles concerning the Borgias—the assumption is straightway stated as a fact. But there were other ways of circumventing awkward commandments, and, unfortunately for the accuracy of these statements of Infessura and Guicciardini, another way was taken in this instance. As early as 1480, Pope Sixtus IV had granted Cesare Borgia—in a Bull dated October 1(1)—dispensation from proving the legitimacy of his birth. This entirely removed the necessity for any such subsequent measures as those which are suggested by these chroniclers.

1 *See the supplement to the Appendix of Thuasne's edition*

of Burchard's Diarium.

Moreover, had Cardinal Roderigo desired to fasten the paternity of Cesare on another, there was ready to his hand Vannozza's actual husband, Giorgio della Croce.(2) When exactly this man became her husband is not to be ascertained. All that we know is that he was so in 1480, and that she was living with him in that year in a house in Piazza Pizzo di Merlo (now Piazza Sforza Cesarini) not far from the house on Banchi Vecchi which Cardinal Roderigo, as Vice-Chancellor, had converted into a palace for himself, and a palace so sumptuous as to excite the wonder of that magnificent age.

2 D'Arignano is as much a fiction as the rest of

Infessura's story.

This Giorgio della Croce was a Milanese, under the protection of Cardinal Roderigo, who had obtained for him a post at the Vatican as apostolic secretary. According to some, he married him to Vannozza in order to afford her an official husband and thus cloak his own relations with her. It is an assumption which you will hesitate to accept. If we know our Cardinal Roderigo at all, he was never the man to pursue his pleasures in a hole-and-corner fashion, nor one to bethink him of a cloak for his amusements. Had he but done so, scandalmongers would have had less to fasten upon in their work of playing havoc with his reputation. What is far more likely is that della Croce owed Cardinal Roderigo's protection and the appointment as apostolic secretary to his own complacency in the matter of his wife's relations with the splendid prelate. However we look at it, the figure cut in this story by della Croce is not heroic.

Between the years 1474 and 1476, Vannozza bore Roderigo two sons, Cesare Borgia (afterwards Cardinal of Valencia and Duke of Valentinois), the central figure of our story, and Giovanni Borgia (afterwards Duke of Gandia).

Lucrezia Borgia, we know from documentary evidence before us, was born on April 19, 1479.

But there is a mystery about the precise respective ages of Vannozza's two eldest sons, and we fear that at this time of day it has become impossible to establish beyond reasonable doubt which was the firstborn; and this in spite of the documents discovered by Gregorovius and his assertion that they remove all doubt and enable him definitely to assert that Giovanni was born in 1474 and Cesare in 1476.

Let us look at these documents. They are letters from ambassadors to their masters; probably correct, and the more credible since they happen to agree and corroborate one another; still, not so utterly and absolutely reliable as to suffice to remove the doubts engendered by the no less reliable documents whose evidence contradicts them.

The first letters quoted by Gregorovius are from the ambassador Gianandrea Boccaccio to his master, the Duke of Ferrara, in 1493. In these he mentions Cesare Borgia as being sixteen to seventeen years of age at the time. But the very manner of writing—"sixteen to seventeen years"—is a common way of vaguely suggesting age rather than positively stating it. So we may pass that evidence over, as of secondary importance.

Next is a letter from Gerardo Saraceni to the Duke of Ferrara, dated October 26, 1501, and it is more valuable, claiming as it does to be the relation of something which his Holiness told the writer. It is in the post-scriptum that this ambassador says: "The Pope gave me to understand that the said Duchess [Lucrezia Borgia] will complete twenty-two years of age next April, and at that same time the Duke of Romagna will complete his twenty-sixth year."(1)

> 1 "Facendomi intendere the epsa Duchessa é di etá di anni ventidui, li quali finiranno a questo Aprile; in el qual tempo anche lo Illmo. Duca di Romagna fornirá anni ventisei."

This certainly fixes the year of Cesare's birth as 1476; but we are to remember that Saraceni is speaking of something that the Pope had recently told him; exactly how recently does not transpire. An error would easily be possible in so far as the age of Cesare is concerned. In so far as the age of Lucrezia is concerned, an error is not only possible, but has actually been committed by Saraceni. At least the age given in his letter is wrong by one year, as we know by a legal document drawn up in February of 1491— Lucrezia's contract of marriage with Don Juan Cherubin de Centelles.(2)

> 2 A contract never executed.

According to this protocol in old Spanish, dated February 26, 1491, Lucrezia completed her twelfth year on April 19, 1491,(3) which definitely and positively gives us the date of her birth as April 19, 1479.

> 3 "Item mes attenent que dita Dona Lucretia a XVIIII de Abril prop. vinent entrará in edat de dotze anys."

A quite extraordinary error is that made by Gregorovius when he says that Lucrezia Borgia was born on April 18, 1480, extraordinary considering that he made it apparently with this very protocol under his eyes, and cites it, in fact (Document IV in the Appendix to his Lucrezia Borgia) as his authority.

To return, however, to Cesare and Giovanni, there is yet another evidence quoted by Gregorovius in support of his contention that the latter was the elder and born in 1474; but it is of the same nature and of no more, nor less, value than those already mentioned.

Worthy of more consideration in view of their greater official and legal character are the Ossuna documents, given in the Supplement of the Appendix in Thuasne's edition of Burchard's Diary, namely:

(a) October 1, 1480.—A Bull from Sixtus IV, already mentioned, dispensing Cesare from proving his legitimacy. In this he is referred to as in his sixth year—"in sexto tuo aetatis anno."

This, assuming Boccaccio's letter to be correct in the matter of April being the month of Cesare's birth, fixes the year of his birth as 1475.

(b) August 16, 1482.—A Bull of Sixtus IV, appointing Roderigo Borgia administrator of Cesare's benefices. In this he is mentioned as being seven years of age (i.e., presumably in his eighth year), which again gives us his birth-year as 1475.

(c) September 12, 1484.—A Bull of Sixtus IV, appointing Cesare treasurer of the Church of Carthage. In this he is mentioned as in his ninth year—"in nono tuo aetatis anno." This is at variance with the other two, and gives us 1476 as the year of his birth.

To these evidences, conflicting as they are, may be added Burchard's mention in his diary under date of September 12, 1491, that Cesare was then seventeen years of age. This would make him out to have been born in 1474.

Clearly the matter cannot definitely be settled upon such evidence as we have. All that we can positively assert is that he was born between the years 1474 and 1476, and we cannot, we think, do better for the purposes of this story than assume his birth-year to have been 1475.

We know that between those same years, or in one or the other of them, was born Giovanni Borgia; but just as the same confusion prevails with regard to his exact age, so is it impossible to determine with any finality whether he was Cesare's junior or senior.

The one document that appears to us to be the most important in this connection is that of the inscription on their mother's tomb. This runs:

FAUSTIAE CATHANAE, CESARE VALENTINAE, JOHANNAE CANDIAE, JUFFREDO SCYLATII, ET LUCRETIA FERRARIAE DUCIB. FILIIS NOBILI PROBITATE INSIGNI, RELIGIONE EXIMIA, ETC., ETC.

If Giovanni was, as is claimed, the eldest of her children, why does his name come second? If Cesare was her second son, why does his name take the first place on that inscription?

It has been urged that if Cesare was the elder of these two, he, and not Giovanni, would have succeeded to the Duchy of Gandia on the death of Pedro Luis—Cardinal Roderigo's eldest son, by an unknown mother. But that does not follow inevitably; for it is to be remembered that Cesare was already destined for an ecclesiastical career, and it may well be that his father was reluctant to change his plans.

Meanwhile the turbulent reign of Sixtus IV went on, until his ambition to increase his dominions had the result of plunging the whole of Italy into war.

Lorenzo de'Medici had thwarted the Pope's purposes in Romagna, coming to the assistance of Città di Castello when this was attacked in the Pope's interest by the warlike Giuliano della Rovere. To avenge himself for this, and to remove a formidable obstacle to his family's advancement, the Pope inspired the Pazzi conspiracy against the lives of the famous masters of Florence. The conspiracy failed; for although Giuliano de'Medici fell stabbed to the heart—before Christ's altar, and at the very moment of the elevation of the Host—Lorenzo escaped with slight hurt, and, by the very risk to which he had been exposed, rallied the Florentines to him more closely than ever.

Open war was the only bolt remaining in the papal quiver, and open war he declared, preluding it by a Bull of Excommunication against the Florentines. Naples took sides with the Pope. Venice and Milan came to the support of Florence, whereupon Milan's attentions were diverted to her own affairs, Genoa being cunningly set in revolt against her.

In 1480 a peace was patched up; but it was short-lived. A few months later war flared out again from the Holy See, against Florence this time, and on the pretext of its having joined the Venetians against the Pope in the late war. A complication now arose, created by the Venetians, who seized the opportunity to forward their own ambitions and increase their territories on the mainland, and upon a pretext of the pettiest themselves declared war upon Ferrara. Genoa and some minor tyrannies were drawn into the quarrel on the one side, whilst on the other Florence, Naples, Mantua, Milan, and Bologna stood by Ferrara. Whilst the papal forces were holding in check the Neapolitans who sought to pass north to aid Ferrara, whilst the Roman Campagna was being harassed by the Colonna, and Milan was engaged with Genoa, the Venetians invested Ferrara, forced her to starvation and to yielding-point. Thereupon the Pope, perceiving the trend of affairs, and that the only likely profit to be derived from the campaign would lie with Venice, suddenly changed sides that he might avoid a contingency so far removed from all his aims.

He made a treaty with Naples, and permitted the Neapolitan army passage through his territories, of which they availed themselves to convey supplies to Ferrara and neutralize the siege. At the same time the Pope excommunicated the Venetians, and urged all Italy to make war upon them.

In this fashion the campaign dragged on to every one's disadvantage and without any decisive battle fought, until at last the peace of Bagnolo was concluded in August of 1484, and the opposing armies withdrew from Ferrara.

The news of it literally killed Sixtus. When the ambassadors declared to him the terms of the treaty he was thrown into a violent rage, and declared the peace to be at once shameful and humiliating. The gout from which he suffered flew to his heart, and on the following day—August 12, 1484—he died.

Two things he did during his reign to the material advantage of the Church, however much he may have neglected the spiritual. He strengthened her hold upon her temporal possessions and he enriched the Vatican by the addition of the Sistine Chapel. For the decoration of this he procured the best Tuscan talent of his day—and of many days—and brought Alessandro Filipeppi (Botticelli), Pietro Vannuccio (Il Perugino), and Domenico Bigordi (IL Ghirlandajo) from Florence to adorn its walls with their frescoes.(1)

> 1 The glory of the Sistine Chapel, however, is Michelangelo's "Last Judgement," which was added later, in the reign of Pope Julius II (Giuliano della Rovere).

In the last years of the reign of Pope Sixtus, Cardinal Roderigo's family had suffered a loss and undergone an increase.

In 1481 Vannozza bore him another son—Giuffredo Borgia, and in the following year died his eldest son (by an unknown mother) Pedro Luis de Borgia, who had reached the age of twenty-two and was betrothed at the time of his decease to the Princess Maria d'Aragona.

In January of that same year, 1482, Cardinal Roderigo had married his daughter Girolama—now aged fifteen—to Giovanni Andrea Cesarini, the scion of a patrician Roman house. The alliance strengthened the bonds of good feeling which for some considerable time had prevailed between the two families. Unfortunately the young couple were not destined to many years of life together, as in 1483 both died.

Of Cesare all that we know at this period is what we learn from the Papal Bulls conferring several benefices upon him. In July 1482 he was granted the revenues from the prebendals and canonries of Valencia; in the following month he was appointed Canon of Valencia and apostolic notary. In April 1484 he was made Provost of Alba, and in September of the same year treasurer of the Church of Carthage. No doubt he was living with his mother, his brothers, and his sister at the house in the Piazza Pizzo di Merlo, where an ample if not magnificent establishment was maintained.

By this time Cardinal Roderigo's wealth and power had grown to stupendous proportions, and he lived in a splendour well worthy of his lofty rank. He was now fifty-three years of age, still retaining the air and vigour of a man in his very prime, which, no doubt, he owed as much as to anything to his abstemious and singularly sparing table-habits. He derived a stupendous income from his numerous abbeys in Italy and Spain, his three bishoprics of Valencia, Porto, and Carthage, and his ecclesiastical offices, among which the Vice-Chancellorship alone yielded him annually eight thousand florins.(1)

> 1 The gold florin, ducat, or crown was equal to ten shillings of our present money, and had a purchasing power of five times that amount.

Volterra refers with wonder to the abundance of his plate, to his pearls, his gold embroideries, and his books, the splendid equipment of his beds, the trappings of his horses, and other similar furnishings in gold, in silver, and in silk. In short, he was the wealthiest prince of the Church of his day, and he lived with a magnificence worthy of a king or of the Pope himself.

Of the actual man, Volterra, writing in 1586, says: "He is of a spirit capable of anything, and of a great intelligence. A ready speaker, and of distinction, notwithstanding his indifferent literary culture; naturally astute, and of marvellous talent in the conduct of affairs."

In the year in which Volterra wrote of Cardinal Roderigo in such terms Vannozza was left a widow by the death of Giorgio della Croce. Her widowhood was short, however, for in the same year—on June 6—she took a second husband, possibly at the instance of Roderigo Borgia, who did not wish to leave her unprotected; that, at least, is the general inference, although there is very little evidence upon which to base it. This second husband was Carlo Canale, a Mantovese scholar who had served Cardinal Francesco Gonzaga in the capacity of chamberlain, and who had come to Rome on the death of his patron.

The marriage contract shows that by this time Vannozza had removed her residence to Piazza Branchis. In addition to this she had by this time acquired a villa with its beautiful gardens and vineyards in the Suburra near S. Pietro in Vincoli. She is also known to have been the proprietor of an inn—the Albergo del Leone—in Via del Orso, opposite the Torre di Nona, for she figures with della Croce in a contract regarding a lease of it in 1483.

With her entrance into second nuptials, her relations with Cardinal Roderigo came to an end, and his two children by her, then in Rome— Lucrezia and Giuffredo—went to take up their residence with Adriana Orsini (née de Mila) at the Orsini Palace on Monte Giordano. She was a cousin of Roderigo's, and the widow of Lodovico Orsini, by whom she had a son, Orso Orsini, who from early youth had been betrothed to Giulia Farnese, the daughter of a patrician family, still comparatively obscure, but destined through this very girl to rise to conspicuous eminence.

For her surpassing beauty this Giulia Farnese has been surnamed La Bella—and as Giulia La Bella was she known in her day—and she has been immortalized by Pinturicchio and Guglielmo della Porta. She sat to the former as a model for his Madonna in the Borgia Tower of the Vatican, and to the latter for the statue of Truth which adorns the tomb of her brother Alessandro Farnese, who became Pope Paul III.

Here in Adriana Orsini's house, where his daughter Lucrezia was being educated, Cardinal Roderigo, now at the mature age of some six-and-fifty years, made the acquaintance and became enamoured of this beautiful golden-headed Giulia, some forty years his junior. To the fact that she presently became his mistress—somewhere about the same time that she became Orso Orsini's wife—is due the sudden rise of the House of Farnese. This began with her handsome, dissolute brother Alessandro's elevation to the purple by her lover, and grew to vast proportions during his subsequent and eminently scandalous occupation of the Papal Throne as Paul III.

In the year 1490 Lucrezia was the only one of Roderigo's children by Vannozza who remained in Rome.

Giovanni Borgia was in Spain, whither he had gone on the death of his brother Pedro Luis, to take posession of the Duchy of Gandia, which the power of his father's wealth and vast influence at the Valencian Court had obtained for that same Pedro Luis. To this Giovanni now succeeded.

Cesare Borgia—now aged fifteen—had for some two years been studying his humanities in an atmosphere of Latinity at the Sapienza of Perugia. There, if we are to believe the praises of him uttered by Pompilio, he was already revealing his unusual talents and a precocious wit. In the preface of the Syllabica on the art of Prosody dedicated to him by Pompilio, the latter hails him as the hope and ornament of the Hous of Borgia— "Borgiae familiae spes et decus."

From Perugia he was moved in 1491 to the famous University of Pisa, a college frequented by the best of Italy. For preceptor he had Giovanni Vera of Arcilla, a Spanish gentleman who was later created a cardinal by Cesare's father. There in Pisa Cesare maintained an establishment of a magnificence in keeping with his father's rank and with the example set him by that same father.

It was Cardinal Roderigo's wish that Cesare should follow an ecclesiastical career; and the studies of canon law which he pursued under Filippo Decis, the most rated lecturer on canon law of his day, were such as peculiarly to fit him for that end and for the highest honours the Church might have to bestow upon him later. At the age of seventeen, while still at Pisa, he was appointed prothonotary of the Church and preconized Bishop of Pampeluna.

Sixtus IV died, as we have seen, in August 1482. The death of a Pope was almost invariably the signal for disturbances in Rome, and they certainly were not wanting on this occasion. The Riario palaces were stormed and looted, and Girolamo Riario—the Pope's "nepot"—threw himself into the castle of Sant' Angelo with his forces.

The Orsini and Colonna were in arms, "so that in a few days incendiarism, robbery, and murder raged in several parts of the city. The cardinals besought the Count to surrender the castle to the Sacred College, withdraw his troops, and deliver Rome from the fear of his forces; and he, that he might win the favour of the future Pope, obeyed, and withdrew to Imola."(1)

1 Macchiavelli, Istorie Fiorentine.

The cardinals, having thus contrived to restore some semblance of order, proceeded to the creation of a new Pontiff, and a Genoese, Giovanni Battista Cibo, Cardinal of Malfetta, was elected and took the name of Innocent VIII.

Again, as in the case of Sixtus, there is no lack of those who charge this Pontiff with having obtained his election by simony. The Cardinals Giovanni d' Aragona (brother to the King of Naples) and Ascanio Sforza (brother of Lodovico, Duke of Milan) are said to have disposed of their votes in the most open and shameless manner, practically putting them up for sale to the highest bidder. Italy rang with the scandal of it, we are told.

Under Innocent's lethargic rule the Church again began to lose much of the vigour with which Sixtus had inspired it. If the reign of Sixtus had been scandalous, infinitely worse was that of Innocent—a sordid, grasping sensualist, without even the one redeeming virtue of strength that had been his predecessor's. Nepotism had characterized many previous pontificates; open paternity was to characterize his, for he was the first Pope who, in flagrant violation of canon law, acknowledged his children for his own. He proceeded to provide for some seven bastards, and that provision appears to have been the only aim and scope of his pontificate.

Not content with raising money by the sale of preferments, Innocent established a traffic in indulgences, the like of which had never been seen before. In the Rome of his day you might, had you the money, buy anything, from a cardinal's hat to a pardon for the murder of your father.

The most conspicuous of his bastards was Francesco Cibo—conspicuous chiefly for the cupidity which distinguished him as it distinguished the Pope his father. For the rest he was a poor-spirited fellow who sorely disappointed Lorenzo de'Medici, whose daughter Maddalena he received in marriage. Lorenzo had believed that, backed by the Pope's influence, Francesco would establish for himself a dynasty in Romagna. But father and son were alike too invertebrate—the one to inspire, the other to execute any such designs as had already been attempted by the nepots of Calixtus III and Sixtus IV.

Under the weak and scandalous rule of Innocent VIII Rome appears to have been abandoned to the most utter lawlessness. Anarchy, robbery, and murder preyed upon the city. No morning dawned without revealing corpses in the streets; and if by chance the murderer was caught, there was pardon for him if he could afford to buy it, or Tor di Nona and the hangman's noose if he could not.

It is not wonderful that when at last Innocent VIII died Infessura should have blessed the day that freed the world of such a monster.

But his death did not happen until 1492. A feeble old man, he had become subject to lethargic or cataleptic trances, which had several times already deceived those in attendance into believing him dead. He grew weaker and weaker, and it became impossible to nourish him upon anything but woman's milk. Towards the end came, Infessura tells us, a Hebrew physician who claimed to have a prescription by which he could save the Pope's life. For his infusion(1) he needed young human blood, and to obtain it he took three boys of the age of ten, and gave them a ducat apiece for as much as he might require of them. Unfortunately he took so much that the three boys incontinently died of his phlebotomy, and the Hebrew was obliged to take to flight to save his own life, for the Pope, being informed of what had taken place, execrated the deed and ordered the physician's arrest. "Judeus quidem aufugit, et Papa sanatus not est," concludes Infessura.

> 1 The silly interpretation of this afforded by later writers, that this physician attempted transfusion of blood—silly, because unthinkable in an age which knew nothing of the circulation of the blood—has already been exploded.

Innocent VIII breathed his last on July 25, 1492.

CHAPTER III
ALEXANDER VI

The ceremonies connected with the obsequies of Pope Innocent VIII lasted—as prescribed—nine days; they were concluded on August 5, 1492, and, says Infessura naïvely, "sic finita fuit eius memoria."

The Sacred College consisted at the time of twenty-seven cardinals, four of whom were absent at distant sees and unable to reach Rome in time for the immuring of the Conclave. The twenty-three present were, in the order of their seniority: Roderigo Borgia, Oliviero Caraffa, Giuliano della Rovere, Battista Zeno, Giovanni Michieli, Giorgio Costa, Girolamo della Rovere, Paolo Fregosi, Domenico della Rovere, Giovanni dei Conti, Giovanni Giacomo Sclafetani, Lorenzo Cibo, Ardicino della Porta, Antoniotto Pallavicino, Maffeo Gerardo, Francesco Piccolomini, Raffaele Riario, Giovanni Battista Savelli, Giovanni Colonna, Giovanni Orsini, Ascanio Maria Sforza, Giovanni de'Medici, and Francesco Sanseverino.

On August 6 they assembled in St. Peter's to hear the Sacred Mass of the Holy Ghost, which was said by Giuliano della Rovere on the tomb of the Prince of the Apostles, and to listen to the discourse "Pro eligendo Pontefice," delivered by the learned and eloquent Bishop of Carthage. Thereafter the Cardinals swore upon the Gospels faithfully to observe their trust, and thereupon the Conclave was immured.

According to the dispatches of Valori, the Ferrarese ambassador in Rome, it was expected that either the Cardinal of Naples (Oliviero Caraffa) or the Cardinal of Lisbon (Giorgio Costa) would be elected to the Pontificate; and according to the dispatch of Cavalieri the ambassador of Modena, the King of France had deposited 200,000 ducats with a Roman banker to forward the election of Giuliano della Rovere. Nevertheless, early on the morning of August 11 it was announced that Roderigo Borgia was elected Pope, and we have it on the word of Valori that the election was unanimous, for he wrote on the morrow to the Council of Eight (the Signory of Florence) that after long contention Alexander VI was created "omnium consensum— ne li manco un solo voto."

The subject of this election is one with which we rarely find an author dealing temperately or with a proper and sane restraint. To vituperate in superlatives seems common to most who have taken in hand this and other episodes in the history of the Borgias. Every fresh writer who comes to the task appears to be mainly inspired by a desire to emulate his forerunners, allowing his pen to riot zestfully in the accumulation of scandalous matter, and seeking to increase if possible its lurid quality by a degree or two. As a rule there is not even an attempt made to put forward evidence in substantiation of anything that is alleged. Wild and sweeping statement takes the place that should be held by calm deduction and reasoned comment.

"He was the worst Pontiff that ever filled St. Peter's Chair," is one of these sweeping statements, culled from the pages of an able, modern, Italian author, whose writings, sound in all that concerns other matters, are strewn with the most foolish extravagances and flagrant inaccuracies in connection with Alexander VI and his family.

To say of him, as that writer says, that "he was the worst Pontiff that ever filled St. Peter's Chair," can only be justified by an utter ignorance of papal history. You have but to compare him calmly and honestly—your mind stripped of preconceptions—with the wretched and wholly contemptible Innocent VIII whom he succeeded, or with the latter's precursor, the terrible Sixtus IV.

That he was better than these men, morally or ecclesiastically, is not to be pretended; that he was worse—measuring achievement by opportunity—is strenuously to be denied. For the rest, that he was infinitely more gifted and infinitely more a man of affairs is not to be gainsaid by any impartial critic.

If we take him out of the background of history in which he is set, and judge him singly and individually, we behold a man who, as a churchman and Christ's Vicar, fills us with horror and loathing, as a scandalous exception from what we are justified in supposing from his office must have been the rule. Therefore, that he may be judged by the standard of his own time if he is to be judged at all, if we are even to attempt to understand him, have we given a sketch of the careers of those Popes who immediately preceded him, with whom as Vice-Chancellor he was intimately associated, and whose examples were the only papal examples that he possessed.

That this should justify his course we do not pretend. A good churchman in his place would have bethought him of his duty to the Master whose Vicar he was, and would have aimed at the sorely needed reform. But we are not concerned to study him as a good churchman. It is by no means clear that we are concerned to study him as a churchman at all. The Papacy had by this time become far less of an ecclesiastical than a political force; the weapons of the Church were there, but they were being employed for the furtherance not of churchly, but of worldly aims. If the Pontiffs in the pages of this history remembered or evoked their spiritual authority, it was but to employ it as an instrument for the advancement of their temporal schemes. And personal considerations entered largely into these.

Self-aggrandizement, insufferable in a cleric, is an ambition not altogether unpardonable in a temporal prince; and if Alexander aimed at self-aggrandizement and at the founding of a permanent dynasty for his family, he did not lack examples in the careers of those among his predecessors with whom he had been associated.

That the Papacy was Christ's Vicarage was a fact that had long since been obscured by the conception that the Papacy was a kingdom of this world. In striving, then, for worldly eminence by every means in his power, Alexander is no more blameworthy than any other. What, then, remains? The fact that he succeeded better than any of his forerunners. But are we on that account to select him for the special object of our vituperation? The Papacy had tumbled into a slough of materialism in which it was to wallow even after the Reformation had given it pause and warning. Under what obligation was Alexander VI, more than any other Pope, to pull it out of that slough? As he found it, so he carried it on, as much a self-seeker, as much a worldly prince, as much a family man and as little a churchman as any of those who had gone immediately before him.

By the outrageous discrepancy between the Papacy's professed and actual aims it was fast becoming an object of execration, and it is Alexander's misfortune that, coming when he did, he has remained as the type of his class.

The mighty of this world shall never want for detractors. The mean and insignificant, writhing under the consciousness of his shortcomings, ministers to his self-love by vilifying the great that he may lessen the gap between himself and them. To achieve greatness is to achieve enemies. It is to excite envy; and as envy no seed can raise up such a crop of hatred.

Does this need labouring? Have we not abundant instances about us of the vulgar tittle-tattle and scandalous unfounded gossip which, born Heaven alone knows on what back-stairs or in what servants' hall, circulates currently to the detriment of the distinguished in every walk of life? And the more conspicuously great the individual, the greater the incentive to slander him, for the interest of the slander is commensurate with the eminence of the personage assailed.

Such to a great extent is the case of Alexander VI. He was too powerful for the stomachs of many of his contemporaries, and he and his son Cesare had a way of achieving their ends. Since that could not be denied, it remained to inveigh loudly against the means adopted; and with pious uplifting of hands and eyes, to cry, "Shame!" and "Horror!" and "The like has never been heard of!" in wilful blindness to what had been happening at the Vatican for generations.

Later writers take up the tale of it. It is a fine subject about which to make phrases, and the passion for phrase-making will at times outweigh the respect for truth. Thus Villari with his "the worst Pontiff that ever filled St. Peter's Chair," and again, elsewhere, echoing what many a writer has said before him from Guicciardini downwards, in utter and diametric opposition to the true facts of the case: "The announcement of his election was received throughout Italy with universal dismay." To this he adds the ubiquitous story of King Ferrante's bursting into tears at the news—"though never before known to weep for the death of his own children."

Let us pause a moment to contemplate the grief the Neapolitan King. What picture is evoked in your minds by that statement of his bursting into tears at Alexander's election? We see—do we not?—a pious, noble soul, horror-stricken at the sight of the Papacy's corruption; a truly sublime figure, whose tears will surely stand to his credit in heaven; a great heart breaking; a venerable head bowed down with lofty, righteous grief, weeping over the grave of Christian hopes. Such surely is the image we are meant to see by Guicciardini and his many hollow echoers.

Turn we now for corroboration of that noble picture to the history of this same Ferrante. A shock awaits us. We find, in this bastard of the great and brilliant Alfonso a cruel, greedy, covetous monster, so treacherous and so fiendishly brutal that we are compelled to extend him the charity of supposing him to be something less than sane. Let us consider but one of his characteristics. He loved to have his enemies under his own supervision, and he kept them so—the living ones caged and guarded, the dead ones embalmed and habited as in life; and this collection of mummies was his pride and delight. More, and worse could we tell you of him. But—ex pede, Herculem.

This man shed tears we are told. Not another word. It is left to our imagination to paint for us a picture of this weeping; it is left to us to conclude that these precious tears were symbolical of the grief of Italy herself; that the catastrophe that provoked them must have been terrible indeed.

But now that we know what manner of man was this who wept, see how different is the inference that we may draw from his sorrow. Can we still imagine it—as we are desired to do—to have sprung from a lofty, Christian piety? Let us track those tears to their very source, and we shall find it to be compounded of rage and fear.

Ferrante saw trouble ahead of him with Lodovico Sforza, concerning a matter which shall be considered in the next chapter, and not at all would it suit him at such a time that such a Pope as Alexander—who, he had every reason to suppose, would be on the side of Lodovico—should rule in Rome.

So he had set himself, by every means in his power, to oppose Roderigo's election. His rage at the news that all his efforts had been vain, his fear of a man of Roderigo's mettle, and his undoubted dread of the consequences to himself of his frustrated opposition of that man's election, may indeed have loosened the tears of this Ferrante who had not even wept at the death of his own children. We say "may" advisedly; for the matter, from beginning to end, is one of speculation. If we leave it for the realm of fact, we have to ask—Were there any tears at all? Upon what authority rests the statement of the Florentine historian? What, in fact, does he say?

"It is well known that the King of Naples, for all that in public he dissembled the pain it caused him, signified to the queen, his wife, with tears—which were Unusual in him even on the death of his children—that a Pope had been created who would be most pernicious to Italy."

So that, when all is said, Ferrante shed his kingly tears to his wife in private, and to her in private he delivered his opinion of the new Pontiff. How, then, came Guicciardini to know of the matter? True, he says, "It is well known"—meaning that he had those tears upon hearsay. It is, of course, possible that Ferrante's queen may have repeated what passed between herself and the king; but that would surely have been in contravention of the wishes of her husband, who had, be it remembered, "dissembled his grief in public." And Ferrante does not impress one as the sort of husband whose wishes his wife would be bold enough to contravene.

It is surprising that upon no better authority than this should these precious tears of Ferrante's have been crystallized in history.

If this trivial instance has been dealt with at such length it is because, for one reason, it is typical of the foundation of so many of the Borgia legends, and, for another, because when history has been carefully sifted for evidence of the "universal dismay with which the election of Roderigo Borgia was received" King Ferrante's is the only case of dismay that comes through the mesh at all. Therefore was it expedient to examine it minutely.

That "universal dismay"—like the tears of Ferrante—rests upon the word of Guicciardini. He says that "men were filled with dread and horror by this election, because it had been effected by such evil ways [con arte si brutte]; and no less because the nature and condition of the person elected were largely known to many."

Guicciardini is to be read with the greatest caution and reserve when he deals with Rome. His bias against, and his enmity of, the Papacy are as obvious as they are notorious, and in his endeavours to bring it as much as possible into discredit he does not even spare his generous patrons, the Medicean Popes—Leo X and Clement VII. If he finds it impossible to restrain his invective against these Pontiffs, who heaped favours and honours upon him, what but virulence can be expected of him when he writes of Alexander VI? He is largely to blame for the flagrant exaggeration of many of the charges brought against the Borgias; that he hated them we know, and that when he wrote of them he dipped his golden Tuscan pen in vitriol and set down what he desired the world to believe rather than what contemporary documents would have revealed to him, we can prove here and now from that one statement of his which we have quoted.

Who were the men who were filled with dismay, horror, or dread at Roderigo's election?

The Milanese? No. For we know that Cardinal Ascanio Sforza, the Duke of Milan's brother, was the most active worker in favour of Roderigo's election, and that this same election was received and celebrated in Milan with public rejoicings.

The Florentines? No. For the Medici were friendly to the House of Borgia, and we know that they welcomed the election, and that from Florence Manfredi—the Ferrarese ambassador—wrote home: "It is said he will be a glorious Pontiff" ("Dicesi che sará glorioso Pontefice").

Were Venice, Genoa, Mantua, Siena, or Lucca dismayed by this election? Surely not, if the superlatively laudatory congratulations of their various ambassadors are of any account.

Venice confessed that "a better pastor could not have been found for the Church," since he had proved himself "a chief full of experience and an excellent cardinal."

Genoa said that "his merit lay not in having been elected, but in having been desired."

Mantua declared that it "had long awaited the pontificate of one who, during forty years, had rendered himself, by his wisdom and justice, capable of any office."

Siena expressed its joy at seeing the summit of eminence attained by a Pope solely upon his merits—"Pervenuto alla dignitá pontificale meramente per meriti proprii."

Lucca praised the excellent choice made, and extolled the accomplishments, the wisdom, and experience of the Pontiff.

Not dismay, then, but actual rejoicing must have been almost universal in Italy on the election of Pope Alexander VI. And very properly—always considering the Pontificate as the temporal State it was then being accounted; for Roderigo's influence was vast, his intelligence was renowned, and had again and again been proved, and his administrative talents and capacity for affairs were known to all. He was well-born, cultured, of a fine and noble presence, and his wealth was colossal, comprising the archbishoprics of Valencia and Porto, the bishoprics of Majorca, Carthage, Agria, the abbeys of Subiaco, the Monastery of Our Lady of Bellefontaine, the deaconry of Sancta Maria in Via Lata, and his offices of Vice-Chancellor and Dean of Holy Church.

We are told that he gained his election by simony. It is very probable that he did. But the accusation has never been categorically established, and until that happens it would be well to moderate the vituperation hurled at him. Charges of that simony are common; conclusive proof there is none. We find Giacomo Trotti, the French ambassador in Milan, writing to the Duke of Ferrara a fortnight after Roderigo's election that "the Papacy has been sold by simony and a thousand rascalities, which is a thing ignominious and detestable."

Ignominious and detestable indeed, if true; but be it remembered that Trotti was the ambassador of France, whose candidate, backed by French influence and French gold, as we have seen, was della Rovere; and, even if his statement was true, the "ignominious and detestable thing" was at least no novelty. Yet Guicciardini, treating of this matter, says: "He gained the Pontificate owing to discord between the Cardinals Ascanio Sforza and Giuliano di San Pietro in Vincoli; and still more because, in a manner without precedent in that age [con esempio nuovo in quella etá] he openly bought the votes of many cardinals, some with money, some with promises of his offices and benefices, which were very great."

Again Guicciardini betrays his bias by attempting to render Roderigo's course, assuming it for the moment to be truly represented, peculiarly odious by this assertion that it was without precedent in that age.

Without precedent! What of the accusations of simony against Innocent VIII, which rest upon a much sounder basis than these against Alexander, and what of those against Sixtus IV? Further, if a simoniacal election was unprecedented, what of Lorenzo Valla's fierce indictment of simony—for which he so narrowly escaped the clutches of the Inquisition some sixty years before this date?

Simony was rampant at the time, and it is the rankest hypocrisy to make this outcry against Alexander's uses of it, and to forget the others.

Whether he really was elected by simony or not depends largely—so far as the evidence available goes—upon what we are to consider as simony. If payment in the literal sense was made or promised, then unquestionably simony there was. But this, though often asserted, still awaits proof. If the conferring of the benefices vacated by a cardinal on his elevation to the Pontificate is to be considered simony, then there never was a Pope yet against whom the charge could not be levelled and established.

Consider that by his election to the Pontificate his Archbishoprics, offices, nay, his very house itself—which at the time of which we write it was customary to abandon to pillage—are vacated; and remember that, as Pope, they are now in his gift and that they must of necessity be bestowed upon somebody. In a time in which Pontiffs are imbued with a spiritual sense of their office and duties, they will naturally make such bestowals upon those whom they consider best fitted to use them for the greater honour and glory of God. But we are dealing with no such spiritual golden age as that when we deal with the Cinquecento, as we have already seen; and, therefore, all that we can expect of a Pope is that he should bestow the preferment he has vacated upon those among the cardinals whom he believes to be devoted to himself. Considering his election in a temporal sense, it is natural that he should behave as any other temporal prince; that he should remember those to whom he owes the Pontificate, and that he should reward them suitably. Alexander VI certainly pursued such a course, and the greatest profit from his election was derived by the Cardinal Sforza who—as Roderigo himself admitted—had certainly exerted all his influence with the Sacred College to gain him the Pontificate. Alexander gave him the vacated Vice-Chancellorship (for which, when all is said, Ascanio Sforza was excellently fitted), his vacated palace on Banchi Vecchi, the town of Nepi, and the bishopric of Agri.

To Orsini he gave the Church of Carthage and the legation of Marche; to Colonna the Abbey of Subiaco; to Savelli the legation of Perugia (from which he afterwards recalled him, not finding him suited to so difficult a charge); to Raffaele Riario went Spanish benefices worth four thousand ducats yearly; to Sanseverino Roderigo's house in Milan, whilst he consented that Sanseverino's nephew—known as Fracassa—should enter the service of the

Church with a condotta of a hundred men-at-arms and a stipend of thirteen thousand ducats yearly.

Guicciardini says of all this that Ascanio Sforza induced many of the cardinals "to that abominable contract, and not only by request and persuasion, but by example; because, corrupt and of an insatiable appetite for riches, he bargained for himself, as the reward of so much turpitude, the Vice-Chancellorships, churches, fortresses [the very plurals betray the frenzy of exaggeration dictated by his malice] and his [Roderigo's] palace in Rome full of furniture of great value."

What possible proof can Guicciardini have—what possible proof can there be—of such a "bargain"? It rests upon purest assumption formed after those properties had changed hands—Ascanio being rewarded by them for his valuable services, and, also—so far as the Vice-Chancellorship was concerned—being suitably preferred. To say that Ascanio received them in consequence of a "bargain" and as the price of his vote and electioneering services is not only an easy thing to say, but it is the obvious thing for any one to say who aims at defaming.

It is surprising that we should find in Guicciardini no mention of the four mule-loads of silver removed before the election from Cardinal Roderigo's palace on Banchi Vecchi to Cardinal Ascanio's palace in Trastevere. This is generally alleged to have been part of the price of Ascanio's services. Whether it was so, or whether, as has also been urged, it was merely removed to save it from the pillaging by the mob of the palace of the cardinal elected to the Pontificate, the fact is interesting as indicating in either case Cardinal Roderigo's assurance of his election.

M. Yriarte does not hesitate to say: "We know to-day, by the dispatches of Valori, the narrative of Girolamo Porzio, and the Diarium of Burchard, the Master of Ceremonies, each of the stipulations made with the electors whose votes were bought."

Now whilst we do know from Valori and Porzio what benefices Alexander actually conferred, we do not know, nor could they possibly have told us, what stipulations had been made which these benefices were insinuated to satisfy.

Burchard's Diarium might be of more authority on this subject, for Burchard was the Master of Ceremonies at the Vatican; but, unfortunately for the accuracy of M. Yriarte's statement, Burchard is silent on the subject, for the excellent reason that there is no diary for the period under consideration. Burchard's narrative is interrupted on the death of Innocent VIII, on July 12, and not resumed until December 2, when it is not retrospective.

There is, it is true, the Diarium of Infessura. But that is of no more authority on such a matter than the narrative of Porzio or the letters of Valori.

Lord Acton—in his essay upon this subject—has not been content to rest the imputation of simony upon such grounds as satisfied M. Yriarte. He has realized that the only testimony of any real value in such a case would be the actual evidence of such cardinals as might be willing to bear witness to the attempt to bribe them. And he takes it for granted—as who would not at this time of day, and in view of such positive statements as abound?—that such evidence has been duly collected; thus, he tells us confidently that the charge rests upon the evidence of those cardinals who refused Roderigo's bribes.

That it most certainly does not. If it did there would be an end to the matter, and so much ink would not have been spilled over it; but no single cardinal has left any such evidence as Lord Acton supposes and alleges. It suffices to consider that, according to the only evidences available—the Casanatense Codices(1) and the dispatches of that same Valori(2) whom M. Yriarte so confidently cites, Roderigo Borgia's election was unanimous. Who, then, were these cardinals who refused his bribes? Or are we to suppose that, notwithstanding that refusal—a refusal which we may justifiably suppose to have been a scandalized and righteously indignant one—they still afforded him their votes?

1 "...essendo concordi tutti i cardinali, quasi da contrari voti rivolti tutti in favore di uno solo, crearono lui sommo ponteflce" (Casanatense MSS). See P. Leonetti, Alessandro VI. 2 "Fu pubblicato il Cardinale Vice-Cancelliere in Sommo Pontefice Alessandro VI(to) nuncupato, el quale dopo una lunga contentione fu creato omnium consensum—ne ii manco un solo voto" (Valori's letter to the Otto di Pratica, August 12, 1492). See Supplement to Appendix in E. Thuasne's edition of Burchard's Diarium.

This charge of simony was levelled with the object of making Alexander VI appear singularly heinous. So much has that object engrossed and blinded those inspired by it, that, of itself, it betrays them. Had their horror been honest, had it sprung from true principles, had it been born of any but a desire to befoul and bespatter at all costs Roderigo Borgia, it is not against him that they would have hurled their denunciations, but against the whole College of Cardinals which took part in the sacrilege and which included three future Popes.(1)

1 *Cardinals Piccolomini, de'Medici, and Giuliano della Rovere.*

Assuming not only that there was simony, but that it was on as wholesale a scale as was alleged, and that for gold—coined or in the form of benefices—Roderigo bought the cardinal's votes, what then? He bought them, true. But they—they sold him their sacred trust, their duty to their God, their priestly honour, their holy vows. For the gold he offered them they bartered these. So much admitted, then surely, in that transaction, those cardinals were the prostitutes! The man who bought so much of them, at least, was on no baser level than were they. Yet invective singles him out for its one object, and so betrays the aforethought malice of its inspiration.

Our quarrel is with that; with that, and with those writers who have taken Alexander's simony for granted—eagerly almost—for the purpose of heaping odium upon him by making him appear a scandalous exception to the prevailing rule.

If, nevertheless, we hold, as we have said, that simony probably did take place, we do so, not so much upon the inconclusive evidence of the fact, as upon the circumstance that it had become almost an established custom to purchase the tiara, and that Roderigo Borgia—since his ambition clearly urged him to the Pontificate—would have been an exception had he refrained.

It may seem that to have disputed so long to conclude by admitting so much is no better than a waste of labour. Not so, we hope. Our aim has been to correct the adjustment of the focus and properly to trim the light in which Roderigo Borgia is to be viewed, to the end that you may see him as he was—neither better nor worse—the creature of his times, of his environment, and of the system in which he was reared and trained. Thus shall you also get a clearer view of his son Cesare, when presently he takes the stage more prominently.

During the seventeen days of the interregnum between the death of Innocent and the election of Alexander the wild scenes usual to such seasons had been taking place in Rome; and, notwithstanding the Cardinal-Chamberlain's prompt action in seizing the gates and bridges, and the patrols' endeavours to maintain order, crime was unfettered to such an extent that some 220 murders are computed to have taken place—giving the terrible average of thirteen a day.

It was a very natural epilogue to the lax rule of the lethargic Innocent. One of the first acts of Alexander's reign was to deal summarily with this lawlessness. He put down violence with a hard hand that knew no mercy. He razed to the ground the house of a murderer caught red-handed, and hanged him above the ruins, and so dealt generally that such order came to prevail as had never before been known in Rome.

Infessura tells us how, in the very month of his election, he appointed inspectors of prisons and four commissioners to administer justice, and that he himself gave audience on Tuesdays and settled disputes, concluding, "et justitiam mirabili modo facere coepit."

He paid all salaries promptly—a striking departure, it would seem, from what had been usual under his predecessor—and the effect of his improved and strenuous legislation was shortly seen in the diminished prices of commodities.

He was crowned Pope on August 6, on the steps of the Basilica of St. Peter, by the Cardinal-Archdeacon Piccolomini. The ceremony was celebrated with a splendour worthy of the splendid figure that was its centre. Through the eyes of Michele Ferno—despite his admission that he is unable to convey a worthy notion of the spectacle—you may see the gorgeous procession to the Lateran in which Alexander VI showed himself to the applauding Romans; the multitude of richly adorned men, gay and festive; the seven hundred priests and prelates, with their familiars the splendid cavalcade of knights and nobles of Rome; the archers and Turkish horsemen, and the Palatine Guard, with its great halberds and flashing shields; the twelve white horses, with their golden bridles, led by footmen; and then Alexander himself on a snow-white horse, "serene of brow and of majestic dignity," his hand uplifted—the Fisherman's Ring upon its forefinger—to bless the kneeling populace. The chronicler flings into superlatives when he comes to praise the personal beauty of the man, his physical vigour and health, "which go to increase the veneration shown him."

Thus in the brilliant sunshine of that Italian August, amid the plaudits of assembled Rome, amid banners and flowers, music and incense, the flash of steel and the blaze of decorations with the Borgian arms everywhere displayed—or, a grazing steer gules—Alexander VI passes to the Vatican, the aim and summit of his vast ambition.

Friends and enemies alike have sung the splendours of that coronation, and the Bull device—as you can imagine—plays a considerable part in those verses, be they paeans or lampoons. The former allude to Borgia as "the Bull," from the majesty and might of the animal that was displayed upon their shield; the latter render it the subject of much scurrilous invective, to which it lends itself as readily. And thereafter, in almost all verse of their epoch, writers ever say "the Bull" when they mean the Borgia.

CHAPTER IV
BORGIA ALLIANCES

At the time of his father's election to the throne of St. Peter, Cesare Borgia—now in his eighteenth year—was still at the University of Pisa.

It is a little odd, considering the great affection for his children which was ever one of Roderigo's most conspicuous characteristics, that he should not have ordered Cesare to Rome at once, to share in the general rejoicings. It has been suggested that Alexander wished to avoid giving scandal by the presence of his children at such a time. But that again looks like a judgement formed upon modern standards, for by the standards of his day one cannot conceive that he would have given very much scandal; moreover, it is to be remembered that Lucrezia and Giuffredo, at least, were in Rome at the time of their father's election to the tiara.

However that may be, Cesare did not quit Pisa until August of that year 1492, and even then not for Rome, but for Spoleto—in accordance with his father's orders—where he took up his residence in the castle. Thence he wrote a letter to Piero de'Medici, which is interesting, firstly, as showing the good relations prevailing between them; secondly, as refuting a story in Guicciardini, wherewith that historian, ready, as ever, to belittle the Borgias, attempts to show him cutting a poor figure. He tells us(1) that, whilst at Pisa, Cesare had occasion to make an appeal to Piero de'Medici in the matter of a criminal case connected with one of his familiars; that he went to Florence and waited several hours in vain for an audience, whereafter he returned to Pisa "accounting himself despised and not a little injured."

1 Istoria d'Italia, tom. V.

No doubt Guicciardini is as mistaken in this as in many another matter, for the letter written from Spoleto expresses his regret that, on the occasion of his passage through Florence (on his way from Pisa to Spoleto), he should not have had time to visit Piero, particularly as there was a matter upon which he desired urgently to consult with him. He recommends to Piero his faithful Remolino, whose ambition it is to occupy the chair of canon law at the University of Pisa, and begs his good offices in that connection.

That Juan Vera, Cesare's preceptor and the bearer of that letter, took back a favourable answer is highly probable, for in Fabroni's Hist. Acad. Pisan we find this Remolino duly established as a lecturer on canon law in the following year.

The letter is further of interest as showing Cesare's full consciousness of the importance of his position; its tone and its signature—"your brother, Cesar de Borgia, Elect of Valencia"—being such as were usual between princes.

The two chief aims of Alexander VI, from the very beginning of his pontificate, were to re-establish the power of the Church, which was then the most despised of the temporal States of Italy, and to promote the fortune of his children. Already on the very day of his coronation he conferred upon Cesare the bishopric of Valencia, whose revenues amounted to an annual yield of sixteen thousand ducats. For the time being, however, he had his hands very full of other matters, and it behoved him to move slowly at first and with the extremest caution.

The clouds of war were lowering heavily over Italy when Alexander came to St. Peter's throne, and it was his first concern to find for himself a safe position against the coming of the threatening storm. The chief menace to the general peace was Lodovico Maria Sforza, surnamed Il Moro,(1) who sat as regent for his nephew, Duke Gian Galeazzo, upon the throne of Milan. That regency he had usurped from Gian Galeazzo's mother, and he was now in a fair way to usurp the throne itself. He kept his nephew virtually a prisoner in the Castle of Pavia, together with his young bride, Isabella of Aragon, who had been sent thither by her father, the Duke of Calabria, heir to the crown of Naples.

> *1 Touching Lodovico Maria's by-name of "Il Moro"—which is generally translated as "The Moor," whilst in one writer we have found him mentioned as "Black Lodovico," Benedetto Varchi's explanation (in his Storia Fiorentina) may be of interest. He tells us that Lodovico was not so called on account of any swarthiness of complexion, as is supposed by Guicciardini, because, on the contrary, he was fair; nor yet on account of his device, showing a Moorish squire, who, brush in hand, dusts the gown of a young woman in regal apparel, with the motto, "Per Italia nettar d'ogni bruttura"; this device of the Moor, he tells us, was a rébus or pun upon the word "moro," which also means the mulberry, and was so meant by Lodovico. The mulberry burgeons at the end of*

winter and blossoms very early. Thus Lodovico symbolized his
own prudence and readiness to seize opportunity betimes.

Gian Galeazzo thus bestowed, Lodovico Maria went calmly about the business of governing, like one who did not mean to relinquish the regency save to become duke. But it happened that a boy was born to the young prisoners at Pavia, whereupon, spurred perhaps into activity by this parenthood and stimulated by the thought that they had now a son's interests to fight for as well as their own, they made appeal to King Ferrante of Naples that he should enforce his grandson-in-law's rights to the throne of Milan. King Ferrante could desire nothing better, for if his grandchild and her husband reigned in Milan, and by his favour and contriving, great should be his influence in the North of Italy. Therefore he stood their friend.

Matters were at this stage when Alexander VI ascended the papal throne.

This election gave Ferrante pause, for, as we have seen, he had schemed for a Pope devoted to his interests, who would stand by him in the coming strife, and his schemes were rudely shaken now. Whilst he was still cogitating the matter of his next move, the wretched Francesco Cibo (Pope Innocent's son) offered to sell the papal fiefs of Cervetri and Anguillara, which had been made over to him by his father, to Gentile Orsini—the head of his powerful house. And Gentile purchased them under a contract signed at the palace of Cardinal Giuliano della Rovere, on September 3, for the sum of forty thousand ducats advanced him by Ferrante.

Alexander protested strongly against this illegal transaction, for Cervetri and Anguillara were fiefs of the Church, and neither had Cibo the right to sell nor Orsini the right to buy them. Moreover, that they should be in the hands of a powerful vassal of Naples such as Orsini suited the Pope as little as it suited Lodovico Maria Sforza. It stirred the latter into taking measures against the move he feared Ferrante might make to enforce Gian Galeazzo's claims.

Lodovico Maria went about this with that sly shrewdness so characteristic of him, so well symbolized by his mulberry badge—a humorous shrewdness almost, which makes him one of the most delightful rogues in history, just as he was one of the most debonair and cultured. He may indeed be considered as one of the types of the subtle, crafty, selfish politician that was the ideal of Macchiavelli.

You see him, then, effacing the tight-lipped, cunning smile from his comely face and pointing out to Venice with a grave, sober countenance how little it can suit her to have the Neapolitan Spaniards ruffling it in the north, as must happen if Ferrante has his way with Milan. The truth of this was so obvious that Venice made haste to enter into a league with him, and into the camp thus formed came, for their own sakes, Mantua, Ferrara, and Siena. The league was powerful enough thus to cause Ferrante to think twice before he took up the cudgels for Gian Galeazzo. If Lodovico could include the Pope, the league's might would be so paralysing that Ferrante would cease to think at all about his grandchildren's affairs.

Foreseeing this, Ferrante had perforce to dry the tears Guicciardini has it that he shed, and, replacing them by a smile, servile and obsequious, repaired, hat in hand, to protest his friendship for the Pope's Holiness.

And so, in December of 1492, came the Prince of Altamura—Ferrante's second son—to Rome to lay his father's homage at the feet of the Pontiff, and at the same time to implore his Holiness to refuse the King of Hungary the dispensation the latter was asking of the Holy See, to enable him to repudiate his wife, Donna Leonora—Ferrante's daughter.

Altamura was received in Rome and sumptuously entertained by the Cardinal Giuliano della Rovere. This cardinal had failed, as we have seen, to gain the Pontificate for himself, despite the French influence by which he had been supported. Writhing under his defeat, and hating the man who had defeated him with a hatred so bitter and venomous that the imprint of it is on almost every act of his life—from the facilities he afforded for the assignment to Orsini of the papal fiefs that Cibo had to sell—he was already scheming for the overthrow of Alexander. To this end he needed great and powerful friends; to this end had he lent himself to the Cibo-Orsini transaction; to this end did he manifest himself the warm well-wisher of Ferrante; to this end did he cordially welcome the latter's son and envoy, and promise his support to Ferrante's petition.

But the Holy Father was by no means as anxious for the friendship of the old wolf of Naples. The matter of the King of Hungary was one that required consideration, and, meanwhile, he may have hinted slyly there was between Naples and Rome a little matter of two fiefs to be adjusted.

Thus his most shrewd Holiness thought to gain a little time, and in that time he might look about him and consider what alliances would suit his interests best.

At this Cardinal della Rovere, in high dudgeon, flung out of Rome and away to his Castle of Ostia to fortify—to wield the sword of St. Paul, since he had missed the keys of St. Peter. It was a shrewd move. He foresaw the injured dignity of the Spanish House of Naples, and Ferrante's wrath at the Pope's light treatment of him and apathy for his interests; and the cardinal knew that with Ferrante were allied the mighty houses of Colonna and Orsini. Thus, by his political divorcement from the Holy See, he flung in his lot with theirs, hoping for red war and the deposition of Alexander.

But surely he forgot Milan and Lodovico Maria, whose brother, Ascanio Sforza, was at the Pope's elbow, the energetic friend to whose efforts Alexander owed the tiara, and who was therefore hated by della Rovere perhaps as bitterly as Alexander himself.

Alexander went calmly about the business of fortifying the Vatican and the Castle of Sant' Angelo, and gathering mercenaries into his service. And, lest any attempt should be made upon his life when he went abroad, he did so with an imposing escort of men-at-arms; which so vexed and fretted King Ferrante, that he did not omit to comment upon it in scathing terms in a letter that presently we shall consider. For the rest, the Pope's Holiness preserved an unruffled front in the face of the hostile preparations that were toward in the kingdom of Naples, knowing that he could check them when he chose to lift his finger and beckon the Sforza into alliance. And presently Naples heard an alarming rumour that Lodovico Maria had, in fact, made overtures to the Pope, and that the Pope had met these advances to the extent of betrothing his daughter Lucrezia to Giovanni Sforza, Lord of Pesaro and cousin to Lodovico.

So back to the Vatican went the Neapolitan envoys with definite proposals of an alliance to be cemented by a marriage between Giuffredo Borgia—aged twelve—and Ferrante's granddaughter Lucrezia of Aragon. The Pope, with his plans but half-matured as yet, temporized, was evasive, and continued to arm and to recruit. At last, his arrangements completed, he abruptly broke off his negotiations with Naples, and on April 25, 1493, publicly proclaimed that he had joined the northern league.

The fury of Ferrante, who realized that he had been played with and outwitted, was expressed in a rabid letter to his ambassador at the Court of Spain.

"This Pope," he wrote, "leads a life that is the abomination of all, without respect for the seat he occupies. He cares for nothing save to aggrandize his children, by fair means or foul, and this is his sole desire. From the beginning of his Pontificate he has done nothing but disturb the peace, molesting everybody, now in one way, now in another. Rome is more full of soldiers than of priests, and when he goes abroad it is with troops of men-at-arms about him, with helmets on their heads and lances by their sides, all his thoughts being given to war and to our hurt; nor does he overlook anything that can be used against us, not only inciting in France the Prince of Salerno and other of our rebels, but befriending every bad character in Italy whom he deems our enemy; and in all things he proceeds with the fraud and dissimulation natural to him, and to make money he sells even the smallest office and preferment."

Thus Ferrante of the man whose friendship he had been seeking some six weeks earlier, and who had rejected his advances. It is as well to know the precise conditions under which that letter was indited, for extracts from it are too often quoted against Alexander. These conditions known, and known the man who wrote it, the letter's proper value is at once apparent.

It was Ferrante's hope, and no doubt the hope of Giuliano della Rovere, that the King of Spain would lend an ear to these grievances, and move in the matter of attempting to depose Alexander; but an event more important than any other in the whole history of Spain—or of Europe, for that matter— was at the moment claiming its full attention, and the trifling affairs of the King of Naples—trifling by comparison—went all unheeded. For this was the year in which the Genoese navigator, Cristofero Colombo, returned to tell of the new and marvellous world he had discovered beyond the seas, and Ferdinand and Isabella were addressing an appeal to the Pope—as Ruler of the World—to establish them in the possession of the discovered continent. Whereupon the Pope drew a line from pole to pole, and granted to Spain the dominion over all lands discovered, or to be discovered, one hundred miles westward of Cape Verde and the Azores.

And thus Ferrante's appeal to Spain against a Pope who showed himself so ready and complaisant a friend to Spain went unheeded by Ferdinand and Isabella. And what time the Neapolitan nursed his bitter chagrin, the alliance between Rome and Milan was consolidated by the marriage of Lucrezia Borgia to Giovanni Sforza, the comely weakling who was Lord of Pesaro and Cotignola.

Lucrezia Borgia's story has been told elsewhere; her rehabilitation has been undertaken by a great historian(1) among others, and all serious-minded students must be satisfied at this time of day that the Lucrezia Borgia of Hugo's tragedy is a creature of fiction, bearing little or no resemblance to the poor lady who was a pawn in the ambitious game played by her father and her brother Cesare, before she withdrew to Ferrara, where eventually she died in child-birth in her forty-first year. We know that she left the duke, her husband, stricken with a grief that was shared by his subjects, to whom she had so deeply endeared herself by her exemplary life and loving rule.(2)

1 *Ferdinand Gregorovius, Lucrezia Borgia.*

2 *See, inter alia, the letters of Alfonso d'Este and Giovanni Gonzaga on her death, quoted in Gregorovius, Lucrezia Borgia.*

Later, in the course of this narrative, where she crosses the story of her brother Cesare, it will be necessary to deal with some of the revolting calumnies concerning her that were circulated, and, in passing, shall be revealed the sources of the malice that inspired them and the nature of the evidence upon which they rest, to the eternal shame alike of those pretended writers of fact and those avowed writers of fiction who, as dead to scruples as to chivalry, have not hesitated to make her serve their base melodramatic or pornographic ends.

At present, however, there is no more than her first marriage to be recorded. She was fourteen years of age at the time, and, like all the Borgias, of a rare personal beauty, with blue eyes and golden hair. Twice before, already, had she entered into betrothal contracts with gentlemen of her father's native Spain; but his ever-soaring ambition had caused him successively to cancel both those unfulfilled contracts. A husband worthy of the daughter of Cardinal Roderigo Borgia was no longer worthy of the daughter of Pope Alexander VI, for whom an alliance must now be sought among Italy's princely houses. And so she came to be bestowed upon the Lord of Pesaro, with a dowry of 30,000 ducats.

Her nuptials were celebrated in the Vatican on June 12, 1493, in the splendid manner worthy of the rank of all concerned and of the reputation for magnificence which the Borgia had acquired. That night the Pope gave a supper-party, at which were present some ten cardinals and a number of ladies and gentlemen of Rome, besides the ambassadors of Ferrara, Venice, Milan, and France. There was vocal and instrumental music, a comedy was performed, the ladies danced, and they appear to have carried their gaieties well into the dawn. Hardly the sort of scene for which the Vatican was the ideal stage. Yet at the time it should have given little or no scandal. But what a scandal was there not, shortly afterwards, in connection with it, and how that scandal was heaped up later, by stories so revolting of the doings of that night that one is appalled at the minds that conceived them and the credulity that accepted them.

Infessura writes of what he heard, and he writes venomously, as he betrays by the bitter sarcasm with which he refers to the fifty silver cups filled with sweetmeats which the Pope tossed into the laps of ladies present at the earlier part of the celebration. "He did it," says Infessura, "to the greater honour and glory of Almighty God and the Church of Rome." Beyond that he ventures into no great detail, checking himself betimes, however, with a suggested motive for reticence a thousand times worse than any formal accusation. Thus: "Much else is said, of which I do not write, because either it is not true, or, if true, incredible."(1)

1 *"Et multa alia dicta sunt; que hic non scribo, que aut non sunt; vel si sunt, incredibilia" (Infessura, Diarium).*

It is amazing that the veil which Infessura drew with those words should have been pierced—not indeed by the cold light of fact, but by the hot eye of prurient imagination; amazing that he should be quoted at all—he who was not present—considering that we have the testimony of what did take place from the pen of an eye-witness, in a letter from Gianandrea Boccaccio, the ambassador of Ferrara, to his master.

At the end of his letter, which describes the proceedings and the wedding-gifts and their presentation, he tells us how the night was spent. "Afterwards the ladies danced, and, as an interlude, a worthy comedy was performed, with much music and singing, the Pope and all the rest of us being present throughout. What else shall I add? It would make a long letter. The whole night was spent in this manner; let your lordship decide whether well or ill."

Is not that sufficient to stop the foul mouth of inventive slander? What need to suggest happenings unspeakable? Yet it is the fashion to quote the last sentence above from Boccaccio's letter in the original—"totam noctem comsumpsimus; judicet modo Ex(ma.) Dominatio vestra si bene o male"—as though decency forbade its translation; and at once this poisonous reticence does its work, and the imagination—and not only that of the unlettered—is fired, and all manner of abominations are speculatively conceived.

Infessura, being absent, says that the comedies performed were licentious ("lascive"). But what comedies of that age were not? It was an age which had not yet invented modesty, as we understand it. That Boccaccio, who was present, saw nothing unusual in the comedy—there was only one, according to him—is proved by his description of it as "worthy" ("una degna commedia.")

M. Yriarte on this same subject(1) is not only petty, but grotesque. He chooses to relate the incident from the point of view of Infessura, whom, by the way, he translates with an amazing freedom,(2) and he makes bold to add regarding Gianandrea Boccaccio that: "It must also be said that the ambassador of Ferrara, either because he did not see everything, or because he was less austere than Infessura, was not shocked by the comedies, etc." ("soit qu'il n'ait pas tout vu, soit qu'il ait été moins austère qu'Infessura, n'est pas choqué....")

1 *La Vie de César Borgia.*

2 Thus in the matter of the fifty silver cups tossed by the Pope into the ladies' laps, "sinum" is the word employed by Infessura—a word which has too loosely been given its general translation of "bosom," ignoring that it equally means "lap" and that "lap" it obviously means in this instance. M. Yriarte, however, goes a step further, and prefers to translate it as "corsage," which at once, and unpleasantly, falsifies the picture; and he adds matter to dot the I's to an extent certainly not warranted even by Infessura.

M. Yriarte, you observe, does not scruple to opine that Boccaccio, who was present, did not see everything; but he has no doubt that Infessura, who was not present, and who wrote from "hearsay," missed nothing.

Alas! Too much of the history of the Borgias has been written in this spirit, and the discrimination in the selection of authorities has ever been with a view to obtaining the more sensational rather than the more truthful narrative.

Although it is known that Cesare came to Rome in the early part of 1493—for his presence there is reported by Gianandrea Boccaccio in March of that year—there is no mention of him at this time in connection with his sister's wedding. Apparently, then, he was not present, although it is impossible to suggest where he might have been at the time.

Boccaccio draws a picture of him in that letter, which is worthy of attention, "On the day before yesterday I found Cesare at home in Trastevere. He was on the point of setting out to go hunting, and entirely in secular habit; that is to say, dressed in silk and armed. Riding together, we talked a while. I am among his most intimate acquaintances. He is man of great talent and of an excellent nature; his manners are those of the son of a great prince; above everything, he is joyous and light-hearted. He is very modest, much superior to, and of a much finer appearance than, his brother the Duke of Gandia, who also is not short of natural gifts. The archbishop never had any inclination for the priesthood. But his benefice yields him over 16,000 ducats."

It may not be amiss—though perhaps no longer very necessary, after what has been written—to say a word at this stage on the social position of bastards in the fifteenth and sixteenth centuries, to emphasize the fact that no stigma attached to Cesare Borgia or to any other member of his father's family on the score of the illegitimacy of their birth.

It is sufficient to consider the marriages they contracted to perceive that, however shocking the circumstances may appear to modern notions, the circumstance of their father being a Pope not only cannot have been accounted extraordinarily scandalous (if scandalous at all) but, on the contrary, rendered them eligible for alliances even princely.

In the fifteenth and sixteenth centuries we see the bastard born of a noble, as noble as his father, displaying his father's arms without debruisement and enjoying his rank and inheritance unchallenged on the score of his birth, even though that inheritance should be a throne—as witness Lucrezia's husband Giovanni, who, though a bastard of the house of Sforza, succeeded, nevertheless, his father in the Tyranny of Pesaro and Cotignola.

Later we shall see this same Lucrezia, her illegitimacy notwithstanding, married into the noble House of Este and seated upon the throne of Ferrara. And before then we shall have seen the bastard Cesare married to a daughter of the royal House of Navarre. Already we have seen the bastard Francesco Cibo take to wife the daughter of the great Lorenzo de'Medici, and we have seen the bastard Girolamo Riario married to Caterina Sforza—a natural daughter of the ducal House of Milan—and we have seen the pair installed in the Tyranny of Imola and Forli. A score of other instances might be added; but these should suffice.

The matter calls for the making of no philosophies, craves no explaining, and, above all, needs no apology. It clears itself. The fifteenth and sixteenth centuries—more just than our own more enlightened times—attributed no shame to the men and women born out of wedlock, saw no reason—as no reason is there, Christian or Pagan—why they should suffer for a condition that was none of their contriving.

To mention it may be of help in visualizing and understanding that direct and forceful epoch, and may even suggest some lenience in considering a Pope's carnal paternity. To those to whom the point of view of the Renaissance does not promptly suggest itself from this plain statement of fact, all unargued as we leave it, we recommend a perusal of Gianpietro de Crescenzi's Il Nobile Romano.

The marriage of Lucrezia Borgia to Giovanni Sforza tightened the relations between the Pope and Milan, as the Pope intended. Meanwhile, however, the crafty and mistrustful Lodovico, having no illusions as to the true values of his allies, and realizing them to be self-seekers like himself, with interests that were fundamentally different from his own, perceived that they were likely only to adhere to him for just so long as it suited their own ends. He bethought him, therefore, of looking about him for other means by which to crush the power of Naples. France was casting longing eyes upon Italy, and it seemed to Lodovico that in France was a ready catspaw. Charles VIII, as the representative of the House of Anjou, had a certain meagre claim upon the throne of Naples; if he could be induced to ride south, lance on thigh, and press that claim there would be an end to the dominion of the House of Aragon, and so an end to Lodovico's fears of a Neapolitan interference with his own occupation of the throne of Milan.

To an ordinary schemer that should have been enough; but as a schemer Lodovico was wholly extraordinary. His plans grew in the maturing, and took in side-issues, until he saw that Naples should be to Charles VIII as the cheese within the mouse-trap. Let his advent into Italy to break the power of Naples be free and open; but, once within, he should find Milan and the northern allies between himself and his retreat, and Lodovico's should it be to bring him to his knees. Thus schemed Lodovico to shiver, first Naples and then France, before hurling the latter back across the Alps. A daring, bold, and yet simple plan of action. And what a power in Italy should not Lodovico derive from its success!

Forthwith he got secretly to work upon it, sending his invitation to Charles to come and make good his claim to Naples, offering the French troops free passage through his territory.(1) And in the character of his invitation he played upon the nature of malformed, ambitious Charles, whose brain was stuffed with romance and chivalric rhodomontades. The conquest of Naples was an easy affair, no more than a step in the glorious enterprise that awaited the French king, for from Naples he could cross to engage the Turk, and win back the Holy Sepulchre, thus becoming a second Charles the Great.

1 See Corlo, Storia di Milano, and Lodovico's letter to Charles VIII, quoted therein, lib. vii.

Thus Lodovico Maria the crafty, to dazzle Charles the romantic, and to take the bull of impending invasion by the very horns.

We have seen the failure of the appeal to Spain against the Pope made by the King of Naples. To that failure was now added the tightening of Rome's relations with Milan by the marriage between Lucrezia Borgia and Giovanni Sforza, and Ferrante—rumours of a French invasion, with Naples for its objective being already in the air—realized that nothing remained him but to make another attempt to conciliate the Pope's Holiness. And this time he went about his negotiations in a manner better calculated to serve his ends, since his need was grown more urgent. He sent the Prince of Altamura again to Rome for the ostensible purpose of settling the vexatious matter of Cervetri and Anguillara and making alliance with the Holy Father, whilst behind Altamura was the Neapolitan army ready to move upon Rome should the envoy fail this time.

But on the terms now put forward, Alexander was willing to negotiate, and so a peace was patched up between Naples and the Holy See, the conditions of which were that Orsini should retain the fiefs for his lifetime, but that they should revert to Holy Church on his death, and that he should pay the Church for the life-lease of them the sum of 40,000 ducats, which already he had paid to Francesco Cibo; that the peace should be consolidated by the marriage of the Pope's bastard, Giuffredo, with Sancia of Aragon, the natural daughter of the Duke of Calabria, heir to the throne of Naples, and that she should bring the Principality of Squillace and the County of Coriate as her dowry.

The other condition demanded by Naples—at the suggestion of Cardinal Giuliano della Rovere—was that the Pope should disgrace and dismiss his ViceChancellor, Ascanio Sforza, which would have shattered the pontifical relations with Milan. To this, however, the Pope would not agree, but he met Naples in the matter to the extent of consenting to overlook Cardinal della Rovere's defection and receive him back into favour.

On these terms the peace was at last concluded in August of 1493, and immediately afterwards there arrived in Rome the Sieur Peron de Basche, an envoy from the King of France charged with the mission to prevent any alliance between Rome and Naples.

The Frenchman was behind the fair. The Pope took the only course possible under the awkward circumstances, and refused to see the ambasssador. Thereupon the offended King of France held a grand council "in which were proposed and treated many things against the Pope and for the reform of the Church."

These royal outbursts of Christianity, these pious kingly frenzies to unseat an unworthy Pontiff and reform the Church, follow always, you will observe, upon the miscarriage of royal wishes.

In the Consistory of September 1493 the Pope created twelve new cardinals to strengthen the Sacred College in general and his own hand in particular.

Amongst these new creations were the Pope's son Cesare, and Alessandro Farnese, the brother of the beautiful Giulia. The grant of the red hat to the latter appears to have caused some scandal, for, owing to the Pope's relations with his sister, to which it was openly said that Farnese owed the purple, he received the by-name of Cardinal della Gonella— Cardinal of the Petticoat.

That was the first important step in the fortunes of the House of Farnese, which was to give dukes to Parma, and reach the throne of Spain (in the person of Isabella Farnese) before becoming extinct in 1758.

BOOK II
THE BULL PASCANT

Roma Bovem invenit tunc, cum fundatur aratro,
Et nunc lapsa suo est ecce renata Bove.

From an inscription quoted by Bernardino Coaxo.

CHAPTER I
THE FRENCH INVASION

You see Cesare Borgia, now in his nineteenth year, raised to the purple with the title of Cardinal-Deacon of Santa Maria Nuova—notwithstanding which, however, he continues to be known in preference, and, indeed, to sign himself by the title of his archbishopric, Cardinal of Valencia.

It is hardly necessary to mention that, although already Bishop of Pampeluna and Archbishop of Valencia, he had received so far only his first tonsure. He never did receive any ecclesiastical orders beyond the minor and revocable ones.

It was said by Infessura, and has since been repeated by a multitude of historians, upon no better authority than that of this writer on hearsay and inveterate gossip, that, to raise Cesare to the purple, Alexander was forced to prove the legitimacy of that young man's birth, and that to this end he procured false witnesses to swear that he was "the son of Vannozza de' Catanei and her husband, Domenico d'Arignano." Already has this been touched upon in an earlier chapter, here it was shown that Vannozza never had a husband of the name of d'Arignano, and it might reasonably be supposed that this circumstance alone would have sufficed to restrain any serious writer from accepting and repeating Infessura's unauthoritative statement.

But if more they needed, it was ready to their hands in the Bull of Sixtus IV of October 1, 1480—to which also allusion has been made—dispensing Cesare from proving his legitimacy: "Super defectum natalium od ordines et quoecumque beneficia."

Besides that, of what avail would any false swearing have been, considering that Cesare was openly named Borgia, that he was openly acknowledged by his father, and that in the very Bull above mentioned he is stated to be the son of Roderigo Borgia?

This is another instance of the lightness, the recklessness with which Alexander VI has been accused of unseemly and illicit conduct, which it may not be amiss to mention at this stage, since, if not the accusation itself, at least the matter that occasioned it belongs chronologically here.

During the first months of his reign—following in the footsteps of predecessors who had made additions to the Vatican—Alexander set about the building of the Borgia Tower. For its decoration he brought Perugino, Pinturicchio, Volterrano, and Peruzzi to Rome. Concerning Pinturicchio and Alexander, Vasari tells us, in his Vita degli Artefici, that over the door of one of the rooms in the Borgia Tower the artist painted a picture of the Virgin Mary in the likeness of Giulia Farnese (who posed to him as the model) with Alexander kneeling to her in adoration, arrayed in full pontificals.

Such a thing would have been horrible, revolting, sacrilegious. Fortunately it does not even amount to a truth untruly told; and well would it be if all the lies against the Borgias were as easy to refute. True, Pinturicchio did paint Giulia Farnese as the Madonna; true also that he did paint Alexander kneeling in adoration—but not to the Madonna, not in the same picture at all. The Madonna for which Giulia Farnese was the model is over a doorway, as Vasari says. The kneeling Alexander is in another room, and the object of his adoration is the Saviour rising from His tomb.

Yet one reputable writer after another has repeated that lie of Vasari's, and shocked us by the scandalous spectacle of a Pope so debauched and lewd that he kneels in pontificals, in adoration, at the feet of his mistress depicted as the Virgin Mary.

In October of that same year of 1493 Cesare accompanied his father on a visit to Orvieto, a journey which appears to have been partly undertaken in response to an invitation from Giulia Farnese's brother Alessandro.

Orvieto was falling at the time into decay and ruin, no longer the prosperous centre it had been less than a hundred years earlier; but the shrewd eye of Alexander perceived its value as a stronghold, to be used as an outpost of Rome or as a refuge in time of danger, and he proceeded to repair and fortify it. In the following summer Cesare was invested with its governorship, at the request of its inhabitants, who sent an embassy to the Pope with their proposal,—by way, no doubt, of showing their gratitude for his interest in the town.

But in the meantime, towards the end of 1493, King Ferrante's uneasiness at the ever-swelling rumours of the impending French invasion was quickened by the fact that the Pope had not yet sent his son Giuffredo to Naples to marry Donna Sancia, as had been contracted. Ferrante feared the intrigues of Milan with Alexander, and that the latter might be induced, after all, to join the northern league. In a frenzy of apprehension, the old king was at last on the point of going to Milan to throw himself at the feet of Lodovico Sforza, who was now his only hope, when news reached him that his ambassadors had been ordered to leave France.

That death-blow to his hopes was a death-blow to the man himself. Upon receiving the news he was smitten by an apoplexy, and upon January 25, 1494, he departed this life without the consolation of being able to suppose that any of his schemes had done anything to avert the impending ruin of his house.

In spite of all Alexander's intercessions and representations, calculated to induce Charles VIII to abandon his descent upon Italy; in spite, no less, of the counsel he received at home from such far-seeing men as had his ear, the Christian King was now determined upon the expedition and his preparations were well advanced. In the month of March he assumed the title of King of Sicily, and sent formal intimation of it to Alexander, demanding his investiture at the hands of the Pope and offering to pay him a heavy annual tribute. Alexander was thus given to choose between the wrath of France and the wrath of Naples, and—to put the basest construction on his motives—he saw that the peril from an enemy on his very frontiers would be more imminent than that of an enemy beyond the Alps. It is also possible that he chose to be guided by his sense of justice and to do in the matter what he considered right. By whatever motive he was prompted, the result was that he refused to accede to the wishes of the Christian King.

The Consistory which received the French ambassador—Peron de Basche—became the scene of stormy remonstrances, Cardinal Giuliano della Rovere, of course, supporting the ambassador and being supported in his act of insubordination by the Vice-Chancellor Ascanio Sforza (who represented his brother Lodovico in the matter) and the Cardinals Sanseverino, Colonna, and Savelli, all attached to French interests. Peron de Basche so far presumed, no doubt emboldened by this support, as to threaten the Pope with deposition if he persisted in his refusal to obey the King of France.

You see once more that kingly attitude, and you shall see it yet again presently and be convinced of its precise worth. In one hand a bribe of heavy annual tribute, in the other a threat of deposition; it was thus they conducted their business with the Holy Father. In this instance his Holiness took the threat, and dismissed the insolent ambassador. Della Rovere, conceiving that in France he had a stouter ally than in Naples, and seeing that he had once more incurred the papal anger by his open enmity, fled back to Ostia; and, not feeling safe there, for the pontifical forces were advancing upon his fortress, took ship to Genoa, and thence to France, to plot the Pope's ruin with the exasperated Charles; and, the charge of simony being the only weapon with which they could attack Alexander's seat upon the papal throne, the charge of simony was once more brandished.

His Holiness took the matter with a becoming and stately calm. He sent his nephew, Giovanni Borgia, to Naples to crown Alfonso, and with him went Giuffredo Borgia to carry out the marriage contract with Alfonso's daughter, and thus strengthen the alliance between Rome and Naples.

By the autumn Charles had crossed the Alps with the most formidable army that had ever been sent out of France, full ninety thousand strong. And so badly was the war conducted by the Neapolitan generals who were sent to hold him in check that the appearance of the French under the very walls of Rome was almost such as to take the Pope by surprise. Charles's advance from the north had been so swift and unhindered that Alexander contemptuously said the French soldiers had come into Italy with wooden spurs and chalk in their hands to mark their lodgings.

Charles had been well received by the intriguing Lodovico Sforza, with whom he visited the Castle of Pavia and the unfortunate Gian Galeazzo, who from long confinement, chagrin, and other causes was now reduced to the sorriest condition. Indeed, on October 22, some days after that visit, the wretched prince expired. Whether or not Lodovico had him poisoned, as has been alleged—a charge, which, after all, rests on no proof, nor even upon the word of any person of reliance—his death most certainly lies at his ambitious uncle's door.

Charles was at Piacenza when the news of Gian Galeazzo's death reached him. Like the good Christian that he accounted himself, he ordered the most solemn and imposing obsequies for the poor youth for whom in life he had done nothing.

Gian Galeazzo left a heart-broken girl-widow and two children to succeed him to the throne he had never been allowed to occupy—the eldest,

Francesco Sforza, being a boy of five. Nevertheless, Lodovico was elected Duke of Milan. Not only did he suborn the Parliament of Milan to that end, but he induced the Emperor to confirm him in the title. To this the Emperor consented, seeking to mask the unscrupulous deed by a pitiful sophism. He expounded that the throne of Milan should originally have been Lodovico's, and never Galeazzo Maria's (Gian Galeazzo's father), because the latter was born before Francesco Sforza had become Duke of Milan, whereas Lodovico was born when he already was so.

The obsequies of Gian Galeazzo completed, Charles pushed on. From Florence he issued his manifesto, and although this confined itself to claiming the kingdom of Naples, and said no word of punishing the Pope for his disobedience in crowning Alfonso and being now in alliance with him, it stirred up grave uneasiness at the Vatican.

The Pope's position was becoming extremely difficult; nevertheless, he wore the boldest possible face when he received the ambassadors of France, and on December 9 refused to grant the letters patent of passage through the Pontifical States which the French demanded. Thereupon Charles advanced threateningly upon Rome, and was joined now by those turbulent barons Orsini, Colonna, and Savelli.

Alexander VI has been widely accused of effecting a volte-face at this stage and betraying his Neapolitan allies; but his conduct, properly considered, can hardly amount to that. What concessions he made to France were such as a wise and inadequately supported man must make to an army ninety thousand strong. To be recklessly and quixotically heroic is not within the function of Popes; moreover, Alexander had Rome to think of, for Charles had sent word that, if he were resisted he would leave all in ruins, whereas if a free passage were accorded him he would do no hurt nor suffer any pillage to be done in Rome.

So the Pope did the only thing consistent with prudence: he made a virtue of necessity and gave way where it was utterly impossible for him to resist. He permitted Charles the passage through his territory which Charles was perfectly able to take for himself if refused. There ensued an interchange of compliments between Pope and King, and early in January Charles entered Rome in such warlike panoply as struck terror into the hearts of all beholders. Of that entrance Paolo Giovio has left us an impressive picture.

The vanguard was composed of Swiss and German mercenaries—tall fellows, these professional warriors, superb in their carriage and stepping in time to the beat of their drums; they were dressed in variegated, close-fitting garments that revealed all their athletic symmetry. A fourth of them were armed with long, square-bladed halberts, new to Italy; the remainder trailed their ten-foot pikes, and carried a short sword at their belts, whilst to every thousand of them there were a hundred arquebusiers. After them came the French infantry, without armour save the officers, who wore steel corselets and head-pieces. These, again, were followed by five thousand Gascon arbalisters, each shouldering his arbalest—a phalanx of short, rude fellows, not to be compared with the stately Swiss. Next came the cavalry, advancing in squadrons, glittering and resplendent in their steel casings; 2,500 of these were in full heavy armour, wielding iron maces and the ponderous lances that were usual also in Italy. Every man-at-arms had with him three horses, mounted by a squire and two valets (four men going to the lance in France). Some 5,000 of the cavalry were more lightly armed, in corselets and head-piece only, and they carried long wooden bows in the English fashion; whilst some were armed with pikes, intended to complete the work of the heavier cavalry. These were followed by 200 knights—the very flower of French chivalry for birth and valour—shouldering their heavy iron maces, their armour covered by purple, gold-embroidered surcoats. Behind them came 400 mounted archers forming the bodyguard of the king.

The misshapen monarch himself was the very caricature of a man, hideous and grotesque as a gargoyle. He was short of stature, spindle-shanked, rachitic and malformed, and of his face, with its colossal nose, loose mouth and shallow brow, Giovio says that "it was the ugliest ever seen on man."

Such was the person of the young king—he was twenty-four years of age at the time—who poured his legions into Rome, and all full-armed as if for work of immediate destruction. Seen, as they were, by torchlight and the blaze of kindled bonfires—for night had fallen long before the rearguard had entered the city—they looked vague, fantastic, and terrifying. But the most awe-inspiring sight of all was kept for the end; it consisted of the thirty-six pieces of artillery which brought up the rear, each piece upon a carriage swiftly drawn by horses, and the longest measuring eight feet, weighing six thousand pounds, and discharging an iron ball as big as a man's head.

The king lay in the Palace of San Marco, where a lodging had been prepared for him, and thither on the day after his entrance came Cesare Borgia, with six Cardinals, from the Castle of Sant' Angelo, whither the Pope had withdrawn, to wait upon his Christian Majesty. Charles immediately revealed the full and exigent nature of his demands. He required the Pope's aid and counsel in the conquest of Naples, upon which he was proceeding; that Cesare Borgia be delivered into his hands as a hostage to ensure the Pope's friendliness; and that the Castle of Sant' Angelo be handed over to him to be used as a retreat in case of need or danger. Further, he demanded that Prince Djem—the brother of Sultan Bajazet, who was in the Pope's hands—should be delivered up to him as a further hostage.

This Djem (Gem, or Zizim, as his name is variously spelled) was the second son of Mahomet II, whose throne he had disputed with his brother Bajazet on their father's death. He had raised an army to enforce his claim, and had not lacked for partisans; but he was defeated and put to flight by his brother. For safety he had delivered himself up to the Knights of Rhodes, whom he knew to be Bajazet's implacable enemies. They made him very welcome, for d'Aubusson, the Grand Master of Rhodes, realized that the possession of the prince's person was a very fortunate circumstance for Christianity, since by means of such a hostage the Turk could be kept in submission. Accordingly d'Aubusson had sent him to France, and wrote: "While Djem lives, and is in our hands, Bajazet will never dare to make war upon Christians, who will thus enjoy great peace. Thus is it salutary that Djem should remain in our power." And in France Djem had been well received and treated with every consideration due to a person of his princely rank.

But he appears to have become a subject of contention among the Powers, several of which urged that he could be of greater service to Christianity in their hands than in those of France. Thus, the King of Hungary had demanded him because, being a neighbour of Bajazet's, he was constantly in apprehension of Turkish raids. Ferdinand of Spain had desired him because the possession of him would assist the Catholic King in the expulsion of the Moors. Ferrante of Naples had craved him because he lived in perpetual terror of a Turkish invasion.

In the end he had been sent to Rome, whither he went willingly under the advice of the Knights of Rhodes, whose prisoner he really considered himself. They had discovered that Bajazet was offering enormous bribes to Charles for the surrender of him, and they feared lest Charles should succumb to the temptation.

So Prince Djem had come to Rome in the reign of Pope Innocent VIII, and there he had since remained, Sultan Bajazet making the Pope an annual allowance of forty thousand ducats for his brother's safe custody. He was a willing prisoner, or rather a willing exile, for, far from being kept a prisoner, he was treated at Rome with every consideration, associating freely with those about the Pontifical Court, and being frequently seen abroad in company with the Pope and the Duke of Gandia.

Now Charles was aware that the Pope, in his dread of a French invasion, and seeing vain all his efforts to dissuade Charles from making his descent upon Italy, had appealed for aid to Bajazet. For so doing he has been severely censured, and with some justice, for the picture of the Head of Christianity making appeal to the infidel to assist him against Christians is not an edifying one. Still, it receives some measure of justification when we reflect what was the attitude of these same Christians towards their Head.

Bajazet himself, thrown into a panic at the thought of Djem falling into the hands of a king who proposed to make a raid upon him, answered the Pope begging his Holiness to "have Djem removed from the tribulations of this world, and his soul transported to another, where he might enjoy a greater peace." For this service he offered the Pope 300,000 ducats, to be paid on delivery of the prince's body; and, if the price was high, so was the service required, for it would have ensured Bajazet a peace of mind he could not hope to enjoy while his brother lived.

This letter was intercepted by Giovanni della Rovere, the Prefect of Sinigaglia, who very promptly handed it to his brother, the Cardinal Giuliano. The cardinal, in his turn, laid it before the King of France, who now demanded of the Pope the surrender of the person of this Djem as a further hostage.

Alexander began by rejecting the king's proposals severally and collectively, but Charles pressed him to reconsider his refusal, and so, being again between the sword and the wall, the Pope was compelled to submit. A treaty was drawn up and signed on January 15, the king, on his side, promising to recognize the Pope and to uphold him in all his rights.

On the following day Charles made solemn act of veneration to the Pontiff in Consistory, kissing his ring and his foot, and professing obedience to him as the kings of France, his forbears, had ever done. Words for deeds!

Charles remained twelve days longer in Rome, and set out at last, on January 28, upon the conquest of Naples. First he went solemnly to take his leave of the Pope, and they parted with every outward mark of a mutual esteem which they most certainly cannot have experienced. When Charles knelt for the Pope's blessing, Alexander raised him up and embraced him; whilst Cesare completed the show of friendliness by presenting Charles with six beautiful chargers.

They set out immediately afterwards, the French king taking with him his hostages, neither of which he was destined to retain for long, with Cesare riding in the place of honour on his right.

The army lay at Marino that night, and on the following at Velletri. In the latter city Charles was met by an ambassador of Spain—Antonio da Fonseca. Ferdinand and Isabella were moved at last to befriend their cousins of Naples, whom all else had now abandoned, and at the same time serve their own interests. Their ambassador demanded that Charles should abandon his enterprise and return to France, or else be prepared for war with Spain.

It is eminently probable that Cesare had knowledge of this ultimatum to Charles, and that his knowledge influenced his conduct. However that may be, he slipped out of Velletri in the dead of that same night disguised as a groom. Half a mile out of the town, Francesco del Sacco, an officer of the Podestá of Velletri, awaited him with a horse, and on this he sped back to Rome, where he arrived on the night of the 30th. He went straight to the house of one Antonio Flores, an auditor of the Tribunal of the Ruota and a person of his confidence, who through his influence and protection was destined to rise to the eminence of the archbishopric of Avignon and Papal Nuncio to the Court of France.

Cesare remained at Flores's house, sending word to the Pope of his presence, but not attempting to approach the Vatican. On the following day he withdrew to the stronghold of Spoleto.

Meanwhile Rome was thrown into a panic by the young cardinal's action and the dread of reprisals on the part of France. The quaking municipality sent representatives to Charles to assure him that Rome had had nothing to do with this breach of the treaty, and to implore him not to visit it upon the city. The king replied by a special embassy to the Pope, and there apparently dropped the matter, for a few days later Cesare reappeared at the Vatican.

Charles, meanwhile, despite the threats of Spain, pushed on to accomplish his easy conquest.

King Alfonso had already fled the kingdom (January 25), abdicating in favour of his brother Federigo. His avowed object was to withdraw to Sicily, retire from the world, and do penance for his sins, for which no doubt there was ample occasion. The real spur was probably—as opined by Commines—cowardice; for, says that Frenchman, "Jamais homme cruel ne fut hardi."

Federigo's defence of the realm consigned to him was not conspicuous, for the French entered Naples almost without striking a blow within twenty days of their departure from Rome.

Scarcely had Charles laid aside his armour when death robbed him of the second hostage he had brought from the Vatican. On February 25, after a week's illness, Prince Djem died of dysentery at the Castle of Capua, whither Charles had sent him.

Rumours that he had been poisoned by the Pope arose almost at once; but, considering that twentyeight days had elapsed since his parting from

Alexander, it was, with the best intentions in the world, rather difficult to make that poisoning credible, until the bright notion was conceived, and made public, that the poison used was a "white powder" of unknown components, which did its work slowly, and killed the victim some time after it had been administered. Thus, by a bold and brazen invention, an impossible falsehood was made to wear a possible aspect.

And in that you have most probably the origin of the famous secret poison of the Borgias. Having been invented to fit the alleged poisoning of Prince Djem, which it was desired to fasten upon the Pope by hook or by crook, it was found altogether too valuable an invention not to be used again. By means of it, it became possible to lay almost any death in the world at the door of Alexander.

Before proceeding to inquire further into this particular case, let us here and now say that, just as to-day there is no inorganic toxin known to science that will either lie fallow for weeks in the human system, suddenly to become active and slay, or yet to kill by slow degrees involving some weeks in the process, so none was known in the Borgian or any other era. Science indeed will tell you that the very notion of any such poison is flagrantly absurd, and that such a toxic action is against all the laws of nature.

But a scientific disquisition is unnecessary. For our present needs arguments of common sense should abundantly suffice. This poison—this white powder—was said to be a secret of the Borgias. If that is so, by what Borgia was the secret of its existence ever divulged? Or, if it never was divulged, how comes it to be known that a poison so secret, and working at such distances of time, was ever wielded by them?

The very nature of its alleged action was such as utterly to conceal the hand that had administered it; yet here, on the first recorded occasion of its alleged use, it was more or less common knowledge if Giovio and Guicciardini are to be believed!

Sagredo(1) says that Djem died at Terracina three days after having been consigned to Charles VIII, of poison administered by Alexander, to whom Bajazet had promised a large sum of money for the deed. The same is practically Giovio's statement, save that Giovio causes him to die at a later date and at Gaeta; Guicciardini and Corio tell a similar story, but inform us that he died in Naples.

1 *In Mem. Storiche dei Monarchi Ottomani.*

It is entirely upon the authority of these four writers that the Pope is charged with having poisoned Djem, and it is noteworthy that in the four narratives we find different dates and three different places given as the date and place of the Turk's death, and more noteworthy still that in not one instance of these four is date or place correctly stated.

Now the place where Djem died, and the date of his death, were public facts about which there was no mystery; they were to be ascertained—as they are still—by any painstaking examiner. His poisoning, on the other hand, was admittedly a secret matter, the truth of which it was impossible to ascertain with utter and complete finality. Yet of this poisoning they know all the secrets, these four nimble writers who cannot correctly tell us where or when the man died!

We will turn from the fictions they have left us—which, alas! have but too often been preferred by subsequent writers to the true facts which lay just as ready to their hands, but of course were less sensational—and we will consider instead the evidence of those contemporaries who do, at least, know the time and place of Djem's decease.

If any living man might have known of a secret poison of the Borgias at this stage, that man was Burchard the Caeremoniarius, and, had he known of it, not for a moment would he have been silent on the point. Yet not a word of this secret poison shall you find in his diaries, and concerning the death of Djem he records that "on February 25 died at the Castle of Capua the said Djem, through meat or drink that disagreed with him."

Panvinio, who, being a Neapolitan, was not likely to be any too friendly to the Pope—as, indeed, he proves again and again—tells us positively that Djem died of dysentry at Capua.(1)

1 Vitis Pontif. Rom.

Sanuto, writing to the Council of Ten, says that Djem took ill at Capua of a catarrh, which "descended to his stomach"; and that so he died.

And now mark Sanuto's reasoning upon his death, which is the very reasoning we should ourselves employ finally to dispose of this chatter of poisoning, did we not find it awaiting quotation, more authoritative therefore than it could be from us, and utterly irrefutable and conclusive in its logic. "This death is very harmful to the King of France, to all Italy, and chiefly to the Pope, who is thereby deprived of 40,000 ducats yearly, which was paid him by his [Djem's] brother for his custody. And the king showed himself greatly grieved by this death, and it was suspected that the Pope had poisoned him, which, however, was not to be believed, as it would have been to his own loss."

Just so—to his own infinite loss, not only of the 40,000 ducats yearly, but of the hold which the custody of Djem gave him upon the Turks.

The reason assigned by those who charged Alexander with this crime was the bribe of 300,000 ducats offered by Bajezet in the intercepted letter. The offer—which, incidentally, had never reached the Pope—was instantly taken as proof of its acceptance—a singular case of making cause follow upon effect, a method all too prevalent with the Borgian chroniclers. Moreover, they entirely overlooked the circumstance that, for Djem's death in the hands of France, the Pope could make no claim upon Bajazet.

Finally—though the danger be incurred of becoming tedious upon this point—they also forgot that, years before, Bajazet had offered such bribes to Charles for the life of Djem as had caused the Knights of Rhodes to remove the Turk from French keeping. Upon that circumstance they might, had it sorted with their inclinations, have set up a stronger case of poisoning against Charles than against the Pope, and they would not have been put to the necessity of inventing a toxin that never had place in any earthly pharmacopoeia.

It is not, by this, suggested that there is any shadow of a case against Charles. Djem died a perfectly natural death, as is established by the only authorities competent to speak upon the matter, and his death was against the interests of everybody save his brother Bajazet; and against nobody's so much as the Pope's.

CHAPTER II
THE POPE AND THE SUPERNATURAL

By the middle of March of that year 1495 the conquest of Naples was a thoroughly accomplished fact, and the French rested upon their victory, took their ease, and made merry in the capital of the vanquished kingdom.

But in the north Lodovico Sforza-now Duke of Milan de facto, as we have seen—set about the second part of the game that was to be played. He had a valuable ally in Venice, which looked none too favourably on the French and was fully disposed to gather its forces against the common foe. The Council of Ten sent their ambassador, Zorzi, to the Pope to propose an alliance.

News reached Charles in Naples of the league that was being formed. He laughed at it, and the matter was made the subject of ridicule in some of the comedies that were being performed for the amusement of his Court. Meanwhile, the intrigue against him went forward; on March 26 his Holiness sent the Golden Rose to the Doge, and on Palm Sunday the league was solemnly proclaimed in St. Peter's. Its terms were vague; there was nothing in it that was directly menacing to Charles; it was simply declared to have been formed for the common good. But in the north the forces were steadily gathering to cut off the retreat of the French, and suddenly Lodovico Sforza threw aside the mask and made an attack upon the French navy at Genoa.

At last Charles awoke to his danger and began to care for his safety. Rapidly he organized the occupation of Naples, and, leaving Montpensier as Viceroy and d'Aubigny as Captain-General, he set out for Rome with his army, intent upon detaching the Pope from the league; for the Pope, being the immediate neighbour of Naples, would be as dangerous as an enemy as he was valuable as an ally to Charles.

He entered Rome on June 1. The Pope, however, was not there to receive him. Alexander had left on May 28 for Orvieto, accompanied by Cesare, the Sacred College, 200 men-at-arms, and 1,000 horse and 3,000 foot, supplied by Venice. At Orvieto, on June 3, the Pontiff received an ambassador from the Emperor, who had joined the league, and on the 4th he refused audience to the ambassador of France, sent to him from Ronciglione, where the King had halted. Charles, insistent, sent again, determined to see the Pope; but Alexander, quite as determined not to see the king, pushed on to Perugia with his escort.

There his Holiness abode until the French and Italians had met on the River Taro and joined battle at Fornovo, of which encounter both sides claimed the victory. If Charles's only object was to win through, then the victory undoubtedly was his, for he certainly succeeded in cutting a way through the Italians who disputed his passage. But he suffered heavily, and left behind him most of his precious artillery, his tents and carriages, and the immense Neapolitan booty he was taking home, with which he had loaded (says Gregorovius) twenty thousand mules. All this fell into the hands of the Italian allies under Gonzaga of Mantua, whilst from Fornovo Charles's retreat was more in the nature of a flight. Thus he won back to France, no whit the better for his expedition, and the only mark of his passage which he left behind him was an obscene ailment, which, with the coming of the French into Italy, first manifested itself in Europe, and which the Italians paid them the questionable compliment of calling "the French disease"— morbo gallico, or il mal francese.

During the Pope's visit to Perugia an incident occurred which is not without importance to students of his character, and of the character left of him by his contemporaries and others.

There lived in Perugia at this time a young nun of the Order of St. Dominic, who walked in the way of St. Catherine of Siena, Colomba da Rieti by name. You will find some marvellous things about her in the Perugian chronicles of Matarazzo, which, for that matter, abound in marvellous things—too marvellous mostly to be true.

When he deals with events happening beyond the walls of his native town Matarazzo, as an historian, is contemptible to a degree second only to that of those who quote him as an authority. When he deals with matters that, so to speak, befell under his very eyes, he is worthy, if not of credit at least of attention, for his "atmosphere" is valuable.

Of this Sister Colomba Matarazzo tells us that she ate not nor drank, save sometimes some jujube fruit, and even these but rarely. "On the day of her coming to Perugia (which happened in 1488), as she was Crossing the Bridge of St. Gianni some young men attempted to lay hands upon her, for she was comely and beautiful; but as they did so, she showed them the jujube fruit which she carried in a white cloth, whereupon they instantly stood bereft of strength and wits."

Next he tells us how she would pass from life for an hour or two, and sometimes for half a day, and her pulse would cease to beat, and she would, seem all dead. And then she would quiver and come to herself again, and prophesy the future, and threaten disaster. And again: "One morning two of her teeth were found to have fallen out, which had happened in fighting with the devil; and, for the many intercessions which she made, and the scandals which she repaired by her prayers, the people came to call her saint."

Notwithstanding all this, and the fact that she lived without nourishment, he tells us that the brothers of St. Francis had little faith in her. Nevertheless, the community built her a very fine monastery, which was richly endowed, and many nuns took the habit of her Order.

Now it happened that whilst at Perugia in his student days, Cesare had witnessed a miracle performed by this poor ecstatic girl; or rather he had arrived on the scene—the Church of St. Catherine of Siena—to find her, with a little naked boy in her lap, the centre of an excited, frenzied crowd, which was proclaiming loudly that the child had been dead and that she had resurrected him. This was a statement which the Prior of the Dominicans did not seem disposed unreservedly to accept, for, when approached with a suggestion that the bells should be rung in honour of the event, he would not admit that he saw any cause to sanction such a course.

In the few years that were sped since then, however, sister Colomba had acquired the great reputation of which Matarazzo tells us, so that, throughout the plain of Tiber, the Dominicans were preaching her fame from convent to convent. In December of 1495 Charles VIII heard of her at Siena, and was stirred by a curiosity which he accounted devotional—the same curiosity that caused one of his gentlemen to entreat Savonarola to perform "just a little miracle" for the King's entertainment. You can picture the gloomy fanatic's reception of that invitation.

The Pope now took the opportunity of his sojourn in Perugia to pay Colomba da Rieti a visit, and there can be no doubt that he did so in a critical spirit. Accompanied by Cesare and some cardinals and gentlemen of his following, he went to the Church of St. Dominic and was conducted to the sister's cell by the Prior—the same who in Cesare's student-days had refused to have the bells rung.

Upon seeing the magnificent figure of the Pontiff filling the doorway of her little chamber, Sister Colomba fell at his feet, and, taking hold of the hem of his gown, she remained prostrate and silent for some moments, when at last she timidly arose. Alexander set her some questions concerning the Divine Mysteries. These she answered readily at first, but, as his questions grew, she faltered, became embarrassed, and fell silent, standing before him white and trembling, no doubt a very piteous figure. The Pope, not liking this, turned to the Prior to demand an explanation, and admonished him sternly: "Caveto, Pater, quia ego Papa sum!"

This had the effect of throwing the Prior into confusion, and he set himself to explain that she was in reality very wonderful, that he himself had not at first believed in her, but that he had seen so much that he had been converted. At this stage Cesare came to his aid, bearing witness, as he could, that he himself had seen the Prior discredit her when others were already hailing her as a saint, wherefore, if he now was convinced, he must have had very good evidence to convince him. We can imagine the Prior's gratitude to the young cardinal for that timely word when he saw himself in danger perhaps of being called to account for fostering and abetting an imposture.

What was Alexander's opinion of her in the end we do not know; but we do know that he was not readily credulous. When, for instance, he heard that the stigmata were alleged to have appeared upon the body of Lucia di Narni he did what might be expected of a sceptic of our own times rather than of a churchman of his superstitious age—he sent his physicians to examine her.

That is but one instance of his common-sense attitude towards supernatural manifestations. His cold, calm judgement caused him to seek, by all available and practical means, to discriminate between the true and the spurious in an age in which men, by their credulity, were but too ready to become the prey of any impostor. It argues a breadth of mind altogether beyond the times in which he had his being. Witches and warlocks, who elsewhere—and even in much later ages, and in Protestant as well as Catholic States—were given to the fire, he contemptuously ignored. The unfortunate Moors and Jews, who elsewhere in Europe were being persecuted by the Holy Inquisition and burnt at the stake as an act of faith for the good of their souls and the greater honour and glory of God, found in Alexander a tolerant protector and in Rome a safe shelter.

These circumstances concerning him are not sufficiently known; it is good to know them for their own sake. But, apart from that, they have a great historical value which it is well to consider. It is not to be imagined that such breadth of views could be tolerated in a Pope in the dawn of the sixteenth century. The times were not ripe for it; men did not understand it; and what men do not understand they thirst to explain, and have a way of explaining in their own fashion and according to their own lights.

A Pope who did such things could not be a good Pope, since such things must be abhorrent to God—as men conceived God then.

To understand this is to understand much of the bad feeling against Alexander and his family, for this is the source of much of it. Because he did not burn witches and magicians it was presently said that he was himself a warlock, and that he practised black magic. It was not, perhaps, wanton calumny; it was said in good faith, for it was the only reason the times could think of that should account for his restraint. Because he tolerated Moors and Jews it was presently said by some that he was a Moor, by others that he was a Jew, and by others still that he was both.

What wonder, then, if the rancorous Cardinal Giuliano della Rovere venomously dubbed him Moor and Jew, and the rabid fanatic Savonarola screamed that he was no Pope at all, that he was not a Christian, nor did he believe in any God?

Misunderstood in these matters, he was believed to be an infidel, and no crime was too impossible to be fastened upon the man who was believed to be that in the Italy of the Cinquecento.

Alexander, however, was very far from being an infidel, very far from not being a Christian, very far from not believing in God, as he has left abundant evidence in the Bulls he issued during his pontificate. It is certainly wrong to assume—and this is pointed out by l'Espinois—that a private life which seems to ignore the commandments of the Church must preclude the possibility of a public life devoted to the service of the Church. This is far from being the case. Such a state of things—such a dual personality—is by no means inconsistent with churchmen of the fifteenth, or, for that matter, of the twentieth century.

The whole truth of the matter is contained in a Portuguese rhyme, which may roughly be translated:

Soundly Father Thomas preaches.

Don't do as he does; do as he teaches.

A debauchee may preach virtue with salutary effect, just as a man may preach hygiene without practising the privations which it entails, or may save you from dyspepsia by pointing out to you what is indigestible without himself abstaining from it.

Such was the case of Alexander VI, as we are justified in concluding from the evidence that remains.

Let us consider the apostolic zeal revealed by his Bull granting America to Spain. This was practically conceded—as the very terms of it will show—on condition that Spain should employ the dominion accorded her over the New World for the purpose of propagating the Christian faith and the conversion and baptism of the heathen. This is strictly enjoined, and emphasized by the command that Spain shall send out God-fearing men who are learned in religion and capable of teaching it to the people of the newly discovered lands.

Thus Alexander invented the missionary.

To King Manuel the Fortunate (of Portugal), who sought his authority for the conquest of Africa, he similarly enjoined that he should contrive that the name of the Saviour be adored there, and the Catholic faith spread and honoured, to the end that the king "might win eternal life and the blessing of the Holy See."

To the soldiers going upon this expedition his Holiness granted the same indulgences as to those who fought in the Holy Land, and he aided the kings of Spain and Portugal in this propagation of Christianity out of the coffers of the Church.

He sent to America a dozen of the children of St. Francis, as apostles to preach the Faith, and he invested them with the amplest powers.

He prosecuted with stern rigour the heretics of Bohemia, who were obscenely insulting Church and Sacraments, and he proceeded similarly against the "Picards" and "Vaudois." Against the Lombard demoniacs, who had grown bold, were banding themselves together and doing great evil to property, to life, and to religion, Alexander raised his mighty arm.

Then there is his Bull of June 1, 1501, against those who already were turning to evil purposes the newly discovered printing-press. In this he inveighed against the printing of matter prejudicial to healthy doctrine, to good manners, and, above all, to the Catholic Faith or anything that should give scandal to the faithful. He threatened the printers of impious works with excommunication should they persist, and enlisted secular weapons to punish them in a temporal as well as a spiritual manner. He ordered the preparation of indexes of all works containing anything hurtful to religion, and pronounced a ban of excommunication against all who should peruse the books so indexed.

Thus Alexander invented the Index Expurgatorius.

There is abundant evidence that he was a fervid celebrant, and of his extreme devotion to the Blessed Virgin—in whose honour he revived the ringing of the Angelus Bell—shall be considered later.

Whatever his private life, it is idle to seek to show that his public career was other than devoted to the upholding of the dignity and honour of the Church.

CHAPTER III
THE ROMAN BARONS

Having driven Charles VIII out of Italy, it still remained for the allies to remove all traces of his passage from Naples and to restore the rule of the House of Aragon. In this they had the aid of Ferdinand and Isabella, who sent an army under the command of that distinguished soldier Gonzalo de Cordoba, known in his day as the Great Captain.

He landed in Calabria in the spring of 1496, and war broke out afresh through that already sorely devastated land. The Spaniards were joined by the allied forces of Venice and the Church under the condotta of the Marquis Gonzaga of Mantua, the leader of the Italians at Fornovo.

Lodovico had detached himself from the league, and again made terms with France for his own safety's sake. But his cousin, Giovanni Sforza, Tyrant of Pesaro—the husband of Lucrezia Borgia—continued in the pontifical army at the head of a condotta of 600 lances. Another command in the same ranks was one of 700 lances under the youthful Giuffredo Borgia, now Prince of Squillace and the husband of Doña Sancia of Aragon, a lady of exceedingly loose morals, who had brought to Rome the habits acquired in the most licentious Court of that licentious age.

The French lost Naples even more easily than they had conquered it, and by July 7 Ferdinand II was able to reenter his capital and reascend his throne. D'Aubigny, the French general, withdrew to France, whilst Montpensier, the Viceroy, retired to Pozzuoli, where he died in the following year.

Nothing could better have suited the purposes of Alexander than the state of things which now prevailed, affording him, as it did, the means to break the power of the insolent Roman barons, who already had so vexed and troubled him. So in the Consistory of June 1 he published a Bull whereby Gentile Virginio Orsini, Giangiordano Orsini, and his bastard Paolo Orsini and Bartolomeo d'Alviano, were declared outlawed for having borne arms with France against the Church, and their possessions were confiscated to the State. This decree was to be enforced by the sword, and, for the purposes of the impending war, the Duke of Gandia was recalled to Rome. He arrived early in August, having left at Gandia his wife Maria Enriquez, a niece of the Royal House of Spain. It was Cesare Borgia who took the initiative in the pomp with which his brother was received in Rome, riding out at the head of the entire Pontifical Court to meet and welcome the young duke.

In addition to being Duke of Gandia, Giovanni Borgia was already Duke of Sessa and Prince of Teano, which further dignities had been conferred upon him on the occasion of his brother Giuffredo's marriage to Donna Sancia. To these the Pope now added the governorship of Viterbo and of the Patrimony of St. Peter, dispossessing Cardinal Farnese of the latter office to bestow it upon this well-beloved son.

In Venice it was being related, a few months later,—in October—that Gandia had brought a woman from Spain for his father, and that the latter had taken her to live with him. The story is given in Sanuto, and of course has been unearthed and served up by most historians and essayists. It cannot positively be said that it is untrue; but it can be said that it is unconfirmed. There is, for instance, no word of it in Burchard's Diarium, and when you consider how ready a chronicler of scandalous matter was this Master of Ceremonies, you will no doubt conclude that, if any foundation there had been for that Venetian story, Burchard would never have been silent on the subject.

The Pope had taken into his pay that distinguished condottiero, Duke Guidobaldo of Urbino, who later was to feel the relentless might of Cesare. To Guidobaldo's command was now entrusted the punitive expedition against the Orsini, and with him was to go the Duke of Gandia, ostensibly to share the leadership, in reality that, under so able a master, he might serve his apprenticeship to the trade of arms. So on October 25 Giovanni Borgia was very solemnly created Gonfalonier of the Church and Captain-General of the pontifical troops. On the same day the three standards were blessed in St. Peter's—one being the Papal Gonfalon bearing the arms of the Church and the other two the personal banners of Guidobaldo and Gandia. The two condottieri attended the ceremony, arrayed in full armour, and received the white truncheons that were the emblems of their command.

On the following day the army set out, accompanied by the Cardinal de Luna as papal legate a latere, and within a month ten Orsini strongholds had surrendered.

So far all had been easy for the papal forces; but now the Orsini rallied in the last three fortresses that remained them—Bracciano, Trevignano, and Anguillara, and their resistance suddenly acquired a stubborn character, particularly that of Bracciano, which was captained by Bartolomeo d'Alviano, a clever, resourceful young soldier who was destined to go far. Thus the campaign, so easily conducted at the outset, received a check which caused it to drag on into the winter. And now the barons received further reinforcements. Vitellozzo Vitelli, the Tyrant of Città di Castello, came to the aid of the Orsini, as did also the turbulent Baglioni of Perugia, the della Rovere in Rome, and all those who were inimical to Alexander VI. On the other hand, however, the barons Colonna and Savelli ranged themselves on the side of the Pope.

Already Trevignano had fallen, and the attack of the pontifical army was concentrated upon Bracciano. Hard pressed, and with all supplies cut off, Bartolomeo d'Alviano was driven to the very verge of surrender, when over the hills came Carlo Orsini, with the men of Vitellozzo Vitelli, to take the papal forces by surprise and put them to utter rout. Guidobaldo was made prisoner, whilst the Duke of Gandia, Fabrizio Colonna, and the papal legate narrowly escaped, and took shelter in Ronciglione, the Pope's son being slightly wounded in the face.

It was a severe and sudden conclusion to a war that had begun under such excellent auspices for the Pontificals. Yet, notwithstanding that defeat, which had left guns and baggage in the hands of the enemy, the Pope was the gainer by the campaign, having won eleven strongholds from the Orsini in exchange for one battle lost.

The barons now prepared to push home their advantage and complete the victory; but the Pope checkmated them by an appeal to Gonzalo de Cordoba, who promptly responded and came with Prospero Colonna to the aid of the Church. He laid siege to Ostia, which was being held for the Cardinal della Rovere, and compelled it to a speedy surrender, thereby bringing the Orsini resistance practically to an end. For the present the might of the barons was broken, and they were forced to pay Alexander the sum of 50,000 ducats to redeem their captured fortresses.

Gonzalo de Cordoba made a triumphal entry into Rome, bringing with him Monaldo da Guerra, the unfortunate defender of Ostia, in chains. He was received with great honour by the Duke of Gandia, accompanied by his brother-in-law, Giovanni Sforza, and they escorted him to the Vatican, where the Pope awaited him.

This was but one of the many occasions just then on which Giovanni Sforza was conspicuous in public in close association with his father-in-law, the Pope. Burchard mentions his presence at the blessing of the candles on the Feast of the Purification, and shows him to us as a candle-bearer standing on the Pope's right hand. Again we see him on Palm Sunday in attendance upon Alexander, he and Gandia standing together on the steps of the pontifical throne in the Sixtine Chapel during the Blessing of the Palms. There and elsewhere Lucrezia's husband is prominently in the public eye during those months of February and March of 1497, and we generally see him sharing, with the Duke of Gandia, the honour of close attendance upon the Pontiff, all of which but serves to render the more marked his sudden disappearance from that scene.

The matter of his abrupt and precipitate flight from Rome is one concerning which it is unlikely that the true and complete facts will ever be revealed. It was public gossip at this time that his marriage with Lucrezia was not a happy one, and that discord marred their life together. Lucrezia's reported grievance upon this subject reads a little vaguely to us now, whatever it may have conveyed at the time. She complained that Giovanni "did not fittingly keep her company,"(1) which may be taken to mean that a good harmony did not prevail between them, or, almost equally well, that there were the canonical grounds for complaint against him as a husband which were afterwards formally preferred and made the grounds for the divorce. It is also possible that Alexander's ambition may have urged him to dissolve the marriage to the end that she might be free to be used again as a pawn in his far-reaching game.

1 "*Che non gli faceva buona compagnia.*"

All that we do know positively is that, one evening in Holy Week, Sforza mounted a Turkish horse, and, on the pretext of going as far as the Church of Sant' Onofrio to take the air, he slipped out of Rome, and so desperately did he ride that, twenty-four hours later, he was home in Pesaro, his horse dropping dead as he reached the town.

Certainly some terrible panic must have urged him, and this rather lends colour to the story told by Almerici in the Memorie di Pesaro. According to this, the Lord of Pesaro's chamberlain, Giacomino, was in Lucrezia's apartments one evening when Cesare was announced, whereupon, by Lucrezia's orders, Giacomino concealed himself behind a screen. The Cardinal of Valencia entered and talked freely with his sister, the essence of his conversation being that the order had been issued for her husband's death.

The inference to be drawn from this is that Giovanni had been given to choose in the matter of a divorce, and that he had refused to be a party to it, whence it was resolved to remove him in a still more effective manner.

Be that as it may, the chroniclers of Pesaro proceed to relate that, after Cesare had left her, Lucrezia asked Giacomino if he had heard what had been said, and, upon being answered in the affirmative, urged him to go at once and warn Giovanni. It was as a consequence of this alleged warning that Giovanni made his precipitate departure.

A little while later, at the beginning of June, Lucrezia left the Vatican and withdrew to the Convent of San Sisto, in the Appian Way, a step which immediately gave rise to speculation and to unbridled gossip, all of which, however, is too vague to be worthy of the least attention. Aretino's advices to the Cardinal Ippolito d'Este suggest that she did not leave the Vatican on good terms with her family, and it is very possible, if what the Pesaro chroniclers state is true, that her withdrawal arose out of her having warned Giovanni of his danger and enabled him to escape.

At about the same time that Lucrezia withdrew to her convent her brother Gandia was the recipient of further honours at the hands of his fond father. The Pope had raised the fief of Benevento to a dukedom, and as a dukedom conferred it upon his son, to him and to his legitimate heirs for ever. To this he added the valuable lordships of Terracina and Pontecorvo.

Cesare, meanwhile, had by no means been forgotten, and already this young cardinal was—with perhaps the sole exception of the Cardinal d'Estouteville—the richest churchman in Christendom. To his many other offices and benefices it was being proposed to add that of Chamberlain of the Holy See, Cardinal Riario, who held the office, being grievously ill and his recovery despaired of. Together with that office it was the Pope's avowed intention to bestow upon Cesare the palace of the late Cardinal of Mantua, and with it, no doubt, he would receive a proportion of the dead cardinal's benefices.

Cesare was twenty-two years of age at the time; tall, of an athletic slenderness, and exceedingly graceful in his movements, he was acknowledged to be the handsomest man of his age. His face was long and pale, his brow lofty, his nose delicately aquiline. He had long auburn hair, and his hazel eyes, large, quick in their movements, and singularly searching in their glance, were alive with the genius of the soul behind them. He inherited from his father the stupendous health and vigour for which Alexander had been remarkable in his youth, and was remarkable still in his old age. The chase had ever been Cesare's favourite pastime, and the wild boar his predilect quarry; and in the pursuit of it he had made good use of his exceptional physical endowments, cultivating them until—like his father before him—he was equal to the endurance of almost any degree of fatigue.

In the Consistory of June 8 he was appointed legate a latere to go to Naples to crown King Federigo of Aragon—for in the meanwhile another change had taken place on the Neapolitan throne by the death of young Ferdinand II, who had been succeeded by his uncle, Federigo, Prince of Altamura.

Cesare made ready for his departure upon this important mission, upon which he was to be accompanied by his brother Giovanni, Duke of Gandia. They were both to be back in Rome by September, when Gandia was to return to Spain, taking with him his sister Lucrezia.

Thus had the Pope disposed; but the Borgia family stood on the eve of the darkest tragedy associated with its name, a tragedy which was to alter all these plans.

CHAPTER IV
THE MURDER OF THE DUKE OF GANDIA

On June 14, 1497, the eve of Cesare and Giovanni Borgia's departure for Naples, their mother Vannozza gave them a farewell supper in her beautiful vineyard in Trastevere. In addition to the two guests of honour several other kinsmen and friends were present, among whom were the Cardinal of Monreale and young Giuffredo Borgia. They remained at supper until an advanced hour of the night, when Cesare and Giovanni took their departure, attended only by a few servants and a mysterious man in a mask, who had come to Giovanni whilst he was at table, and who almost every day for about a month had been in the habit of visiting him at the Vatican.

The brothers and these attendants rode together into Rome and as far as the Vice-Chancellor Ascanio Sforza's palace in the Ponte Quarter. Here Giovanni drew rein, and informed Cesare that he would not be returning to the Vatican just yet, as he was first "going elsewhere to amuse himself." With that he took his leave of Cesare, and, with one single exception—in addition to the man in the mask—dismissed his servants. The latter continued their homeward way with the cardinal, whilst the Duke, taking the man in the mask upon the crupper of his horse and followed his single attendant, turned and made off in the direction of the Jewish quarter.

In the morning it was found that Giovanni had not yet returned, and his uneasy servants informed the Pope of his absence and of the circumstances of it. The Pope, however, was not at all alarmed. Explaining his son's absence in the manner so obviously suggested by Giovanni's parting words to Cesare on the previous night, he assumed that the gay young Duke was on a visit to some complacent lady and that presently he would return.

Later in the day, however, news was brought that his horse had been found loose in the streets, in the neighbourhood of the Cardinal of Parma's palace, with only one stirrup-leather, the other having clearly been cut from the saddle, and, at the same time, it was related that the servant who had accompanied him after he had separated from the rest had been found at dawn in the Piazza della Giudecca mortally wounded and beyond speech, expiring soon after his removal to a neighbouring house.

Alarm spread through the Vatican, and the anxious Pope ordered inquiries to be made in every quarter where it was possible that anything might be learned. It was in answer to these inquiries that a boatman of the Schiavoni—one Giorgio by name—came forward with the story of what he had seen on the night of Wednesday. He had passed the night on board his boat, on guard over the timber with which she was laden. She was moored along the bank that runs from the Bridge of Sant' Angelo to the Church of Santa Maria Nuova.

He related that at about the fifth hour of the night, just before daybreak, he had seen two men emerge from the narrow street alongside the Hospital of San Girolamo, and stand on the river's brink at the spot where it was usual for the scavengers to discharge their refuse carts into the water. These men had looked carefully about, as if to make sure that they were not being observed. Seeing no one astir, they made a sign, whereupon a man well mounted on a handsome white horse, his heels armed with golden spurs, rode out of that same narrow street. Behind him, on the crupper of his horse, Giorgio beheld the body of a man, the head hanging in one direction and the legs in the other. This body was supported there by two other men on foot, who walked on either side of the horseman.

Arrived at the water's edge, they turned the horse's hind-quarters to the river; then, taking the body between them, two of them swung it well out into the stream. After the splash, Giorgio had heard the horseman inquire whether they had thrown well into the middle, and had heard him receive the affirmative answer—"Signor, Si." The horseman then sat scanning the surface a while, and presently pointed out a dark object floating, which proved to be their victim's cloak. The men threw stones at it, and so sank it, whereupon they turned, and all five departed as they had come.

Such is the boatman's story, as related in the Diarium of Burchard. When the Pope had heard it, he asked the fellow why he had not immediately gone to give notice of what he had witnessed, to which this Giorgio replied that, in his time, he had seen over a hundred bodies thrown into the Tiber without ever anybody troubling to know anything about them.

This story and Gandia's continued absence threw the Pope into a frenzy of apprehension. He ordered the bed of the river to be searched foot by foot. Some hundreds of boatmen and fishermen got to work, and on that same afternoon the body of the ill-fated Duke of Gandia was brought up in one of the nets. He was not only completely dressed—as was to have been expected from Giorgio's story—but his gloves and his purse containing thirty ducats were still at his belt, as was his dagger, the only weapon he had carried; the jewels upon his person, too, were all intact, which made it abundantly clear that his assassination was not the work of thieves.

His hands were still tied, and there were from ten to fourteen wounds on his body, in addition to which his throat had been cut.

The corpse was taken in a boat to the Castle of Sant' Angelo, where it was stripped, washed, and arrayed in the garments of the Captain-General of the Church. That same night, on a bier, the body covered with a mantle of brocade, the face "looking more beautiful than in life," he was carried by torchlight from Sant' Angelo to Santa Maria del Popolo for burial, quietly and with little pomp.

The Pope's distress was terrible. As the procession was crossing the Bridge of Sant' Angelo, those who stood there heard his awful cries of anguish, as is related in the dispatches of an eye-witness quoted by Sanuto. Alexander shut himself up in his apartments with his passionate sorrow, refusing to see anybody; and it was only by insistence that the Cardinal of Segovia and some of the Pope's familiars contrived to gain admission to his presence; but even then, not for three days could they induce him to taste food, nor did he sleep.

At last he roused himself, partly in response to the instances of the Cardinal of Segovia, partly spurred by the desire to avenge the death of his child, and he ordered Rome to be ransacked for the assassins; but, although the search was pursued for two months, it proved utterly fruitless.

That is the oft-told story of the death of the Duke of Gandia. Those are all the facts concerning it that are known or that ever will be known. The rest is speculation, and this speculation follows the trend of malice rather than of evidence.

Suspicion fell at first upon Giovanni Sforza, who was supposed to have avenged himself thus upon the Pope for the treatment he had received. There certainly existed that reasonable motive to actuate him, but not a particle of evidence against him.

Next rumour had it that Cardinal Ascanio Sforza's was the hand that had done this work, and with this rumour Rome was busy for months. It was known that he had quarrelled violently with Gandia, who had been grossly insulted by a chamberlain of Ascanio's, and who had wiped out the insult by having the man seized and hanged.

Sanuto quotes a letter from Rome on July 21, which states that "it is certain that Ascanio murdered the Duke of Gandia." Cardinal Ascanio's numerous enemies took care to keep the accusation alive at the Vatican, and Ascanio, in fear for his life, had left Rome and fled to Grottaferrata. When summoned to Rome, he had refused to come save under safeconduct. His fears, however, appear to have been groundless, for the Pope attached no importance to the accusation against him, convinced of his innocence, as he informed him.

Thereupon public opinion looked about for some other likely person upon whom to fasten its indictment, and lighted upon Giuffredo Borgia, Gandia's youngest brother. Here, again, a motive was not wanting. Already has mention been made of the wanton ways of Giuffredo's Neapolitan wife, Doña Sancia. That she was prodigal of her favours there is no lack of evidence, and it appears that, amongst those she admitted to them, was the dead duke. Jealousy, then, it was alleged, was the spur that had driven Giuffredo to the deed; and that the rumour of this must have been insistent is clear when we find the Pope publicly exonerating his youngest son.

Thus matters stood, and thus had public opinion spoken, when in the month of August the Pope ordered the search for the murderer to cease. Bracci, the Florentine ambassador, explains this action of Alexander's. He writes that his Holiness knew who were the murderers, and that he was taking no further steps in the matter in the hope that thus, conceiving themselves to be secure, they might more completely discover themselves.

Bracci's next letter bears out the supposition that he writes from inference, and not from knowledge. He repeats that the investigations have been suspended, and that to account for this some say what already he has written, whilst others deny it; but that the truth of the matter is known to none.

Later in the year we find the popular voice denouncing Bartolomeo d'Alviano and the Orsini. Already in August the Ferrarese ambassador, Manfredi, had written that the death of the Duke of Gandia was being imputed to Bartolomeo d'Alviano, and in December we see in Sanuto a letter from Rome which announces that it is positively stated that the Orsini had caused the death of Giovanni Borgia.

These various rumours were hardly worth mentioning for their own values, but they are important as showing how public opinion fastened the crime in turn upon everybody it could think of as at all likely to have had cause to commit it, and more important still for the purpose of refuting what has since been written concerning the immediate connection of Cesare Borgia with the crime in the popular mind.

Not until February of the following year was the name of Cesare ever mentioned in connection with the deed. The first rumour of his guilt synchronized with that of his approaching renunciation of his ecclesiastical career, and there can be little doubt that the former sprang from the latter.

The world conceived that it had discovered on Cesare's part a motive for the murder of his brother. That motive—of which so very much has been made—shall presently be examined. Meanwhile, to deal with the actual rumour, and its crystallization into history. The Ferrarese ambassador heard it in Venice on February 12, 1498. Capello seized upon it, and repeated it two and a half years later, stating on September 28, 1500: "etiam amazó il fratello."

And there you have the whole source of all the unbridled accusations subsequently launched against Cesare, all of which find a prominent place in Gregorovius's Geschichte der Stadt Rom, whilst the rumours accusing others, which we have mentioned here, are there slurred over.

One hesitates to attack the arguments and conclusions of the very eminent author of that mighty History of Rome in the Middle Ages, but conscience and justice demand that his chapter upon this subject be dealt with as it deserves.

The striking talents of Gregorovius are occasionally marred by the egotism and pedantry sometimes characteristic of the scholars of his nation. He is too positive; he seldom opines; he asserts with finality the things that only God can know; occasionally his knowledge, transcending the possible, quits the realm of the historian for that of the romancer, as for instance—to cite one amid a thousand—when he actually tells us what passes in Cesare Borgia's mind at the coronation of the King of Naples. In the matter of authorities, he follows a dangerous and insidious eclecticism, preferring those who support the point of view which he has chosen, without a proper regard for their intrinsic values.

He tells us definitely that, if Alexander had not positive knowledge, he had at least moral conviction that it was Cesare who had killed the Duke of Gandia. In that, again, you see the God-like knowledge which he usurps; you see him clairvoyant rather than historical. Starting out with the positive assertion that Cesare Borgia was the murderer, he sets himself to prove it by piling up a mass of worthless evidence, whose worthlessness it is unthinkable he should not have realized.

"According to the general opinion of the day, which in all probability was correct, Cesare was the murderer of his brother."

Thus Gregorovius in his Lucrezia Borgia. A deliberate misstatement! For, as we have been at pains to show, not until the crime had been fastened upon everybody whom public opinion could conceive to be a possible assassin, not until nearly a year after Gandia's death did rumour for the first time connect Cesare with the deed. Until then the ambassadors' letters from

Rome in dealing with the murder and reporting speculation upon possible murderers never make a single allusion to Cesare as the guilty person.

Later, when once it had been bruited, it found its way into the writings of every defamer of the Borgias, and from several of these it is taken by Gregorovius to help him uphold that theory.

Two motives were urged for the crime. One was Cesare's envy of his brother, whom he desired to supplant as a secular prince, fretting in the cassock imposed upon himself which restrained his unbounded ambition. The other—and no epoch but this one under consideration, in its reaction from the age of chivalry, could have dared to level it without a careful examination of its sources—was Cesare's jealousy, springing from the incestuous love for their sister Lucrezia, which he is alleged to have disputed with his brother. Thus, as l'Espinois has pointed out, to convict Cesare Borgia of a crime which cannot absolutely be proved against him, all that is necessary is that he should be charged with another crime still more horrible of which even less proof exists.

This latter motive, it is true, is rejected by Gregorovius. "Our sense of honesty," he writes, "repels us from attaching faith to the belief spread in that most corrupt age." Yet the authorities urging one motive are commonly those urging the other, and Gregorovius quotes those that suit him, without considering that, if he is convinced they lie in one connection, he has not the right to assume them truthful in another.

The contemporary, or quasi-contemporary writers upon whose "authority" it is usual to show that Cesare Borgia was guilty of both those revolting crimes are: Sanazzaro, Capello, Macchiavelli, Matarazzo, Sanuto, Pietro Martire d'Anghiera, Guicciardini, and Panvinio.

A formidable array! But consider them, one by one, at close quarters, and take a critical look at what they actually wrote:

SANAZZARO was a Neapolitan poet and epigrammatist, who could not—his times being what they were—be expected to overlook the fact that in these slanderous rumours of incest was excellent matter for epigrammatical verse. Therefore, he crystallized them into lines which, whilst doing credit to his wit, reveal his brutal cruelty. No one will seriously suppose that such a man would be concerned with the veracity of the matter of his verses— even leaving out of the question his enmity towards the House of Borgia, which will transpire later. For him a ben trovato was as good matter as a truth, or better. He measured its value by its piquancy, by its adaptability to epigrammatic rhymes.

Conceive the heartlessness of the man who, at the moment of Alexander's awful grief at the murder of his son—a grief which so moved even his enemies that the bitter Savonarola, and the scarcely less bitter Cardinal della Rovere, wrote to condole with him—could pen that terrible epigram:

Piscatorem hominum ne te non, Sexte, putemus,

Piscaris notum retibus ecce tuum.

Consider the ribaldry of that, and ask yourselves whether this is a man who would immolate the chance of a witticism upon the altar of Truth.

It is significant that Sanazzaro, for what he may be worth, confines himself to the gossip of incest. Nowhere does he mention that Cesare was the murderer, and we think that his silence upon the matter, if it shows anything, shows that Cesare's guilt was not so very much the "general opinion of the day," as Gregorovius asks us to believe.

CAPPELLO was not in Rome at the time of the murder, nor until three years later, when he merely repeated the rumour that had first sprung up some eight months after the crime.

The precise value of his famous "relation" (in which this matter is recorded, and to which we shall return in its proper place) and the spirit that actuated him is revealed in another accusation of murder which he levels at Cesare, an accusation which, of course, has also been widely disseminated upon no better authority than his own. It is Capello who tells us that Cesare stabbed the chamberlain Perrotto in the Pope's very arms; he adds the details that the man had fled thither for shelter from Cesare's fury, and that the blood of him, when he was stabbed, spurted up into the very face of the Pope. Where he got the story is not readily surmised—unless it be assumed that he evolved it out of his feelings for the Borgias. The only contemporary accounts of the death of this Perrotto—or Pedro Caldes, as was his real name—state that he fell by accident into the Tiber and was drowned.

Burchard, who could not have failed to know if the stabbing story had been true, and would not have failed to report it, chronicles the fact that Perrotto was fished out of Tiber, having fallen in six days earlier—"non libenter." This statement, coming from the pen of the Master of Ceremonies at the Vatican, requires no further corroboration. Yet corroboration there actually is in a letter from Rome of February 20, 1498, quoted by Marino Sanuto in his Diarii. This states that Perrotto had been missing for some days, no one knowing what had become of him, and that now "he has been found drowned in the Tiber."

We mention this, in passing, with the twofold object of slaying another calumny, and revealing the true value of Capello, who happens to be the chief "witness for the prosecution" put forward by Gregorovius. "Is it not of great significance," inquires the German historian, "that the fact should have been related so positively by an ambassador who obtained his knowledge from the best sources?"

The question is frivolous, for the whole trouble in this matter is that there were no sources at all, in the proper sense of the word—good or bad. There was simply gossip, which had been busy with a dozen names already.

MACCHIAVELLI includes a note in his Extracts from Letters to the Ten, in which he mentions the death of Gandia, adding that "at first nothing was known, and then men said it was done by the Cardinal of Valencia."

There is nothing very conclusive in that. Besides, incidentally it may be mentioned, that it is not clear when or how these extracts were compiled by Macchiavelli (in his capacity of Secretary to the Signory of Florence) from the dispatches of her ambassadors. But it has been shown—though we are hardly concerned with that at the moment—that these extracts are confused by comments of his own, either for his own future use or for that of another.

MATARAZZO is the Perugian chronicler of whom we have already expressed the only tenable opinion. The task he set himself was to record the contemporary events of his native town—the stronghold of the blood-dripping Baglioni. He enlivened it by every scrap of scandalous gossip that reached him, however alien to his avowed task. The authenticity of this scandalmongering chronicle has been questioned; but, even assuming it to be authentic, it is so wildly inaccurate when dealing with matters happening beyond the walls of Perugia as to be utterly worthless.

Matarazzo relates the story of the incestuous relations prevailing in the Borgia family, and with an unsparing wealth of detail not to be found elsewhere; but on the subject of the murder he has a tale to tell entirely different from any other that has been left us. For, whilst he urges the incest as the motive of the crime, the murderer, he tells us, was Giovanni Sforza, the outraged husband; and he gives us the fullest details of that murder, time and place and exactly how committed, and all the other matters which have never been brought to light.

It is all a worthless, garbled piece of fiction, most obviously; as such it has ever been treated; but it is as plausible as it is untrue, and, at least, as authoritative as any available evidence assigning the guilt to Cesare.

SANUTO we accept as a more or less careful and painstaking chronicler, whose writings are valuable; and Sanuto on the matter of the murder confines himself to quoting the letter of February 1498, in which the accusation against Cesare is first mentioned, after having given other earlier letters which accuse first Ascanio and then Orsini far more positively than does the latter letter accuse Cesare.

On the matter of the incest there is no word in Sanuto; but there is mention of Doña Sancia's indiscretions, and the suggestion that, through jealousy on her account, it was rumoured that the murder had been committed — another proof of how vague and ill-defined the rumours were.

PIETRO MARTIRE D'ANGHIERA writes from Burgos, in Spain, that he is convinced of the fratricide. It is interesting to know of that conviction of his; but difficult to conceive how it is to be accepted as evidence.

If more needs to be said of him, let it be mentioned that the letter in which he expresses that conviction is dated April 1497 — two months before the murder took place! So that even Gregorovius is forced to doubt the authenticity of that document.

GUICCIARDINI is not a contemporary chronicler of events as they happened, but an historian writing some thirty years later. He merely repeats what Capello and others have said before him. It is for him to quote authorities for what he writes, and not to be set up as an authority. He is not reliable, and he is a notorious defamer of the Papacy, sparing nothing that will serve his ends. He dilates with gusto upon the accusation of incest.

Lastly, PANVINTO is in the same category as Guicciardini. He was not born until some thirty years after these events, and his History of the Popes was not written until some sixty years after the murder of the Duke of Gandia. This history bristles with inaccuracies; he never troubles to verify his facts, and as an authority he is entirely negligible.

In the valuable Diarium of Burchard there is unfortunately a lacuna at this juncture, from the day after the murder (of which he gives the full particulars to which we have gone for our narrative of that event) until the month of August following. And now we may see Gregorovius actually using silence as evidence. He seizes upon that lacuna, and goes so far as to set up the tentative explanation that Burchard "perhaps purposely interrupted his Diary that he might avoid mentioning the fratricide."

If such were the case, it would be a strange departure from Burchard's invariable rule, which is one of cold, relentless, uncritical chronicling of events, no matter what their nature. Besides, any significance with which that lacuna might be invested is discounted by the fact that such gaps are of fairly common occurrence in the course of Burchard's record. Finally it remains to be shown that the lacuna in question exists in the original diaries, which have yet to be discovered.

So much for the valuable authorities, out of which—and by means of a selection which is not quite clearly defined—Gregorovius claims to have proved that the murderer of the Duke of Gandia was his brother Cesare Borgia, Cardinal of Valencia.(1)

1 *It is rather odd that, in the course of casting about for a possible murderer of Gandia, public opinion should never have fastened upon Cardinal Alessandro Farnese. He had lately been stripped of the Patrimony of St. Peter that the governorship of this might be bestowed upon Gandia; his resentment had been provoked by that action of the Pope's, and the relations between himself and the Borgias were strained in consequence. Possibly there was clear proof that he could have had no connection with the crime.*

Now to examine more closely the actual motives given by those authorities and by later, critical writers, for attributing the guilt to Cesare.

In September of the year 1497, the Pope had dissolved the marriage of his daughter Lucrezia and Giovanni Sforza, and the grounds for the dissolution were that the husband was impotens et frigidus natura— admitted by himself.(2)

2 *"El S. de Pesaro ha scripto qua de sua mano non haverla mai cognosciuta et esser impotente, alias la sententia non se potea dare. El prefato S. dice pero haver scripto cosi per obedire el Duca de Milano et Aschanio" (Collenuccio's letter from Rome to the Duke of Ferrara, Dec. 25, 1497).*

If you know anything of the Italy of to-day, you will be able to conceive for yourself how the Italy of the fifteenth century must have held her sides and pealed her laughter at the contemptible spectacle of an unfortunate who afforded such reason to be bundled out of a nuptial bed. The echo of that mighty burst of laughter must have rung from Calabria to the Alps, and well may it have filled the handsome weakling who was the object of its cruel ridicule with a talion fury. The weapons he took up wherewith to defend himself were a little obvious. He answered the odious reflections upon his virility by a wholesale charge of incest against the Borgia family; he screamed that what had been said of him was a lie invented by the Borgias to serve their own unutterable ends.(1) Such was the accusation with which the squirming Lord of Pesaro retaliated, and, however obvious, yet it was not an accusation that the world of his day would lightly cast aside, for all that the perspicacious may have rated it at its proper value.

1 *"Et mancho se e curato de fare prova de qua con Done per poterne chiarire el Rev. Legato che era qua, sebbene sua Excellentia tastandolo sopra cio gli ne abbia facto offerta." And further: "Anzi haverla conosciuta infinite volte, ma chel Papa non geiha tolta per altro se non per usare con lei" (Costabili's letter from Milan to the Duke of Ferrara, June 23, 1497).*

What is of great importance to students of the history of the Borgias is that this was the first occasion on which the accusation of incest was raised. Of course it persisted; such a charge could not do otherwise. But now that we see in what soil it had its roots we shall know what importance to attach to it.

Not only did it persist, but it developed, as was but natural. Cesare and the dead Gandia were included in it, and presently it suggested a motive— not dreamed of until then—why Cesare might have been his brother's murderer.

Then, early in 1498, came the rumour that Cesare was intending to abandon the purple, and later Writers, from Capello down to our own times, have chosen to see in Cesare's supposed contemplation of that step a motive so strong for the crime as to prove it in the most absolutely conclusive manner. In no case could it be such proof, even if it were admitted as a motive. But is it really so to be admitted? Did such a motive exist at all? Does it really follow—as has been taken for granted—that Cesare must have remained an ecclesiastic had Gandia lived? We cannot see that it does. Indeed, such evidence as there is, when properly considered, points in the opposite direction, even if no account is taken of the fact that this was not the first occasion on which it was proposed that Cesare should abandon the ecclesiastical career, as is shown by the Ferrarese ambassador's dispatches of March 1493.

It is contended that Gandia was a stumbling-block to Cesare, and that Gandia held the secular possessions which Cesare coveted; but if that were really the case why, when eventually (some fourteen months after Gandia's death) Cesare doffed the purple to replace it by a soldier's harness, did he not assume the secular possessions that had been his brother's?

His dead brother's lands and titles went to his dead brother's son, whilst Cesare's career was totally different, as his aims were totally different, from any that had been Gandia's, or that might have been Gandia's had the latter lived. True, Cesare became Captain-General of the Church in his dead brother's place; but for that his brother's death was not necessary. Gandia had neither the will nor the intellect to undertake the things that awaited Cesare. He was a soft-natured, pleasure-loving youth, whose way of life was already mapped out for him. His place was at Gandia, in Spain, and, whilst he might have continued lord of all the possessions that were his, it would have been Cesare's to become Duke of Valentinois, and to have made himself master of Romagna, precisely as he did.

In conclusion, Gandia's death no more advanced, than his life could have impeded, the career which Cesare afterwards made his own, and to say that Cesare murdered him to supplant him is to set up a theory which the subsequent facts of Cesare's life will nowise justify.

It is idle of Gregorovius to say that the logic of the crime is inexorable— in its assigning the guilt to Cesare—fatuous of him to suppose that, as he claims, he has definitely proved Cesare to be his brother's murderer.

There is much against Cesare Borgia, but it never has been proved, and never will be proved, that he was a fratricide. Indeed the few really known facts of the murder all point to a very different conclusion—a conclusion more or less obvious, which has been discarded, presumably for no better reason than because it was obvious.

Where was all this need to go so far afield in quest of a probable murderer imbued with political motives? Where the need to accuse in turn every enemy that Gandia could possibly possess before finally fastening upon his own brother?

Certain evidence is afforded by the known facts of the case, scant as they are. It may not amount to much, but at least it is sufficient to warrant a plausible conclusion, and there is no justification for discarding it in favour of something for which not a particle of evidence is forthcoming.

There is, first of all, the man in the mask to be accounted for. That he is connected with the crime is eminently probable, if not absolutely certain.

It is to be remembered that for a month—according to Burchard— he had been in the habit of visiting Gandia almost daily. He comes to Vannozza's villa on the night of the murder. Is it too much to suppose that he brought a message from some one from whom he was in the habit of bringing messages?

He was seen last on the crupper of Gandia's horse as the latter rode away towards the Jewish quarter.(1) Gandia himself announced that he was bound on pleasure—going to amuse himself. Even without the knowledge which we possess of his licentious habits, no doubt could arise as to the nature of the amusement upon which he was thus bound at dead of night; and there are the conclusions formed in the morning by his father, when it was found that Gandia had not returned.

1 *The Ghetto was not yet in existence. It was not built until 1556,*
under Paul IV.

Is it so very difficult to conceive that Gandia, in the course of the assignation to which he went, should have fallen into the hands of an irate father, husband, or brother? Is it not really the obvious inference to draw from the few facts that we possess? That it was the inference drawn by the Pope and clung to even some time after the crime and while rumours of a different sort were rife, is shown by the perquisition made in the house of Antonio Pico della Mirandola, who had a daughter whom it was conceived might have been the object of the young duke's nocturnal visit, and whose house was near the place where Gandia was flung into the Tiber.

We could hazard speculations that would account for the man in the mask, but it is not our business to speculate save where the indications are fairly clear.

Let us consider the significance of Gandia's tied hands and the wounds upon his body in addition to the mortal gash across his throat. To what does this condition point? Surely not to a murder of expediency so much as to a fierce, lustful butchery of vengeance. Surely it suggests that Gandia may have been tortured before his throat was cut. Why else were his wrists pinioned? Had he been swiftly done to death there would have been no need for that. Had hired assassins done the work they would not have stayed to pinion him, nor do we think they would have troubled to fling him into the river; they would have slain and left him where he fell.

The whole aspect of the case suggests the presence of the master, of the personal enemy himself. We can conceive Gandia's wrists being tied, to the end that this personal enemy might do his will upon the wretched young man, dealing him one by one the ten or fourteen wounds in the body before making an end of him by cutting his throat. We cannot explain the pinioned wrists in any other way. Then the man on the handsome white horse, the man whom the four others addressed as men address their lord. Remember his gold spurs—a trifle, perhaps; but hired assassins do not wear gold spurs, even though their bestriding handsome white horses may be explainable.

Surely that was the master, the personal enemy himself—and it was not Cesare, for Cesare at the time was at the Vatican.

There we must leave the mystery of the murder of the Duke of Gandia; but we leave it convinced that, such scant evidence as there is, points to an affair of sordid gallantry, and nowise implicates his brother Cesare.

CHAPTER V
THE RENUNCIATION OF THE PURPLE

At the Consistory of June 19, 1497 the Sacred College beheld a broken-hearted old man who declared that he had done with the world, and that henceforth life could offer him nothing that should endear it to him.

"A greater sorrow than this could not be ours, for we loved him exceedingly, and now we can hold neither the Papacy nor any other thing as of concern. Had we seven Papacies, we would give them all to restore the duke to life." So ran his bitter lament.

He denounced his course of life as not having been all that it should have been, and appeared to see in the murder of his son a punishment for the evil of his ways. Much has been made of this, and quite unnecessarily. It has been taken eagerly as an admission of his unparalleled guilt. An admission of guilt it undoubtedly was; but what man is not guilty? and how many men—ay, and saints even—in the hour of tribulation have cried out that they were being made to feel the wrath of God for the sins that no man is without?

If humanity contains a type that would not have seen in such a cause for sorrow a visitation of God, it is the type of inhuman monster to which we are asked to believe that Alexander VI belonged. A sinner unquestionably he was, and a great one; but a human sinner, and not an incarnate devil, else there could have been no such outcry from him in such an hour as this.

He announced that henceforth the spiritual needs of the Church should be his only care. He inveighed against the corruption of the ecclesiastical estate, confessing himself aware of how far it had strayed from the ancient discipline and from the laws that had been framed to bridle licence and cupidity, which were now rampant and unchecked; and he proclaimed his intention to reform the Curia and the Church of Rome. To this end he appointed a commission consisting of the Cardinal-Bishops Oliviero Caraffa and Giorgio Costa, the Cardinal-Priests Antonietto Pallavicino and Gianantonio Sangiorgio, and the Cardinal-Deacons Francesco Piccolomini and Raffaele Riario.

There was even a suggestion that he was proposing to abdicate, but that he was prevailed upon to do nothing until his grief should have abated and his judgement be restored to its habitual calm. This suggestion, however, rests upon no sound authority.

Letters of condolence reached him on every hand. Even his arch-enemy, Cardinal Giuliano della Rovere, put aside his rancour in the face of the Pope's overwhelming grief—and also because it happened to consort with his own interests, as will presently transpire. He wrote to Alexander from France that he was truly pained to the very soul of him in his concern for the Pope's Holiness—a letter which, no doubt, laid the foundations to the reconciliation that was toward between them.

Still more remarkable was it that the thaumaturgical Savonarola should have paused in the atrabilious invective with which he was inflaming Florence against the Pope, should have paused to send him a letter of condolence in which he prayed that the Lord of all mercy might comfort his Holiness in his tribulation.

That letter is a singular document; singularly human, yielding a singular degree of insight into the nature of the man who penned it. A whole chapter of intelligent speculation upon the character of Savonarola, based upon a study of externals, could not reveal as much of the mentality of that fanatical demagogue as the consideration of just this letter.

The sympathy by which we cannot doubt it to have been primarily inspired is here overspread by the man's rampant fanaticism, there diluted by the prophecies from which he cannot even now refrain; and, throughout, the manner is that of the pulpit-thumping orator. The first half of his letter is a prelude in the form of a sermon upon Faith, all very trite and obvious; and the notion of this excommunicated friar holding forth to the Pope's Holiness in polemical platitudes delivered with all the authority of inspired discoveries of his own is one more proof that at the root of fanaticism in all ages and upon all questions, lies an utter lack of a sense of fitness and proportion. Having said that "the just man liveth in the Lord by faith," and that "the Lord in His mercy passeth over all our sins," he proclaims that he announces things of which he is assured, and for which he is ready to suffer all persecutions, and begs his Holiness to turn a favourable eye upon the work of faith in which he is labouring, and to give heed no more to the impious, promising the Holy Father that thus shall the Lord bestow upon him the essence of joy instead of the spirit of grief. Having begun, as we have seen, with an assurance that "the Lord in His mercy passeth over all our sins," he concludes by prophesying, with questionable logic, that "the thunders of His wrath will ere long be heard." Nor does he omit to mention—with an apparent arrogance that again betrays that same want of a sense of proportion—that all his predictions are true.

His letter, however, and that of Cardinal della Rovere, among so many others, show us how touched was the world by the Pope's loss and overwhelming grief, how shocked at the manner in which this had been brought about.

The commission which Alexander had appointed for the work of reform had meanwhile got to work, and the Cardinal of Naples edited the articles of a constitution which was undoubtedly the object of prolonged study and consideration, as is revealed by the numerous erasures and emendations which it bears. Unfortunately—for reasons which are not apparent—it was never published by Alexander. Possibly by the time that it was concluded the aggrandizement of the temporal power was claiming his entire attention to the neglect of the spiritual needs of the Holy See. It is also possible— as has been abundantly suggested—that the stern mood of penitence had softened with his sorrow, and was now overpast.

Nevertheless, it may have been some lingering remnant of this fervour of reform that dictated the severe punishment which fell that year upon the flagitious Bishop of Cosenza. A fine trade was being driven in Rome by the sale of forged briefs of indulgence. Raynaldus cites a Bull on that score addressed by Alexander, in the first year of his pontificate, to the bishops of Spain, enjoining them to visit with punishment all who in that kingdom should be discovered to be pursuing such a traffic. On September 4, 1497, Burchard tells us, three servants of the Pontifical Secretary, the Archbishop of Cosenza (Bartolomeo Florido) were arrested in consequence of the discovery of twenty forged briefs issued by them. In their examination they incriminated their master the archbishop, who was consequently put upon his trial and found guilty. Alexander deposed, degraded, and imprisoned him in Sant' Angelo in a dark room, where he was supplied with oil for his lamp and bread and water for his nourishment until he died. His underlings were burnt in the Campo di Fiori in the following month.

The Duke of Gandia left a widow and two children—Giovanni, a boy of three years of age, and Isabella, a girl of two. In the interests of her son, the widowed duchess applied to the Governor of Valencia in the following September for the boy's investiture in the rights of his deceased father. This was readily granted upon authority from Rome, and so the boy Giovanni was recognized as third Duke of Gandia, Prince of Sessa and Teano, and Lord of Cerignola and Montefoscolo, and the administration of his estates during his minority was entrusted to his uncle, Cesare Borgia.

The Lordship of Benevento—the last grant made to Giovanni Borgia—was not mentioned; nor was it then nor ever subsequently claimed by the widow. It is the one possession of Gandia's that went to Cesare, who was confirmed in it by the King of Naples.

The Gandia branch of the Borgia family remained in Spain, prospered and grew in importance, and, incidentally, produced St. Francis de Borgia. This Duke of Gandia was Master of the Household to Charles V, and thus a man of great worldly consequence; but it happened that he was so moved by the sight of the disfigured body of his master's beautiful queen that he renounced the world and entered the Society of Jesus, eventually becoming its General. He died in 1562, and in the fulness of time was canonized.

Cesare's departure for Naples as legate a latere to anoint and crown Federigo of Aragon was naturally delayed by the tragedy that had assailed his house, and not until July 22 did he take his leave of the Pope and set out with an escort of two hundred horse.

Naples was still in a state of ferment, split into two parties, one of which favoured France and the other Aragon, so that disturbances were continual. Alexander expressed the hope that Cesare might appear in that distracted kingdom in the guise of an "angel of peace," and that by his coronation of King Federigo he should set a term to the strife that was toward.

The city of Naples itself was now being ravaged by fever, and in consequence of this it was determined that Cesare should repair instead to Capua, where Federigo would await him. Arrived there, however, Cesare fell ill, and the coronation ceremony again suffered a postponement until August 10. Cesare remained a fortnight in the kingdom, and on August 22 set out to return to Rome, and his departure appears to have been a matter of relief to Federigo, for so impoverished did the King of Naples find himself that the entertainment of the legate and his numerous escort had proved a heavy tax upon his flabby purse.

On the morning of September 6 all the cardinals in Rome received a summons to attend at the Monastery of Santa Maria Nuova to welcome the returned Cardinal of Valencia. In addition to the Sacred College all the ambassadors of the Powers were present, and, after the celebration of the Mass, the entire assembly proceeded to the Vatican, where the Pope was waiting to receive his son. When the young cardinal presented himself at the foot of the papal throne Alexander opened his arms to him, embraced, and kissed him, speaking no word.

This rests upon the evidence of two eye-witnesses,(1) and the circumstance has been urged and propounded into the one conclusive piece of evidence that Cesare had murdered his brother, and that the Pope knew it. In this you have some more of what Gregorovius terms "inexorable logic." He kissed him, but he spake no word to him; therefore, they reason, Cesare murdered Gandia. Can absurdity be more absurd, fatuity more fatuous? Lucus a non lucendo! To square the circle should surely present no difficulty to these subtle logicians.

1 *"Non dixit verbum Pape Valentinus, nec Papa sibi, sed eo deosculato, descendit de solio" (Burchard's Diarium, and "Solo lo bació," in letter from Rome in Sanuto's Diarii)*

It was, as we have seen, in February of 1498 that it was first rumoured that Cesare intended to put off the purple; and that the rumour had ample foundation was plain from the circumstance that the Pope was already laying plans whose fulfilment must be dependent upon that step, and seeking to arrange a marriage for Cesare with Carlotta of Aragon, King Federigo of Naples's daughter, stipulating that her dowry should be such that Cesare, in taking her to wife, should become Prince of Altamura and Tarentum.

But Federigo showed himself unwilling, possibly in consideration of the heavy dowry demanded and of the heavy draft already made by the Borgias—through Giuffredo Borgia, Prince of Squillace—upon this Naples which the French invasion had so impoverished. He gave out that he would not have his daughter wedded to a priest who was the son of a priest and that he would not give his daughter unless the Pope could contrive that a cardinal might marry and yet retain his hat.

It all sounded as if he were actuated by nice scruples and high principles; but the opinion is unfortunately not encouraged when we find him, nevertheless, giving his consent to the marriage of his nephew Alfonso to Lucrezia Borgia upon the pronouncement of her divorce from Giovanni Sforza. The marriage, let us say in passing, was celebrated at the Vatican on June 20, 1498, Lucrezia receiving a dowry of 40,000 ducats. But the astute Alexander saw to it that his family should acquire more than it gave, and contrived that Alfonso should receive the Neapolitan cities of Biselli and Quadrata, being raised to the title of Prince of Biselli.

Nevertheless, there was a vast difference between giving in marriage a daughter who must take a weighty dowry out of the kingdom and receiving a daughter who would bring a handsome dowry with her. And the facts suggest that such was the full measure of Federigo's scruples.

Meanwhile, to dissemble his reluctance to let Cesare have his daughter to wife, Federigo urged that he must first take the feeling of Ferdinand and Isabella in this matter.

While affairs stood thus, Charles VIII died suddenly at Amboise in April of that year 1498. Some work was being carried out there by artists whom he had brought from Naples for the purpose, and, in going to visit this, the king happened to enter a dark gallery, and struck his forehead so violently against the edge of a door that he expired the same day—at the age of twenty-eight. He was a poor, malformed fellow, as we have seen, and "of little understanding," Commines tells us, "but so good that it would have been impossible to have found a kinder creature."

With him the Valois dynasty came to an end. He was succeeded by his cousin, the Duke of Orleans, who, upon his coronation at Rheims, assumed the title of King of France and the Two Sicilies and Duke of Milan—a matter which considerably perturbed Federigo of Aragon and Lodovico Sforza. Each of these rulers saw in that assumption of his own title by Louis XII a declaration of enmity, the prelude to a declaration of open war; wherefore, deeming it idle to send their ambassadors to represent them at the Court of France, they refrained from doing so.

Louis XII's claim upon the Duchy of Milan was based upon his being the grandson of Valentina Visconti, and, considering himself a Visconti, he naturally looked upon the Sforza dominion as no better than a usurpation which too long had been left undisturbed. To disturb it now was the first aim of his kingship. And to this end, as well as in another matter, the friendship of the Pope was very desirable to Louis.

The other matter concerned his matrimonial affairs. No sooner did he find himself King of France than he applied to Rome for the dissolution of his marriage with Jeanne de Valois, the daughter of Louis XI. The grounds he urged were threefold: Firstly, between himself and Jeanne there existed a relationship of the fourth degree and a spiritual affinity, resulting from the fact that her father, Louis XI, had held him at the baptismal font—which before the Council of Trent did constitute an impediment to marriage. Secondly, he had not been a willing party to the union, but had entered into it as a consequence of intimidation from the terrible Louis XI, who had threatened his life and possessions if not obeyed in this. Thirdly, Jeanne laboured under physical difficulties which rendered her incapable of maternity.

Of such a nature was the appeal he made to Alexander, and Alexander responded by appointing a commission presided over by the Cardinal of Luxembourg, and composed of that same cardinal and the Bishops of Albi and Ceuta, assisted by five other bishops as assessors, to investigate the king's grievance. There appears to be no good reason for assuming that the inquiry was not conducted fairly and honourably or that the finding of the bishops and ultimate annulment of the marriage was not in accordance with their consciences. We are encouraged to assume that all this was indeed so, when we consider that Jeanne de Valois submitted without protest to the divorce, and that neither then nor subsequently at any time did she prefer any complaint, accepting the judgement, it is presumable, as a just and fitting measure.

She applied to the Pope for permission to found a religious order, whose special aim should be the adoration and the emulation of the perfections of the Blessed Virgin, a permission which Alexander very readily accorded her. He was, himself, imbued with a very special devotion for the Mother of the Saviour. We see the spur of this special devotion of his in the votive offering of a silver effigy to her famous altar of the Santissima Nunziata in Florence, which he had promised in the event of Rome being freed from Charles VIII. Again, after the accident of the collapse of a roof in the Vatican, in which he narrowly escaped death, it is to Santa Maria Nuova that we see him going in procession to hold a solemn thanksgiving service to Our Lady. In a dozen different ways did that devotion find expression during his pontificate; and be it remembered that Catholics owe it to Alexander VI that the Angelus-bell is rung thrice daily in honour of the Blessed Virgin.

To us this devotion to the Mother of Chastity on the part of a churchman openly unchaste in flagrant subversion of his vows is a strange and incongruous spectacle. But the incongruity of it is illumining. It reveals Alexander's simple attitude towards the sins of the flesh, and shows how, in common with most churchmen of his day, he found no conscientious difficulty in combining fervid devotion with perfervid licence. Whatever it may seem by ours, by his lights—by the light of the examples about him from his youth, by the light of the precedents afforded him by his predecessors in St. Peter's Chair—his conduct was a normal enough affair, which can have afforded him little with which to reproach himself.

In the matter of the annulment of the marriage of Louis XII it is to be conceded that Alexander made the most of the opportunity it afforded him. He perceived that the moment was propitious for enlisting the services of the King of France to the achievement of his own ends, more particularly to further the matter of the marriage of Cesare Borgia with Carlotta of Aragon, who was being reared at the Court of France. Accordingly Alexander desired the Bishop of Ceuta to lay his wishes in the matter before the Christian King, and, to the end that Cesare might find a fitting secular estate awaiting him when eventually he emerged from the clergy, the Pope further suggested to Louis, through the bishop's agency, that Cesare should receive the investiture of the counties of Valentinois and Dyois in Dauphiny. On the face of it this wears the look of inviting bribery. In reality it scarcely amounted to so much, although the opportunism that prompted the request is undeniable. Yet it is worthy of consideration that in what concerned the counties of Valentinois and Dyois, the Pope's suggestion constituted a wise political step. These territories had been in dispute between France and the Holy See for a matter of some two hundred years, during which the Popes had been claiming dominion over them. The claims had been admitted by Louis XI, who had relinquished the counties to the Church; but shortly after his death the Parliament of Dauphiny had restored them to the crown of France. Charles VIII and Innocent VIII had wrangled over them, and an arbitration was finally projected, but never held.

Alexander now perceived a way to solve the difficulty by a compromise which should enrich his son and give the latter a title to replace that of cardinal which he was to relinquish. So his proposal to Louis XII was that the Church should abandon its claim upon the territories, whilst the king, raising Valentinois to the dignity of a duchy, should so confer it upon Cesare Borgia.

Although the proposal was politically sound, it constituted at the same time an act of flagrant nepotism. But let us bear in mind that Alexander did not lack a precedent for this particular act. When Louis XI had surrendered Valentinois to Sixtus IV, this Pope had bestowed it upon his nephew Girolamo, thereby vitiating any claim that the Holy See might subsequently have upon the territory. We judge it—under the circumstances that Louis XI had surrendered it to the Church—to be a far more flagrant piece of nepotism than was Alexander's now.

Louis XII, nothing behind the Pope in opportunism, saw in the concession asked of him the chance of acquiring Alexander's good-will. He consented, accompanying his consent by a request for a cardinal's hat for Georges d'Amboise, Bishop of Rouen, who had been his devoted friend in less prosperous times, and the sharer of his misfortunes under the previous reign, and was now his chief counsellor and minister. In addition he besought—dependent, of course, upon the granting of the solicited divorce—a dispensation to marry Anne of Brittany, the beautiful widow of Charles VIII. This was Louis's way of raising the price, as it were, of the concession and services asked of him; yet, that there might be no semblance of bargaining, his consent to Cesare's being created Duke of Valentinois was simultaneous with his request for further favours.

With the Royal Patents conferring that duchy upon the Pope's son, Louis de Villeneuve reached Rome on August 7, 1498. On the same day the young cardinal came before the Sacred College, assembled in Consistory, to crave permission to doff the purple.

After the act of adoration of the Pope's Holiness, he humbly submitted to his brother cardinals that his inclinations had ever been in opposition to his embracing the ecclesiastical dignity, and that, if he had entered upon it at all, this had been solely at the instances of his Holiness, just as he had persevered in it to gratify him; but that, his inclinations and desires for the secular estate persisting, he implored the Holy Father, of his clemency, to permit him to put off his habit and ecclesiastical rank, to restore his hat and benefices to the Church, and to grant him dispensation to return to the world and be free to contract marriage. And he prayed the very reverend cardinals to use their good offices on his behalf, adding to his own their intercessions to the Pope's Holiness to accord him the grace he sought.

The cardinals relegated the decision of the matter to the Pope. Cardinal Ximenes alone—as the representative of Spain—stood out against the granting of the solicited dispensation, and threw obstacles in the way of it. In this, no doubt, he obeyed his instructions from Ferdinand and Isabella, who saw to the bottom of the intrigue with France that was toward, and of the alliance that impended between Louis XII and the Holy See—an alliance not at all to the interests of Spain.

The Pope made a speedy rout of the cardinal's objections with the most apostolic and irresistible of all weapons. He pointed out that it was not for him to hinder the Cardinal of Valencia's renunciation of the purple, since that renunciation was clearly become necessary for the salvation of his soul—"Pro salutae animae suae"—to which, of course, Ximenes had no answer.

But, with the object of conciliating Spain, this ever-politic Pope indicated that, if Cesare was about to become a prince of France, his many ecclesiastical benefices, yielding some 35,000 gold florins yearly, being mostly in Spain, would be bestowed upon Spanish churchmen, and he further begged Ximenes to remember that he already had a "nephew" at the Court of Spain in the person of the heir of Gandia, whom he particularly commended to the favour of Ferdinand and Isabella.

Thus was Cesare Borgia's petition granted, and his return to the world accomplished. And, by a strange chance of homonymy, his title remained unchanged despite his change of estate. The Cardinal of Valencia, in Spain, became the Duke of Valence—or Valentinois—in France and in Italy Valentino remained Valentino.

BOOK III
THE BULL RAMPANT

"Cum numine Caesaris omen"
(motto on Cesare Borgia's sword.)

CHAPTER I
THE DUCHESS OF VALENTINOIS

King Louis XII dispatched the Sieur de Sarenon by sea, with a fleet of three ships and five galleys, to the end that he should conduct the new duke to France, which fleet was delayed so that it did not drop its anchors at Ostia until the end of September.

Meanwhile, Cesare's preparations for departure had been going forward, and were the occasion of a colossal expenditure on the part of his sire. For the Pope desired that his son, in going to France to assume his estate, and for the further purposes of marrying a wife, of conveying to Louis the dispensation permitting his marriage with Anne of Brittany, and of bearing the red hat to Amboise, should display the extraordinary magnificence for which the princes of cultured and luxurious Italy were at the time renowned.

His suite consisted of fully a hundred attendants, what with esquires, pages, lacqueys and grooms, whilst twelve chariots and fifty sumpter-mules were laden with his baggage. The horses of his followers were all sumptuously caparisoned with bridles and stirrups of solid silver; and, for the rest, the splendour of the liveries, the weapons and the jewels, and the richness of the gifts he bore with him were the amazement even of that age of dazzling displays.

In Cesare's train went Ramiro de Lorqua, the Master of his Household; Agabito Gherardi, his secretary; and his Spanish physician, Gaspare Torella—the only medical man of his age who had succeeded in discovering a treatment for the pudendagra which the French had left in Italy, and who had dedicated to Cesare his learned treatise upon that disease.

As a body-guard, or escort of honour, Cesare took with him thirty gentlemen, mostly Romans, among whom were Giangiordano Orsini, Pietro Santa Croce, Mario di Mariano, Domenico Sanguigna, Giulio Alberini, Bartolomeo Capranica, and Gianbattista Mancini—all young, and all members of those patrician families which Alexander VI had skilfully attached to his own interest.

The latest of these was the Orsini family, with which an alliance was established by the marriage celebrated at the Vatican on September 28 of that same year between Fabio Orsini and Girolama Borgia, a niece of the Pope's.

Cesare's departure took place on October 1, in the early morning, when he rode out with his princely retinue, and followed the Tiber along Trastevere, without crossing the city. He was mounted on a handsome charger, caparisoned in red silk and gold brocade—the colours of France, in which he had also dressed his lacqueys. He wore a doublet of white damask laced with gold, and carried a mantle of black velvet swinging from his shoulders. Of black velvet, too, was the cap on his auburn head, its sable colour an effective background for the ruddy effulgence of the great rubies—"as large as beans"—with which it was adorned.

Of the gentlemen who followed him, the Romans were dressed in the French mode, like himself, whilst the Spaniards adhered to the fashions of their native Spain.

He was escorted as far as the end of the Banchi by four cardinals, and from a window of the Vatican the Pope watched the imposing cavalcade and followed it with his eyes until it was lost to view, weeping, we are told, for very joy at the contemplation of the splendour and magnificence which it had been his to bestow upon his beloved son—"the very heart of him," as he wrote to the King of France in that letter of which Cesare was the bearer.

On October 12 the Duke of Valentinois landed at Marseilles, where he was received by the Bishop of Dijon, whom the king had sent to meet him, and who now accompanied the illustrious visitor to Avignon. There Cesare was awaited by the Cardinal Giuliano della Rovere. This prelate was now anxious to make his peace with Alexander—and presently we shall look into the motives that probably inspired him, a matter which has so far, we fancy, escaped criticism for reasons that we shall also strive to make apparent. To the beginnings of a reconciliation with the Pontiff afforded by his touching letter of condolence on the death of the Duke of Gandia, he now added a very cordial reception and entertainment of Cesare; and throughout his sojourn in France the latter received at the hands of della Rovere the very friendliest treatment, the cardinal missing no opportunity of working in the duke's interests and for the advancement of his ends.

The Pope wrote to the cardinal commending Cesare to his good graces, and the cardinal replied with protestations which he certainly proceeded to make good.

Della Rovere was to escort Cesare to the king, who was with his Court then at Chinon, awaiting the completion of the work that was being carried out at his Castle of Blois, which presently became his chief residence. But Cesare appears to have tarried in Avignon, for he was still there at the end of October, nor did he reach Chinon until the middle of December. The pomp of his entrance was a thing stupendous. We find a detailed relation of it in Brantôme, translated into prose form some old verses which, he tells us, that he found in the family treasury. He complains of their coarseness, and those who are acquainted with the delightful old Frenchman's own frankness of expression may well raise their brows at that criticism of his. Whatever the coarse liberties taken with the subject—of which we are not allowed more than an occasional glimpse—and despite the fact that the relation was in verse, which ordinarily makes for the indulgence of the rhymer's fancy— the description appears to be fairly accurate, for it corresponds more or less with the particulars given in Sanuto.

At the head of the cavalcade went twenty-four sumpter-mules, laden with coffers and other baggage under draperies embroidered with Cesare's arms—prominent among which would be the red bull, the emblem of his house, and the three-pointed flame, his own particular device. Behind these came another twenty-four mules, caparisoned in the king's colours of scarlet and gold, to be followed in their turn by sixteen beautiful chargers led by hand, similarly caparisoned, and their bridles and stirrups of solid silver. Next came eighteen pages on horseback, sixteen of whom were in scarlet and yellow, whilst the remaining two were in cloth of gold. These were followed by a posse of lacqueys in the same liveries and two mules laden with coffers draped with cloth of gold, which contained the gifts of which Cesare was the bearer. Behind these rode the duke's thirty gentlemen, in cloth of gold and silver, and amongst them came the duke himself.

Cesare was mounted on a superb war-horse that was all empanoplied in a cuirass of gold leaves of exquisite workmanship, its head surmounted by a golden artichoke, its tail confined in a net of gold abundantly studded with pearls. The duke was in black velvet, through the slashings of which appeared the gold brocade of the undergarment. Suspended from a chain said by Brantôme's poet to be worth thirty thousand ducats, a medallion of diamonds blazed upon his breast, and in his black velvet cap glowed those same wonderful rubies that we saw on the occasion of his departure from Rome. His boots were of black velvet, laced with gold thread that was studded with gems.

The rear of the cavalcade was brought up by more mules and the chariots bearing his plate and tents and all the other equipage with which a prince was wont to travel.

It is said by some that his horse was shod with solid gold, and there is also a story—pretty, but probably untrue—that some of his mules were shod in the same metal, and that, either because the shoes were loosely attached of intent, or because the metal, being soft, parted readily from the hoofs, these golden shoes were freely cast and left as largesse for those who might care to take them.

The Bishop of Rouen—that same Georges d'Amboise for whom he was bringing the red hat—the Seneschal of Toulouse and several gentlemen of the Court went to meet him on the bridge, and escorted him up through the town to the castle, where the king awaited him. Louis XII gave him a warm and cordial welcome, showing him then and thereafter the friendliest consideration. Not so, however, the lady he was come to woo. It was said in Venice that she was in love with a young Breton gentleman in the following of Queen Anne. Whether this was true, and Carlotta acted in the matter in obedience to her own feelings, or whether she was merely pursuing the instructions she had received from Naples, she obstinately and absolutely refused to entertain or admit the suit of Cesare.

Della Rovere, on January 18, wrote to the Pope from Nantes, whither the Court had moved, a letter in which he sang the praises of the young Duke of Valentinois.

"By his modesty his readiness, his prudence, and his other virtues he has known how to earn the affections of every one." Unfortunately, there was one important exception, as the cardinal was forced to add: "The damsel, either out of her own contrariness, or because so induced by others, which is easier to believe, constantly refuses to hear of the wedding."

Della Rovere was quite justified in finding it easier to believe that Carlotta was acting upon instructions from others, for, when hard pressed to consent to the alliance, she demanded that the Neapolitan ambassador should himself say that her father desired her to do so—a statement which, it seems, the ambassador could not bring himself to make.

Baffled by the persistence of that refusal, Cesare all but returned a bachelor to Italy. So far, indeed, was his departure a settled matter that in February of 1489, at the Castle of Loches, he received the king's messages for the Pope. Yet Louis hesitated to let him go without having bound his Holiness to his own interests by stronger bonds.

In the task of tracing the annals of the Borgias, the honest seeker after truth is compelled to proceed axe in hand that he may hack himself a way through the tangle of irresponsible or malicious statements that have grown up about this subject, driving their roots deep into the soil of history. Not a single chance does malignity, free or chartered, appear to have missed for the invention of flagitious falsehoods concerning this family, or for the no less flagitious misinterpretation of known facts.

Amid a mass of written nonsense dealing with Cesare's sojourn in France is the oft-repeated, totally unproven statement that he withheld from Louis the dispensation enabling the latter to marry Anne of Brittany, until such time as he should have obtained from Louis all that he desired of him—in short, that he sold him the dispensation for the highest price he could extract. The only motive served by this statement is once more to show Alexander and his son in the perpetration of simoniacal practices, and the statement springs, beyond doubt, from a passage in Macchiavelli's Extracts from Dispatches to the Ten. Elsewhere has been mentioned the confusion prevailing in those extracts, and their unreliability as historical evidences. That circumstance can be now established. The passage in question runs as follows:

"This dispensation was given to Valentinois when he went to France without any one being aware of its existence, with orders to sell it dearly to the king, and not until satisfied of the wife and his other desires. And, whilst these things were toward, the king learnt from the Bishop of Ceuta that the dispensation already existed, and so, without having received or even seen it the marriage was celebrated, and for revealing this the Bishop of Ceuta was put to death by order of Valentinois."

Now, to begin with, Macchiavelli admits that what passed between Pope and duke was secret. How, then, does he pretend to possess these details of it? But, leaving that out of the question, his statement—so abundantly repeated by later writers—is traversed by every one of the actual facts of the case.

That there can have been no secret at all about the dispensation is made plain by the fact that Manfredi, the Ferrarese ambassador, writes of it to Duke Ercole on October 2—the day after Cesare's departure from Rome. And as for the death of Fernando d'Almeida Bishop of Ceuta, this did not take place then, nor until two years later (on January 7, 1499) at the siege of Forli, whither he had gone in Cesare's train—as is related in Bernardi's Chronicles and Bonoli's history of that town.

To return to the matter of Cesare's imminent departure unwed from France, Louis XII was not the only monarch to whom this was a source of anxiety. Keener far was the anxiety experienced on that score by the King of Naples, who feared that its immediate consequence would be to drive the Holy Father into alliance with Venice, which was paying its court to him at the time and with that end in view. Eager to conciliate Alexander in this hour of peril, Federigo approached him with alternative proposals, and offered to invest Cesare in the principalities of Salerno and Sanseverino, which had been taken from the rebel barons. To this the Pope might have consented, but that, in the moment of considering it, letters reached him from Cesare which made him pause.

Louis XII had also discovered an alternative to the marriage of Cesare with Carlotta, and one that should more surely draw the Pope into the alliance with Venice and himself.

Among the ladies of the Court of Queen Anne—Louis had now been wedded a month—there were, besides Carlotta, two other ladies either of whom might make Cesare a suitable duchess. One of these was a niece of the king's, the daughter of the Comte de Foix; the other was Charlotte d'Albret, a daughter of Alain d'Albret, Duc de Guyenne, and sister to the King of Navarre. Between these two Cesare was now given to choose by Louis, and his choice fell upon Charlotte.

She was seventeen years of age and said to be the most beautiful maid in France, and she had been reared at the honourable and pious Court of Jeanne de Valois, whence she had passed into that of Anne of Brittany, which latter, says Hilarion de Coste,(1) was "a school of virtue, an academy of honour."

1 *Éloges et vies des Reynes, Princesses, etc.*

Negotiations for her hand were opened with Alain, who, it is said, was at first unwilling, but in the end won over to consent. Navarre had need of the friendship of the King of France, that it might withstand the predatory humours of Castille; and so, for his son's sake, Alain could not long oppose the wishes of Louis. Considering closely the pecuniary difficulties under which this Alain d'Albret was labouring and his notorious avarice, one is tempted to conclude that such difficulties as he may have made were dictated by his reduced circumstances, his impossibility, or unwillingness, to supply his daughter with a dowry fitting her rank, and an unworthy desire to drive in the matter the best bargain possible. And this is abundantly confirmed by the obvious care and hard-headed cunning with which the Sieur d'Albret investigated Cesare's circumstances and sources of revenue to verify their values to be what was alleged.

Eventually he consented to endow her with 30,000 livres Tournois (90,000 francs) to be paid as follows: 6,000 livres on the celebration of the marriage, and the balance by annual instalments of 1,500 livres until cleared off. This sum, as a matter of fact, represented her portion of the inheritance from her deceased mother, Françoise de Bretagne, and it was tendered subject to her renouncing all rights and succession in any property of her father's or her said deceased mother's.

Thus is it set forth in the contract drawn up by Alain at Castel-Jaloux on March 23, 1499, which contract empowers his son Gabriel and one Regnault de St. Chamans to treat and conclude the marriage urged by the king between the Duke of Valentinois and Alain's daughter, Charlotte d'Albret. But that was by no means all. Among other conditions imposed by Alain, he stipulated that the Pope should endow his daughter with 100,000 livres Tournois, and that for his son, Amanieu d'Albret, there should be a cardinal's hat—for the fulfilment of both of which conditions Cesare took it upon himself to engage his father.

On April 15 the treaty between France and Venice was signed at Blois. It was a defensive and offensive alliance directed against all, with the sole exception of the reigning Pontiff, who should have the faculty to enter into it if he so elected. This was the first decisive step against the House of Sforza, and so secretly were the negotiations conducted that Lodovico Sforza's first intimation of them resulted from the capture in Milanese territory of a courier from the Pope with letters to Cesare in France. From these he learnt, to his dismay, not only of the existence of the league, but that the Pope had joined it. The immediate consequence of this positive assurance that Alexander had gone over to Sforza's enemies was Ascanio Sforza's hurried departure from Rome on July 13.

In the meantime Cesare's marriage had followed almost immediately upon the conclusion of the treaty. The nuptials were celebrated on May 12, and on the 19th he received at the hands of the King of France the knightly

Order of St. Michael, which was then the highest honour that France could confer. When the news of this reached the Pope he celebrated the event in Rome with public festivities and illuminations.

Of Cesare's courtship we have no information. The fact that the marriage was purely one of political expediency would tend to make us conceive it as invested with that sordid lovelessness which must so often attend the marriages of princes. But there exists a little data from which we may draw certain permissible inferences. This damsel of seventeen was said to be the loveliest in France, and there is more than a suggestion in Le Feron's De Gestis Regnum Gallorum, that Cesare was by no means indifferent to her charms. He tells us that the Duke of Valentinois entered into the marriage very heartily, not only for the sake of its expediency, but for "the beauty of the lady, which was equalled by her virtues and the sweetness of her nature."

Cesare, we have it on more than one authority, was the handsomest man of his day. The gallantry of his bearing merited the approval of so fastidious a critic in such matters as Baldassare Castiglione, who mentions it in his Il Cortigiano. Of his personal charm there is also no lack of commendation from those who had his acquaintance at this time. Added to this, his Italian splendour and flamboyance may well have dazzled a maid who had been reared amid the grey and something stern tones of the Court of Jeanne de Valois.

And so it may well be that they loved, and that they were blessed in their love for the little space allotted them in each other's company. The sequel justifies in a measure the assumption. Just one little summer out of the span of their lives—brief though those lives were—did they spend together, and it is good to find some little evidence that, during that brief season at least, they inhabited life's rose-garden.

In September—just four short months after the wedding-bells had pealed above them—the trumpets of war blared out their call to arms. Louis's preparations for the invasion of Milan were complete and he poured his troops through Piedmont under the command of Giangiacomo Trivulzio.

Cesare was to accompany Louis into Italy. He appointed his seventeen-year-old duchess governor and administrator of his lands and lordships in France and Dauphiny under a deed dated September 8, and he made her heiress to all his moveable possessions in the event of his death. Surely this bears some witness, not only to the prevailing of a good understanding between them, but to his esteem of her and the confidence he reposed in her mental qualities. The rest her later mourning of him shows.

Thus did Cesare take leave of the young wife whom he was never to see again. Their child—born in the following spring—he was never to see at all. The pity of it! Ambition-driven, to fulfil the destiny expected of him, he turned his back upon that pleasant land of Dauphiny where the one calm little season of his manhood had been spent, where happiness and peace might have been his lifelong portion had he remained. He set his face towards Italy and the storm and stress before him, and in the train of King Louis he set out upon the turbulent meteoric course that was to sear so deep and indelible a brand across the scroll of history.

CHAPTER II
THE KNELL OF THE TYRANTS

In the hour of his need Lodovico Sforza found himself without friends or credit, and he had to pay the price of the sly, faithless egotistical policy he had so long pursued with profit.

His far-reaching schemes were flung into confusion because a French king had knocked his brow against a door, and had been succeeded by one who conceived that he had a legal right to the throne of Milan, and the intent and might to enforce it, be the right legal or not. It was in vain now that Lodovico turned to the powers of Italy for assistance, in vain that his cunning set fresh intrigues afoot. His neighbours had found him out long since; he had played fast and loose with them too often, and there was none would trust him now.

Thus he found himself isolated, and in no case to withstand the French avalanche which rolled down upon his duchy. The fall of Milan was a matter of days; of resistance there was practically none. Town after town threw up its gates to the invaders, and Lodovico, seeing himself abandoned on all sides, sought in flight the safety of his own person.

Cesare took no part in the war, which, after all, was no war—no more than an armed progress. He was at Lyons with the King, and he did not move into Italy until Louis went to take possession of his new duchy.

Amid the acclamations of the ever-fickle mob, hailing him as its deliverer, Louis XII rode triumphantly into Milan on October 6, attended by a little host of princes, including the Prince of Savoy, the Dukes of Montferrat and Ferrara, and the Marquis of Mantua. But the place of honour went to Cesare Borgia, who rode at the king's side, a brilliant and arresting figure. This was the occasion on which Baldassare Castiglione—who was in the Marquis of Mantua's suite—was moved to such praise of the appearance and gallant bearing of the duke, and of the splendid equipment of his suite, which outshone those of all that little host of attendant princes.

From this time onward Cesare signs himself "Cesare Borgia of France," and quarters on his shield the golden lilies of France with the red bull of the House of Borgia.

The conditions on which Alexander VI joined the league of France and Venice became apparent at about this time. They were to be gathered from the embassy of his nephew, the Cardinal Giovanni Borgia, to Venice in the middle of September. There the latter announced to the Council of Ten that the Pope's Holiness aimed at the recovery to the Church of those Romagna tyrannies which originally were fiefs of the Holy See and held by her vicars, who, however, had long since repudiated the Pontifical authority, refused the payment of their tributes, and in some instances had even gone so far as to bear arms against the Church.

With one or two exceptions the violent and evil misgovernment of these turbulent princelings was a scandal to all Italy. They ruled by rapine and murder, and rendered Romagna little better than a nest of brigands. Their state of secession from the Holy See arose largely out of the nepotism practised by the last Popes—a nepotism writers are too prone to overlook when charging Alexander with the same abuse. Such Popes as Sixtus IV and Innocent VIII had broken up the States of the Church that they might endow their children and their nephews. The nepotism of such as these never had any result but to impoverish the Holy See; whilst, on the other hand, the nepotism of Alexander—this Pope who is held up to obloquy as the archetype of the nepotist—had a tendency rather to enrich it. It was not to the States of the Church, not by easy ways of plundering the territories of the Holy See, that he turned to found dominions and dynasties for his children. He went beyond and outside of them, employing princely alliances as the means to his ends. Gandia was a duke in Spain; Giuffredo a prince in Naples, and Cesare a duke in France. For none of these could it be said that territories had been filched from Rome, whilst the alliances made for them were such as tended to strengthen the power of the Pope, and, therefore, of the Church.

The reconsolidation of the States of the Church, the recovery of her full temporal power, which his predecessors had so grievously dissipated, had ever been Alexander's aim; Louis XII afforded him, at last, his opportunity, since with French aid the thing now might be attempted.

His son Cesare was the Hercules to whom was to be given the labour of cleaning out the Augean stable of the Romagna.

That Alexander may have been single-minded in his purpose has never been supposed. It might, indeed, be to suppose too much; and the general assumption that, from the outset, his chief aim was to found a powerful State for his son may be accepted. But let us at least remember that such had been the aims of several Popes before him. Sixtus IV and Innocent VIII had similarly aimed at founding dynasties in Romagna for their families, but, lacking the talents and political acuteness of Alexander and a son of the mettle and capacity of Cesare Borgia, the feeble trail of their ambition is apt to escape attention. It is also to be remembered that, whatever Alexander's ulterior motive, the immediate results of the campaign with which he inspired his son were to reunite to the Church the States which had fallen away from her, and to re-establish her temporal sway in the full plenitude of its dominion. However much he may have been imbued with the desire to exalt and aggrandize his children politically, he did nothing that did not at the same time make for the greater power and glory of the Church.

His formidable Bull published in October set forth how, after trial, it had been found that the Lords or Vicars of Rimini, Pesaro, Imola, Forli, Camerino and Faenza, with other feudatories of the Holy See (including the duchy of Urbino) had never paid the yearly tribute due to the Church, wherefore he, by virtue of his apostolic authority, deprived them of all their rights, and did declare them so deprived.

It has been said again and again that this Bull amounting to a declaration of war, was no more than a pretext to indulge his rapacity; but surely it bears the impress of a real grievance, and, however blameable the results that followed out of it, for the measure itself there were just and ample grounds.

The effect of that Bull, issued at a moment when Cesare stood at arms with the might of France at his back, ready to enforce it, was naturally to throw into a state of wild dismay these Romagna tyrants whose acquaintance we shall make at closer quarters presently in the course of following Cesare's campaign. Cesare Borgia may have been something of a wolf; but you are not to suppose that the Romagna was a fold of lambs.

Giovanni Sforza—Cesare's sometime brother-inlaw, and Lord of Pesaro—flies in hot haste to Venice for protection. There are no lengths to which he will not go to thwart the Borgias in their purpose, to save his tyranny from falling into the power of this family which he hates most rabidly, and of which he says that, having robbed him of his honour, it would now deprive him of his possessions. He even offers to make a gift of his dominions to the Republic.

There was much traders' blood in Venice, and, trader-like, she was avid of possessions. You can surmise how she must have watered at the mouth to see so fine a morsel cast thus into her lap, and yet to know that the consumption of it might beget a woeful indigestion. Venice shook her head regretfully. She could not afford to quarrel with her ally, King Louis, and so she made answer—a thought contemptuously, it seems—that Giovanni should have made his offer while he was free to do so.

The Florentines exerted themselves to save Forli from the fate that threatened it. They urged a league of Bologna, Ferrara, Forli, Piombino, and Siena for their common safety—a proposal which came to nothing, probably because Ferrara and Siena, not being threatened by the Bull, saw no reason why, for the sake of others, they should call down upon themselves the wrath of the Borgias and their mighty allies.

Venice desired to save Faenza, whose tyrant, Manfredi, was also attainted for non-payment of his tributes, and to this end the Republic sent an embassy to Rome with the moneys due. But the Holy Father refused the gold, declaring that it was too late for payment.

Forli's attempt to avert the danger was of a different sort, and not exerted until this danger—in the shape of Cesare himself—stood in arms beneath her walls. Two men, both named Tommaso—though it does not transpire that they were related—one a chamberlain of the Palace of Forli, the other a musician, were so devoted to the Countess Sforza-Riario, the grim termagant who ruled the fiefs of her murdered husband, Girolamo Riario, as to have undertaken an enterprise from which they cannot have hoped to emerge with their lives. It imported no less than the murder of the Pope. They were arrested on November 21, and in the possession of one of them was found a hollow cane containing a letter "so impregnated with poison that even to unfold it would be dangerous." This letter was destined for the Holy Father.

The story reads like a gross exaggeration emanating from men who, on the subject of poisoning, display the credulity of the fifteenth century, so ignorant in these matters and so prone to the fantastic. And our minds receive a shock upon learning that, when put to the question, these messengers actually made a confession—upon which the story rests—admitting that they had been sent by the countess to slay the Pope, in the hope that thus Forli might be saved to the Riarii. At first we conclude that those wretched men, examined to the accompaniment of torture, confessed whatever was required of them, as so frequently happened in such cases. Such, indeed, is the very explanation advanced by more than one writer, coupled with the suggestion, in some instances, that the whole affair was trumped up by the Pope to serve his own ends.

They will believe the wildest and silliest of poisoning stories (such as those of Djem and Cardinal Giovanni Borgia) which reveal the Borgias as the poisoners; but, let another be accused and the Borgias be the intended victims, and at once they grow rational, and point out to you the wildness of the statement, the impossibility of its being true. Yet it is a singular fact that a thorough investigation of this case of the Countess Sforza-Riario's poisoned letter reveals it to be neither wild nor impossible but simply diabolical. The explanation of the matter is to be found in Andrea Bernardi's Chronicles of Forli. He tells us exactly how the thing was contrived, with a precision of detail which we could wish to see emulated by other contemporaries of his who so lightly throw out accusations of poisoning. He informs us that a deadly and infectious disease was rampant in Forli in that year 1499, and that, before dispatching her letter to the Pope, the Countess caused it to be placed upon the body of one who was sick of this infection—thus hoping to convey it to his Holiness.(1)

1 *"Dite litre lei le aveva fate tocare et tenere adose ad uno nostro infetado."—Andrea Bernardi (Cronache di Forli).*

Alexander held a thanksgiving service for his escape at Santa Maria della Pace, and Cardinal Raffaele Riario fled precipitately from Rome, justly fearful of being involved in the papal anger that must fall upon his house.

By that time, however, Cesare had already taken the field. The support of Louis, conqueror of Milan, had been obtained, and in this Cardinal Giuliano della Rovere had once more been helpful to the Borgias.

His reconciliation with the Pope, long since deserved by the services he had rendered the House of Borgia in forwarding Cesare's aims, as we have seen, was completed now by an alliance which bound the two families together. His nephew, Francesco della Rovere, had married Alexander's niece, Angela Borgia.

There is a letter from Giuliano to the Pope, dated October 12, 1499, in which he expresses his deep gratitude in the matter of this marriage, which naturally redounded to the advantage of his house, and pledges himself to exert all the influence which he commands with Louis XII for the purpose of furthering the Duke of Valentinois' wishes. So well does he keep this promise that we see him utterly abandoning his cousins the Riarii, who were likely to be crushed under the hoofs of the now charging bull, and devoting himself strenuously to equip Cesare for that same charge. So far does he go in this matter that he is one of the sureties—the other being the Cardinal Giovanni Borgia—for the loan of 45,000 ducats raised by Cesare in Milan towards the cost of his campaign.

This is the moment in which to pause and consider this man, who, because he was a bitter enemy of Alexander's, and who, because earlier he had covered the Pope with obloquy and insult and is to do so again later, is hailed as a fine, upright, lofty, independent, noble soul.

Not so fine, upright, or noble but that he can put aside his rancour when he finds that there is more profit in fawning than in snarling; not so independent but that he can become a sycophant who writes panegyrics of Cesare and letters breathing devotion to the Pope, once he has realized that thus his interests will be better served. This is the man, remember, who dubbed Alexander a Jew and a Moor; this the man who agitated at the Courts of France and Spain for Alexander's deposition from the Pontificate on the score of the simony of his election; this the man whose vituperations of the Holy Father are so often quoted, since—coming from lips so honest— they must, from the very moment that he utters them, be merited. If only the historian would turn the medal about a little, and allow us a glimpse of the reverse as well as of the obverse, what a world of trouble and misconceptions should we not be spared!

Della Rovere had discovered vain his work of defamation, vain his attempts to induce the Kings of France and Spain to summon a General Council and depose the man whose seat he coveted, so he had sought to make his peace with the Holy See. The death of Charles VIII, and the succession of a king who had need of the Pope's friendship and who found a friend in Alexander, rendered it all the more necessary that della Rovere should set himself to reconquer, by every means in his power, the favour of Alexander.

And so you see this honourable, upright man sacrificing his very family to gain that personal end. Where now is that stubbornly honest conscience of his which made him denounce Alexander as no Christian and no Pope? Stifled by self-interest. It is as well that this should be understood, for this way lies the understanding of many things.

The funds for the campaign being found, Cesare received from Louis three hundred lances captained by Yves d'Allègre and four thousand foot, composed of Swiss and Gascons, led by the Bailie of Dijon. Further troops were being assembled for him at Cesena—the one fief of Romagna that remained faithful to the Church—by Achille Tiberti and Ercole Bentivogli, and to these were to be added the Pontifical troops that would be sent to him; so that Cesare found himself ultimately at the head of a considerable army, some ten thousand strong, well-equipped and supported by good artillery.

Louis XII left Milan on November 7—one month after his triumphal entrance—and set out to return to France, leaving Trivulzio to represent him as ruler of the Milanese. Two days later Cesare's army took the road, and he himself went with his horse by way of Piacenza, whilst the foot, under the

Bailie of Dijon, having obtained leave of passage through the territories of Ferrara and Cremona, followed the Po down to Argenta.

Thus did Cesare Borgia—personally attended by a caesarian guard, wearing his livery—set out upon the conquest of the Romagna. Perhaps at no period of his career is he more remarkable than at this moment. To all trades men serve apprenticeships, and to none is the apprenticeship more gradual and arduous than to the trade of arms. Yet Cesare Borgia served none. Like Minerva, springing full-grown and armed into existence, so Cesare sprang to generalship in the hour that saw him made a soldier. This was the first army in which he had ever marched, yet he marched at the head of it. In his twenty-four years of life he had never so much as witnessed a battle pitched; yet here was he riding to direct battles and to wrest victories. Boundless audacity and swiftest intelligence welded into an amazing whole!

CHAPTER III
IMOLA AND FORLI

Between his departure from Milan and his arrival before Imola, where his campaign was to be inaugurated, Cesare paid a flying visit to Rome and his father, whom he had not seen for a full year. He remained three days at the Vatican, mostly closeted with the Pope's Holiness. At the end of that time he went north again to rejoin his army, which by now had been swelled by the forces that had joined it from Cesena, some Pontifical troops, and a condotta under Vitellozzo Vitelli.

The latter, who was Lord of Castello, had gone to Milan to seek justice at the hands of Louis XII against the Florentines, who had beheaded his brother Paolo—deservedly, for treason in the conduct of the war against Pisa. This Vitellozzo was a valuable and experienced captain. He took service with Cesare, spurred by the hope of ultimately finding a way to avenge himself upon the Florentines, and in Cesare's train he now advanced upon Imola and Forli.

The warlike Countess Caterina Sforza-Riario had earlier been granted by her children full administration of their patrimony during their minority. To the defence of this she now addressed herself with all the resolution of her stern nature. Her life had been unfortunate, and of horrors she had touched a surfeit. Her father, Galeazzo Sforza, was murdered in Milan Cathedral by a little band of patriots; her brother Giangaleazzo had died, of want or poison, in the Castle of Pavia, the victim of her ambitious uncle, Lodovico; her husband, Girolamo Riario, she had seen butchered and flung naked from a window of the very castle which she now defended; Giacomo Feo, whom she had secretly married in second nuptials, was done to death in Forli, under her very eyes, by a party of insurrectionaries. Him she had terribly avenged. Getting her men-at-arms together, she had ridden at their head into the quarter inhabited by the murderers, and there ordered—as Macchiavelli tells us—the massacre of every human being that dwelt in it, women and children included, whilst she remained at hand to see it done. Thereafter she took a third husband, in Giovanni di Pierfrancesco de'Medici, who died in 1498. By him this lusty woman had a son whose name was to ring through Italy as that of one of the most illustrious captains of his day—Giovanni delle Bande Nere.

Such was the woman whom Sanuto has called "great-souled, but a most cruel virago," who now shut herself into her castle to defy the Borgia.

She had begun by answering the Pope's Bull of attainder with the statement that, far from owing the Holy See the tribute which it claimed, the Holy See was actually in her debt, her husband, Count Girolamo Riario, having been a creditor of the Church for the provisions made by him in his office of Captain-General of the Pontifical forces. This subterfuge, however, had not weighed with Alexander, whereupon, having also been frustrated in her attempt upon the life of the Pope's Holiness, she had proceeded to measures of martial resistance. Her children and her treasures she had dispatched to Florence that they might be out of danger, retaining of the former only her son Ottaviano, a young man of some twenty years; but, for all that she kept him near her, it is plain that she did not account him worthy of being entrusted with the defence of his tyranny, for it was she, herself, the daughter of the bellicose race of Sforza, who set about the organizing of this.

Disposing of forces that were entirely inadequate to take the field against the invader, she entrenched herself in her fortress of Forli, provisioning it to withstand a protracted siege and proceeding to fortify it by throwing up outworks and causing all the gates but one to be built up.

Whilst herself engaged upon military measures she sent her son Ottaviano to Imola to exhort the Council to loyalty and the defence of the city. But his mission met with no success. Labouring against him was a mighty factor which in other future cases was to facilitate Cesare's subjection of the Romagna. The Riarii—in common with so many other of the Romagna tyrants—had so abused their rule, so ground the people with taxation, so offended them by violence, and provoked such deep and bitter enmity that in this hour of their need they found themselves deservedly abandoned by their subjects. The latter were become eager to try a change of rulers, in the hope of finding thus an improved condition of things; a worse, they were convinced, would be impossible.

So detested were the Riarii and so abhorred the memory they left behind them in Imola that for years afterwards the name of Cesare Borgia was blessed there as that of a minister of divine justice ("tanquam minister divina justitiae") who had lifted from them the harsh yoke by which they had been oppressed.

And so it came to pass that, before ever Cesare had come in sight of Imola, he was met by several of its gentlemen who came to offer him the town, and he received a letter from the pedagogue Flaminio with assurances that, if it should be at all possible to them, the inhabitants would throw open the gates to him on his approach. And Flaminio proceeded to implore the duke that should he, nevertheless, be constrained to have recourse to arms to win admittance, he should not blame the citizens nor do violence to the city by putting it to pillage, assuring him that he would never have a more faithful, loving city than Imola once this should be in his power.

The duke immediately sent forward Achille Tiberti with a squadron of horse to demand the surrender of the town. And the captain of the garrison of Imola replied that he was ready to capitulate, since that was the will of the people. Three days later—on November 27—Cesare rode in as conqueror.

The example of the town, however, was not followed by the citadel. Under the command of Dionigio di Naldo the latter held out, and, as the duke's army made its entrance into Imola, the castellan signified his resentment by turning his cannon upon the town itself, with such resolute purpose that many houses were set on fire and demolished. This Naldo was one of the best reputed captains of foot of his day, and he had seen much service under the Sforza; but his experience could avail him little here.

On the 28th Cesare opened the attack, training his guns upon the citadel; but it was not until a week later that, having found a weak spot in the walls on the side commanding the town, he opened a breach through which his men were able to force a passage, and so possess themselves of a half-moon. Seeing the enemy practically within his outworks, and being himself severely wounded in the head, Naldo accounted it time to parley. He begged a three-days' armistice, pledging himself to surrender at the end of that time should he not receive reinforcements in the meanwhile; and to this arrangement the duke consented.

The good faith of Naldo has been questioned, and it has been suggested that his asking for three days' grace was no better than a cloak to cover his treacherous sale of the fortress to the besieger. It seems, however, to be no more than one of those lightly-uttered, irresponsible utterances with which the chronicles of the time abound, for Naldo had left his wife and children at Forli in the hands of the Countess, as hostages for his good faith, and this renders improbable the unsupported story of his baseness.

On December 7, no reinforcements having reached him, Naldo made formal surrender of the citadel, safe-conduct having been granted to his garrison.

A week later there arrived at Imola Cesare's cousin, the Cardinal Giovanni Borgia, whom the Pope had constituted legate in Bologna and the Romagna in place of the Cardinal Ascanio Sforza, and whom he had sent to support Cesare's operations with ecclesiastical authority. Cardinal

Giovanni, as the Pope's representative, received in the Church of San Domenico the oath of fealty of the city to the Holy See. This was pledged by four representative members of the Council of Thirty; and by that act the conquest and subjection of the town became a fully accomplished fact.

The lesser strongholds of the territory threw up their gates one by one before the advancing enemy, until only Forli remained to be taken. Cesare pushed forward to reduce it.

On his way he passed through Faenza, whose tyrant, Manfredi, deeming himself secure in the protection of Venice and in view of the circumstance that the republic had sent to Rome the arrears of tribute due from his fief, and anxious to conciliate the Pope, received and entertained Cesare very cordially.

At Forli the case of Imola was practically repeated. Notwithstanding that the inhabitants were under the immediate eye of the formidable countess, and although she sent her brother, Alessandro Sforza, to exhort the people and the Council to stand by her, the latter, weary as the rest of the oppressive tyranny of her family, dispatched their representatives to Cesare to offer him the town.

The Countess's valour was of the sort that waxes as the straits become more desperate. Since the town abandoned and betrayed her, she would depend upon her citadel, and by a stubborn resistance make Cesare pay as dearly as possible for the place. To the danger which she seems almost eager to incur for her own part, this strong-minded, comely matron will not subject the son she has kept beside her until now; and so she packs Ottaviano off to Florence and safety. That done, she gives her mutinous subjects a taste of her anger by attempting to seize half a dozen of the principal citizens of Forli. As it happened, not only did this intent miscarry, but it went near being the means of involving her in battle even before the duke's arrival; for the people, getting wind of the affair, took up arms to defend their threatened fellow-citizens.

She consoled herself, however, by seizing the persons of Nicolo Tornielli and Lodovico Ercolani, whom the Council had sent to inform her that their representatives had gone to Cesare with the offer of the town. Further, to vent her rage and signify her humour, she turned her cannon upon the Communal Palace and shattered the tower of it.

Meanwhile Cesare advanced. It was again Tiberti who now rode forward with his horse to demand the surrender of Forli. This was accorded as readily as had been that of Imola, whereupon Cesare came up to take possession in person; but, despite the cordial invitation of the councillors, he refused to enter the gates until he had signed the articles of capitulation.

On December 19, under a deluge of rain, Cesare, in full armour, the banner of the Church borne ahead of him, rode into Forli with his troops. He was housed in the palace of Count Luffo Nomaglie (one of the gentlemen whom Caterina had hoped to capture), and his men were quartered through the town. These foreign soldiers of his seem to have got a little out of hand here at Forli, and they committed a good many abuses, to the dismay and discomfort of the Citizens.

Sanuto comments upon this with satisfaction, accounting the city well served for having yielded herself up like a strumpet. It is a comment more picturesque than just, for obviously Forli did not surrender through pusillanimity, but to the end that it might be delivered from the detestable rule of the Riarii.

The city occupied, it now remained to reduce the fortress and bring its warrior-mistress to terms. Cesare set about this at once, nor allowed the Christmas festivities to interfere with his labours, but kept his men at work to bring the siege-guns into position. On Christmas Day the countess belatedly attempted a feeble ruse in the hope of intimidating them. She flew from her battlements a banner, bearing the device of the lion of St. Mark, thinking to trick Cesare into the belief that she had obtained the protection of Venice, or, perhaps, signifying thus that she threw herself into the arms of the republic, making surrender of her fiefs to the Venetians to the end that she might spite a force which she could not long withstand—as Giovanni Sforza had sought to do.

But Cesare, nowise disturbed by that banner, pursued his preparations, which included the mounting of seven cannons and ten falconets in the square before the Church of St. John the Baptist. When all was ready for the bombardment, he made an effort to cause her to realize the hopelessness of her resistance and the vain sacrifice of life it must entail. He may have been moved to this by the valour she displayed, or it may have been that he obeyed the instincts of generalship which made him ever miserly in the matter of the lives of his soldiers. Be that as it may, with intent to bring her to a reasonable view of the situation, he rode twice to the very edge of the ditch to parley with her; but all that came of his endeavours was that on the occasion of his second appeal to her, he had a narrow escape of falling a victim to her treachery, and so losing his life.

She came down from the ramparts, and, ordering the lowering of the bridge, invited him to meet her upon it that there they might confer more at their ease, having, meanwhile, instructed her castellan to raise the bridge again the moment the duke should set foot upon it. The castellan took her instructions too literally, for even as the duke did set one foot upon it there was a grind and clank of machinery, and the great structure swung up and clattered into place. The duke remained outside, saved by a too great eagerness on the part of those who worked the winches, for had they waited but a second longer they must have trapped him.

Cesare returned angry to Forli, and set a price upon Caterina's head—20,000 ducats if taken alive, 10,000 if dead; and on the morrow he opened fire. For a fortnight this was continued without visible result, and daily the countess was to be seen upon the walls with her castellan, directing the defences. But on January 12, Cesare's cannon having been concentrated upon one point, a breach was opened at last. Instantly the waiting citizens, who had been recruited for the purpose, made forward with their faggots, heaping them up in the moat until a passage was practicable. Over this went Cesare's soldiers to force an entrance.

A stubborn fight ensued within the ravelin, where the duke's men were held in check by the defenders, and not until some four hundred corpses choked that narrow space did the besieged give ground before them.

Like most of the Italian fortresses of the period, the castle of Forli consisted of a citadel within a citadel. In the heart of the main fabric—but cut off from it again by its own moat—arose the great tower known as the Maschio. This was ever the last retreat of the besieged when the fortress itself had been carried by assault, and, in the case of the Maschio of the Citadel of Forli, so stout was its construction that it was held to be practically invulnerable.

Had the countess's soldiers made their retreat in good order to this tower, where all the munitions and provisions were stored, Cesare would have found the siege but in the beginning; but in the confusion of that grim hour, besieged and besiegers, Borgian and Riarian, swept forward interlocked, a writhing, hacking, bleeding mob of men-at-arms. Thus they flung themselves in a body across the bridge that spanned the inner moat, and so into the Maschio, whilst the stream of Cesare's soldiers that poured uninterruptedly across in the immediate wake of that battling mass rendered it impossible for the defenders to take up the bridge.

Within the tower the carnage went on, and the duke's men hacked their way through what remained of the Forlivese until they had made themselves masters of that inner stronghold whither Caterina had sought her last refuge.

A Burgundian serving under the Bailie of Dijon was the first to come upon her in the room to which she had fled with a few attendants and a handful of men, amongst whom were Alessandro Sforza, Paolo Riario, and Scipione Riario—this last an illegitimate son of her first husband's, whom she had adopted. The Burgundian declared her his prisoner, and held her for the price that had been set upon her head until the arrival of Cesare, who entered the citadel with his officers a little while after the final assault had been delivered.

Cesare received and treated her with the greatest courtesy, and, seeing her for the moment destitute, he presented her with a purse containing two hundred ducats for her immediate needs. Under his escort she left the castle, and was conducted, with her few remaining servants, to the Nomaglie Palace to remain in the Duke's care, his prisoner. Her brother and the other members of her family found with her were similarly made prisoners.

After her departure the citadel was given over to pillage, and all hell must have raged in it if we may judge from an incident related by Bernardi in his chronicles. A young clerk, named Evangelista da Monsignane, being seized by a Burgundian soldier who asked him if he had any money, produced and surrendered a purse containing thirteen ducats, and so got out of the mercenaries' clutches, but only to fall into the hands of others, one of whom again declared him a prisoner. The poor youth, terrified at the violence about him, and eager to be gone from that shambles, cried out that, if they would let him go, he would pay them a ransom of a hundred ducats.

Thereupon "Surrender to me!" cried one of the soldiers, and, as the clerk was about to do so, another, equally greedy for the ransom, thrust himself forward. "No. Surrender to me, rather," demanded this one.

The first insisted that the youth was his prisoner, whereupon the second brandished his sword, threatening to kill Evangelista. The clerk, in a panic, flung himself into the arms of a monk who was with him, crying out for mercy, and there in the monk's arms he was brutally slain, "to put an end," said his murderer, "to the dispute."

Forlimpopoli surrendered a few days later to Yves d'Allègre, whom Cesare had sent thither, whilst in Forli, as soon as he had reduced the citadel, and before even attempting to repair the damage done, the duke set about establishing order and providing for the dispensation of justice, exerting to that end the rare administrative ability which not even his bitterest detractors have denied him.

He sent a castellan to Forlimpopoli and fetched from Imola a Podestà for Forli.(1) He confirmed the Council of Forty that ruled Forli—being ten for each quarter of the city—and generally made sound and wise provision for the town's well-being, which we shall presently see bearing fruit.

1 It was customary throughout Italy that the Podestà, or chief magistrate, should never be a native of the town—rarely of the

State—in which he held his office. Thus, having no local interests or relationships, he was the likelier to dispense justice with desirable single-mindedness.

Next the repairing of the fortress claimed his attention, and he disposed for this, entrusting the execution of his instructions to Ramiro de Lorqua, whom he left behind as governor. In the place where the breach was opened by his cannon he ordered the placing of a marble panel bearing his arms; and there it is to be seen to this day: Dexter, the sable bars of the House of Lenzol; Sinister, the Borgia bull in chief, and the lilies of France; and, superimposed, an inescutcheon bearing the Pontifical arms.

All measures being taken so far as Forli was concerned, Cesare turned his attention to Pesaro, and prepared to invade it. Before leaving, however, he awaited the return of his absent cousin, the Cardinal Giovanni Borgia, who, as papal legate, was to receive the oath of fealty of the town; but, instead of the cardinal whom he was expecting, came a messenger with news of his death of fever at Fossombrone.

Giovanni Borgia had left Forli on December 28 to go to Cesena, with intent, it was said, to recruit to his cousin's army those men of Rimini, who, exiled and in rebellion against their tyrant Malatesta, had sought shelter in that Pontifical fief. Thence he had moved on to Urbino, where—in the ducal palace—he awaited news of the fall of Forli, and where, whilst waiting, he fell ill. Nevertheless, when the tidings of Cesare's victory reached him, he insisted upon getting to horse, to repair to Forli; but, discovering himself too ill to keep the saddle, he was forced to abandon the journey at Fossombrone, whilst the outcome of the attempt was an aggravation of the fever resulting in the cardinal's death.

Cesare appears to have been deeply grieved by the loss of Giovanni, and there is every cause to suppose that a sincere attachment prevailed between the cousins. Yet Cesare has been charged with his death, and accused of having poisoned him, and, amidst the host of silly, baseless accusations levelled against Cesare, you shall find none more silly or baseless than this. In other instances of unproven crimes with which he has been charged there may be some vestiges of matter that may do duty for evidence or be construed into motives; here there is none that will serve one purpose or the other, and the appalling and rabid unscrupulousness, the relentless malice of Borgian chroniclers is in nothing so completely apparent as in this accusation.

Sanuto mentions the advices received, and the rumours which say that Cesare murdered him through jealousy, knowing him beloved by the Pope, seeing him a legate, and fearing that he might come to be given the governorship of some Romagna fief.

When Gandia died and Cesare was accused of having murdered him, the motive advanced was that Cesare, a papal legate, resented a brother who was a duke. Now, Cesare, being a duke, resents a cousin's being a papal legate. You will observe that, if this method of discovering motives is pursued a little further, there is no man who died in Cesare's life-time whom Cesare could not be shown to have had motives for murdering.

Sillier even than Sanuto's is the motive with which Giovio attempts to bolster up the accusation which he reports: "He [Cesare] poisoned him because he [Giovanni] favoured the Duke of Gandia."

That, apparently, was the best that Giovio could think of. It is hardly intelligible—which is perhaps inevitable, for it is not easy to be intelligible when you don't quite know, yourself, what you mean, which must have been Giovio's case.

The whole charge is so utterly foolish, stupid, and malicious that it would scarcely be worth mentioning, were it not that so many modern writers have included this among the Borgia crimes. As a matter of fact— and as a comparison of the above-cited dates will show—eighteen days had elapsed between Giovanni Borgia's leaving Cesare at Forli and his succumbing at Urbino—which in itself disposes of the matter. It may be mentioned that this is a circumstance which those foolish or deliberately malicious calumniators either did not trouble to ascertain or else thought it wiser to slur over. Although, had they been pressed, there was always the death of Djem to be cited and the fiction of the slow-working poison specially invented to meet and explain his case.

The preparations for the invasion of Pesaro were complete, and it was determined that on January 22 the army should march out of Forli; but on the night of the 21st a disturbance occurred. The Swiss under the Bailie of Dijon became mutinous—they appear throughout to have been an ill-conditioned lot—and they clamoured now for higher pay if they were to go on to Pesaro, urging that already they had served the Duke of Valentinois as far as they had pledged themselves to the King of France.

Towards the third hour of the night the Bailie himself, with these mutineers at his heels, presented himself at the Nomaglie Palace to demand that the Countess Sforza-Riario should be delivered into his hands. His claim was that she was his prisoner, since she had been arrested by a soldier of his own, and that her surrender was to France, to which he added—a thought inconsequently, it seems—that the French law forbade that women should be made prisoners. Valentinois, taken utterly by surprise, and without the force at hand to resist the Bailie and his Swiss, was compelled to submit and to allow the latter to carry the countess off to his own lodging; but he dispatched a messenger to Forlimpopoli with orders for the immediate return of Allègre and his horse, and in the morning, after Mass, he had the army drawn up in the market-place; and so, backed by his Spanish, French, and Italian troops, he faced the threatening Swiss.

The citizens were in a panic, expecting to see battle blaze out at any moment, and apprehensive of the consequences that might ensue for the town.

The Swiss had grown more mutinous than ever overnight, and they now refused to march until they were paid. It was Cesare's to quell and restore them to obedience. He informed them that they should be paid when they reached Cesena, and that, if they were retained thereafter in his employ, their pay should be on the improved scale which they demanded. Beyond that he made no concessions. The remainder of his harangue was matter to cow them into submission, for he threatened to order the ringing of the alarm-bells, and to have them cut to pieces by the people of Forli whom their gross and predatory habits had already deeply offended.

Order was at last restored, and the Bailie of Dijon was compelled to surrender back the countess to Cesare. But their departure was postponed until the morrow. On that day, January 23, after receiving the oath of fealty from the Anziani in the Church of San Mercuriale, the duke marched his army out of Forli and took the road to Pesaro.

Caterina Sforza Riario went with him. Dressed in black and mounted upon a white horse, the handsome amazon rode between Cesare Borgia and Yves d'Allègre.

At Cesena the duke made a halt, and there he left the countess in the charge of d'Allègre whilst he himself rode forward to overtake the main body of his army, which was already as far south as Cattolica. As for Giovanni Sforza, despite the fact that the Duke of Urbino had sent some foot to support him, he was far more likely to run than to fight, and in fact he had already taken the precaution of placing his money and valuables in safety and was disposing, himself, to follow them. But it happened that there was not yet the need. Fate—in the shape of his cousin Lodovico of Milan—postponed the occasion.

On the 26th Cesare lay at Montefiori, and there he was reached by couriers sent at all speed from Milan by Trivulzio. Lodovico Sforza had raised an army of Swiss and German mercenaries to reconquer his dominions, and the Milanese were opening their arms to receive him back, having already discovered that, in exchanging his rule for that of the French, they had but exchanged King Log for King Stork. Trivulzio begged for the instant return of the French troops serving under Cesare, and Cesare, naturally compelled to accede, was forced to postpone the continuance of his campaign, a matter which must have been not a little vexatious at such a moment.

He returned to Cesena, where, on the 27th, he dismissed Yves d'Allègre and his men, who made all haste back to Milan, so that Cesare was left with a force of not more than a thousand foot and five hundred horse. These, no doubt, would have sufficed him for the conquest of Pesaro, but Giovanni Sforza, encouraged by his cousin's return, and hopeful now of assistance, would certainly entrench himself and submit to a siege which must of necessity be long-drawn, since the departure of the French had deprived Cesare of his artillery.

Therefore the duke disposed matters for his return to Rome instead, and, leaving Ercole Bentivogli with five hundred horse and Gonsalvo de Mirafuente with three hundred foot to garrison Forli, he left Cesena with the remainder of his forces, including Vitelli's horse, on January 30. With him went Caterina Sforza-Riario, and of course there were not wanting those who alleged that, during the few days at Cesena he had carried his conquest of her further than the matter of her territories(1)—a rumour whose parent was, no doubt, the ribald jest made in Milan by Trivulzio when he heard of her capture.

1 "Teneva detta Madona (la qual é belissima dona, fiola del Ducha Galeazo di Milan) di zorno e di note in la sna camera, con la quale—judicio omnium—si deva piacer" (Sanuto's Diarii).

He conducted her to Rome—in golden chains, "like another Palmyra," it is said—and there she was given the beautiful Belvedere for her prison until she attempted an escape in the following June; whereupon, for greater safety, she was transferred to the Castle of Sant' Angelo. There she remained until May of 1501, when, by the intervention of the King of France, she was set at liberty and permitted to withdraw to Florence to rejoin her children. In the city of the lilies she abode, devoting herself to good works until she ended her turbulent, unhappy life in 1509.

The circumstance that she was not made to pay with her life for her attempt to poison the Pope is surely something in favour of the Borgias, and it goes some way towards refuting the endless statements of their fierce and vindictive cruelty. Of course, it has been urged that they spared her from fear of France; but, if that is admitted, what then becomes of the theory of that secret poison which might so well have been employed in such a case as this?

CHAPTER IV
GONFALONIER OF THE CHURCH

Although Cesare Borgia's conquest of Imola and Forli cannot seriously be accounted extraordinary military achievements—save by consideration of the act that this was the first campaign he had conducted—yet in Rome the excitement caused by his victory was enormous. Possibly this is to be assigned to the compelling quality of the man's personality, which was beginning to manifest and assert itself and to issue from the shadow into which it had been cast hitherto by that of his stupendous father.

The enthusiasm mounted higher and higher whilst preparations were being made for his reception, and reached its climax on February 26, when, with overpowering pomp, he made an entrance into Rome that was a veritable triumph.

Sanuto tells us that, as news came of his approach, the Pope, in his joyous impatience and excitement, became unable to discharge the business of his office, and no longer would give audience to any one. Alexander had ever shown himself the fondest of fathers to his children, and now he overflowed with pride in this son who already gave such excellent signs of his capacity as a condottiero, and justified his having put off the cassock to strap a soldier's harness to his lithe and comely body.

Cardinals Farnese and Borgia, with an imposing suite, rode out some way beyond the gates of Santa Maria del Popolo to meet the duke. At the gate itself a magnificent reception had been prepared him, and the entire Pontifical Court, prelates, priests, ambassadors of the Powers, and officials of the city and curia down to the apostolic abbreviators and secretaries, waited to receive him.

It was towards evening—between the twenty-second and the twenty-third hours—when he made his entrance. In the van went the baggage-carts, and behind these marched a thousand foot in full campaign apparel, headed by two heralds in the duke's livery and one in the livery of the King of France. Next came Vitellozzo's horse followed by fifty mounted gentlemen-at-arms—the duke's Caesarean guard—immediately preceding Cesare himself.

The handsome young duke—"bello e biondo"—was splendidly mounted, but very plainly dressed in black velvet with a simple gold chain for only ornament, and he had about him a hundred guards on foot, also in black velvet, halbert on shoulder, and a posse of trumpeters in a livery that displayed his arms. In immediate attendance upon him came several cardinals on their mules, and behind these followed the ambassadors of the Powers, Cesare's brother Giuffredo Borgia, and Alfonso of Aragon, Duke of Biselli and Prince of Salerno—Lucrezia's husband and the father of her boy Roderigo, born some three months earlier. Conspicuous, too, in Cesare's train would be the imposing figure of the formidable Countess Sforza-Riario, in black upon her white horse, riding in her golden shackles between her two attendant women.

As the procession reached the Bridge of Sant' Angelo a salute was thundered forth by the guns from the castle, where floated the banners of Cesare and of the Church. The press of people from the Porta del Popolo all the way to the Vatican was enormous. It was the year of the Papal Jubilee, and the city was thronged, with pilgrims from all quarters of Europe who had flocked to Rome to obtain the plenary indulgence offered by the Pope. So great was the concourse on this occasion that the procession had the greatest difficulty in moving forward, and the progress through the streets, packed with shouting multitudes, was of necessity slow. At last, however, the Bridge of Sant' Angelo being crossed, the procession pushed on to the Vatican along the new road inaugurated for the Jubilee by Alexander in the previous December.

From the loggia above the portals of the Vatican the Pope watched his son's imposing approach, and when the latter dismounted at the steps his Holiness, with his five attendant cardinals, descended to the Chamber of the Papagallo—the papal audiencechamber, contiguous to the Borgia apartments—to receive the duke. Thither sped Cesare with his multitude of attendants, and at sight of him now the Pope's eyes were filled with tears of joy. The duke advanced gravely to the foot of the throne, where he fell upon his knees, and was overheard by Burchard to express to his father, in their native Spanish, all that he owed to the Pope's Holiness, to which Alexander replied in the same tongue. Then Cesare stooped and kissed the Pope's feet and then his hand, whereupon Alexander, conquered no doubt by the paternal instincts of affection that were so strong in him, raised his son and took him fondly in his arms.

The festivities in honour of Cesare's return were renewed in Rome upon the morrow, and to this the circumstance that the season was that of carnival undoubtedly contributed and lent the displays a threatrical character which might otherwise have been absent. In these the duke's victories were made the subject of illustration. There was a procession of great chariots in Piazza Navona, with groups symbolizing the triumphs of the ancient Caesar, in the arrangement of which, no doubt, the assistance had been enlisted of that posse of valiant artists who were then flocking to Rome and the pontifical Court.

Yriarte, mixing his facts throughout with a liberal leaven of fiction, tells us that "this is the precise moment in which Cesare Borgia, fixing his eyes upon the Roman Caesar, takes him definitely for his model and adopts the device 'Aut Caesar, aut nihil.'"

Cesare Borgia never adopted that device, and never displayed it. In connection with him it is only to be found upon the sword of honour made for him when, while still a cardinal, he went to crown the King of Naples. It is not at all unlikely that the inscription of the device upon that sword— which throughout is engraved with illustrations of the career of Julius Caesar—may have been the conceit of the sword-maker as a rather obvious play upon Cesare's name.(1) Undoubtedly, were the device of Cesare's own adoption we should find it elsewhere, and nowhere else is it to be found.

1 The scabbard of this sword is to be seen in the South Kensington Museum; the sword itself is in the possession of the Caetani family.

Shortly after Cesare's return to Rome, Imola and Forli sent their ambassadors to the Vatican to beseech his Holiness to sign the articles which those cities had drawn up and by virtue of which they created Cesare their lord in the place of the deposed Riarii.

It is quite true that Alexander had announced that, in promoting the Romagna campaign, he had for object to restore to the Church the States which had rebelliously seceded from her. Yet there is not sufficient reason to suppose that he was flagrantly breaking his word in acceding to the request of which those ambassadors were the bearers and in creating his son Count of Imola and Forli. Admitted that this was to Cesare's benefit and advancement, it is still to be remembered that those fiefs must be governed for the Church by a Vicar, as had ever been the case.

That being so, who could have been preferred to Cesare for the dignity, seeing that not only was the expulsion of the tyrants his work, but that the inhabitants themselves desired him for their lord? For the rest, granted his exceptional qualifications, it is to be remembered that the Pope was his father, and—setting aside the guilt and scandal of that paternity—it is hardly reasonable to expect a father to prefer some other to his son for a stewardship for which none is so well equipped as that same son. That Imola and Forli were not free gifts to Cesare, detached, for the purpose of so making them, from the Holy See, is clear from the title of Vicar with which Cesare assumed control of them, as set forth in the Bull of investiture.

In addition to his receiving the rank of Vicar and Count of Imola and Forli, it was in this same month of March at last—and after Cesare may be said to have earned it—that he received the Gonfalon of the Church. With the unanimous concurrence of the Sacred College, the Pope officially appointed him Captain-General of the Pontifical forces—the coveting of which position was urged, it will be remembered, as one of his motives for his alleged murder of the Duke of Gandia three years earlier.

On March 29 Cesare comes to St. Peter's to receive his new dignity and the further honour of the Golden Rose which the Pope is to bestow upon him—the symbol of the Church Militant and the Church Triumphant.

Having blessed the Rose, the Pope is borne solemnly into St. Peter's, preceded by the College of Cardinals. Arrived before the High Altar, he puts off his tiara—the conical, richly jewelled cap, woven from the plumage of white peacocks—and bareheaded kneels to pray; whereafter he confesses himself to the Cardinal of Benevento, who was the celebrant on this occasion. That done, he ascends and takes his seat upon the Pontifical Throne, whither come the cardinals to adore him, while the organ peals forth and the choir gives voice. Last of all comes Cesare, dressed in cloth of gold with ermine border, to kneel upon the topmost step of the throne, whereupon the Pope, removing his tiara and delivering it to the attendant Cardinal of San Clemente, pronounces the beautiful prayer of the investiture. That ended, the Pope receives from the hands of the Cardinal of San Clemente the splendid mantle of gonfalonier, and sets it about the duke's shoulders with the prescribed words: "May the Lord array thee in the garment of salvation and surround thee with the cloak of happiness." Next he takes from the hands of the Master of the Ceremonies—that same Burchard whose diary supplies us with these details—the gonfalonier's cap of scarlet and ermine richly decked with pearls and surmounted by a dove—the emblem of the Holy Spirit—likewise wrought in pearls. This he places upon Cesare's auburn head; whereafter, once more putting off his tiara, he utters the prescribed prayer over the kneeling duke.

That done, and the Holy Father resuming his seat and his tiara, Cesare stoops to kiss the Pope's feet, then rising, goes in his gonfalonier apparel, the cap upon his head, to take his place among the cardinals. The organ crashes forth again; the choir intones the "Introito ad altare Deum"; the celebrant ascends the altar, and, having offered incense, descends again and the Mass begins.

The Mass being over, and the celebrant having doffed his sacred vestments and rejoined his brother cardinals, the Cardinal of San Clemente repairs once more to the Papal Throne, preceded by two chamberlains who carry two folded banners, one bearing the Pope's personal arms, the other the arms of Holy Church. Behind the cardinal follows an acolyte with the censer and incense-boat and another with the holy water and the aspersorio, and behind these again two prelates with a Missal and a candle. The Pope rises, blesses the folded banners and incenses them, having received the censer from the hands of a priest who has prepared it. Then, as he resumes his seat, Cesare steps forward once more, and, kneeling, places both hands upon the Missal and pronounces in a loud, clear voice the words of the oath of fealty to St. Peter and the Pope, swearing ever to protect the latter and his successors from harm to life, limb, or possessions. Thereafter the Pope takes the blessed banners and gives the charge of them to Cesare, delivering into his hands the white truncheon symbolic of his office, whilst the Master of Ceremonies hands the actual banners to the two deputies, who in full armour have followed to receive them, and who attach them to the lances provided for the purpose.

The investiture is followed by the bestowal of the Golden Rose, whereafter Cesare, having again kissed the Pope's feet and the Ring of the Fisherman on his finger, has the cap of office replaced upon his head by Burchard himself, and so the ceremonial ends.

The Bishop of Isernia was going to Cesena to assume the governorship of that Pontifical fief, and, profiting by this, Cesare appointed him his lieutenant-general in Romagna, with authority over all his other officers there and full judicial powers. Further, he desired him to act as his deputy and receive the oath of fealty of the duke's new subjects.

Meanwhile, Cesare abode in Rome, no doubt impatient of the interruption which his campaign had suffered, and which it seemed must continue yet awhile. Lodovico Sforza had succeeded in driving the French out of his dominions as easily as he, himself, had been driven out by them a few months earlier. But Louis XII sent down a fresh army under La Trémouille, and Lodovico, basely betrayed by his Swiss mercenaries at Novara in April, was taken prisoner.

That was the definite end of the Sforza rule in Milan. For ten years the crafty, scheming Lodovico was left to languish a prisoner in the Castle of Loches, at the end of which time he miserably died.

Immediately upon the return of the French to Milan, the Pope asked for troops that Cesare might resume his enterprise not only against Pesaro, Faenza, and Rimini, but also against Bologna, where Giovanni Bentivogli had failed to support—as in duty bound—the King of France against Lodovico Sforza. But Bentivogli repurchased the forfeited French protection at the price of 40,000 ducats, and so escaped the impending danger; whilst Venice, it happened, was growing concerned to see no profit accruing to herself out of this league with France and Rome; and that was a matter which her trader spirit could not brook. Therefore, Venice intervened in the matter of Rimini and Faenza, which she protected in somewhat the same spirit as the dog protected the straw in the manger. Next, when, having conquered the Milanese, Louis XII turned his thoughts to the conquest of Naples, and called upon Venice to march with him as became a good ally, the Republic made it quite clear that she was not disposed to move unless there was to be some profit to herself. She pointed out that Mantua and Ferrara were in the same case as Bologna, for having failed to lend assistance to the French in the hour of need, and proposed to Louis XII the conquest and division of those territories.

Thus matters stood, and Cesare had perforce to await the conclusion of the Pisan War in which the French were engaged, confident, however, that, once that was at an end, Louis, in his anxiety to maintain friendly relations with the Pope, would be able to induce Venice to withdraw her protection from Rimini and Faenza. So much accomplished for him, he was now in a position to do the rest without the aid of French troops if necessary. The Jubilee—protracted for a further year, so vast and continuous was the concourse of the faithful, 200,000 of whom knelt in the square before St. Peter's on Easter Day to receive the Pope's blessing—was pouring vast sums of money into the pontifical coffers, and for money men were to be had in plenty by a young condottiero whose fame had been spreading ever since his return from the Romagna. He was now the hope of the soldiers of fortune who abounded in Italy, attracted thither from all quarters by the continual opportunities for employment which that tumultuous land afforded.

It is in speaking of him at about this time, and again praising his personal beauty and fine appearance, that Capello says of him that, if he lives, he will be one of Italy's greatest captains.

Such glimpses as in the pages of contemporary records we are allowed of Cesare during that crowded time of the Papal Jubilee are slight and fleeting. On April 13 we see him on horseback accompanying the Pope through Rome in the cavalcade that visited the four Basilicas to win the indulgence offered, and, as usual, he is attended by his hundred armed grooms in black.

On another occasion we behold him very differently engaged—giving an exhibition of his superb physical gifts, his strength, his courage, and his matchless address. On June 24, at a bull-fight held in Rome—Spanish tauromachia having been introduced from Naples, where it flourished under the Aragon dominion—he went down into the arena, and on horseback, armed only with a light lance, he killed five wild bulls. But the masterstroke he reserved for the end. Dismounting, and taking a doublehanded sword to the sixth bull that was loosed against him, he beheaded the great beast at one single stroke, "a feat which all Rome considered great."

Thus sped the time of waiting, and meanwhile he gathered about him a Court not only of captains of fortune, but of men of art and letters, whom he patronized with a liberality—indeed, a prodigality—so great that it presently became proverbial, and, incidentally, by its proportions provoked his father's disapproval. In the brilliant group of men of letters who enjoyed his patronage were such writers as Justolo, Sperulo, and that unfortunate poet Serafino Cimino da Aquila, known to fame and posterity as the great Aquilano. And it would be, no doubt, during these months that Pier di Lorenzo painted that portrait of Cesare which Vasari afterwards saw in Florence, but which, unfortunately, is not now known to exist. Bramante, too, was of his Court at this time, as was Michelangelo Buonarroti, whose superb group of "Mercy," painted for Cardinal de Villiers, had just amazed all Rome. With Pinturicchio, and Leonardi da Vinci—whom we shall see later beside Cesare—Michelangelo was ever held in the highest esteem by the duke.

The story of that young sculptor's leap into fame may not be so widely known but that its repetition may be tolerated here, particularly since, remotely at least, it touches Cesare Borgia.

When, in 1496, young Buonarroti, at the age of twenty-three, came from Florence to Rome to seek his fortune at the opulent Pontifical Court, he brought a letter of recommendation to Cardinal Sforza-Riario. This was the time of the great excavations about Rome; treasures of ancient art were daily being rescued from the soil, and Cardinal Sforza-Riario was a great dilletante and collector of the antique. With pride of possession, he conducted the young sculptor through his gallery, and, displaying his statuary to him, inquired could he do anything that might compare with it. If the cardinal meant to use the young Florentine cavalierly, his punishment was immediate and poetic, for amid the antiques Michelangelo beheld a sleeping Cupid which he instantly claimed as his own work. Riario was angry; no doubt suspicious, too, of fraud. This Cupid was—as its appearance showed—a genuine antique, which the cardinal had purchased from a Milanese dealer for two hundred ducats. Michelangelo, in a passion, named the dealer—one Baldassare—to whom he had sent the statue after treating it, with the questionable morality of the cinquecentist, so as to give it the appearance of having lain in the ground, to the end that Baldassare might dispose of it as an antique.

His present fury arose from his learning the price paid by the cardinal to Baldassare, from whom Michelangelo had received only thirty ducats. In his wrath he demanded—very arbitrarily it seems—the return of his statue. But to this the cardinal would not consent until Baldassare had been arrested and made to disgorge the money paid him. Then, at last, Sforza-Riario complied with Michelangelo's demands and delivered him his Cupid—a piece of work whose possession had probably ceased to give any pleasure to that collector of the antique.

But the story was bruited abroad, and cultured Rome was agog to see the statue which had duped so astute a judge as Sforza-Riario. The fame of the young sculptor spread like a ripple over water, and it was Cesare Borgia—at that time still Cardinal of Valencia who bought the Cupid. Years later he sent it to Isabella d'Este, assuring her that it had not its equal among contemporary works of art.

CHAPTER V
THE MURDER OF ALFONSO OF ARAGON

We come now to the consideration of an event which, despite the light that so many, and with such assurance, have shed upon it, remains wrapped in uncertainty, and presents a mystery second only to that of the murder of the Duke of Gandia.

It was, you will remember, in July of 1498 that Lucrezia took a second husband in Alfonso of Aragon, the natural son of Alfonso II of Naples and nephew of Federigo, the reigning king. He was a handsome boy of seventeen at the time of his marriage—one year younger than Lucrezia—and, in honour of the event and in compliance with the Pope's insistence, he was created by his uncle Duke of Biselli and Prince of Salerno. On every hand the marriage was said to be a love-match, and of it had been born, in November of 1499, the boy Roderigo.

On July 15, 1500, at about the third hour of the night, Alfonso was assaulted and grievously wounded—mortally, it was said at first—on the steps of St. Peter's.

Burchard's account of the affair is that the young prince was assailed by several assassins, who wounded him in the head, right arm, and knee. Leaving him, no doubt, for dead, they fled down the steps, at the foot of which some forty horsemen awaited them, who escorted them out of the city by the Pertusa Gate. The prince was residing in the palace of the Cardinal of Santa Maria in Portico, but so desperate was his condition that those who found him upon the steps of the Basilica bore him into the Vatican, where he was taken to a chamber of the Borgia Tower, whilst the Cardinal of Capua at once gave him absolution in articulo mortis.

The deed made a great stir in Rome, and was, of course, the subject of immediate gossip, and three days later Cesare issued an edict forbidding, under pain of death, any man from going armed between Sant' Angelo and the Vatican.

News of the event was carried immediately to Naples, and King Federigo sent his own physician, Galieno, to treat and tend his nephew. In the care of that doctor and a hunchback assistant, Alfonso lay ill of his wounds until August 17, when suddenly be died, to the great astonishment of Rome, which for some time had believed him out of danger. In recording his actual death, Burchard is at once explicit and reticent to an extraordinary degree. "Not dying," he writes, "from the wound he had taken, he was yesterday strangled in his bed at the nineteenth hour."

Between the chronicling of his having been wounded on the steps of St. Peter's and that of his death, thirty-three days later, there is no entry in Burchard's diary relating to the prince, nor anything that can in any way help the inquirer to a conclusion; whilst, on the subject of the strangling, not another word does the Master of Ceremonies add to what has above been quoted. That he should so coldly—almost cynically—state that Alfonso was strangled, without so much as suggesting by whom, is singular in one who, however grimly laconic, is seldom reticent—notwithstanding that he may have been so accounted by those who despaired of finding in his diary the confirmation of such points of view as they happen to have chosen and of such matters as it pleased them to believe and propagate.

That same evening Alfonso's body was borne, without pomp, to St. Peter's, and placed in the Chapel of Santa Maria delle Febbre. It was accompanied by Francesco Borgia, Archbishop of Cosenza.

The doctor who had been in attendance upon the deceased and the hunchback were seized, taken to Sant' Angelo and examined, but shortly thereafter set at liberty.

So far we are upon what we may consider safe ground. Beyond that we cannot go, save by treading the uncertain ways of speculation, and by following the accounts of the various rumours circulated at the time. Formal and absolutely positive evidence of the author of Alfonso's murder there is none.

The Venetian ambassador, the ineffable, gossipmongering Paolo Capello, whom we have seen possessed of the fullest details concerning the Duke of Gandia's death—although he did not come to Rome until two and a half years after the crime—is again as circumstantial in this instance. You see in this Capello the forerunner of the modern journalist of the baser sort, the creature who prowls in quest of scraps of gossip and items of scandal, and who, having found them, does not concern himself greatly in the matter of their absolute truth so that they provide him with sensational "copy." It is this same Capello, bear in mind, who gives us the story of Cesare's murdering in the Pope's very arms that Pedro Caldes who is elsewhere shown to have fallen into Tiber and been drowned, down to the lurid details of the blood's spurting into the Pope's face.

His famous Relazione to the Senate in September of 1500 is little better than an epitome of all the scandal current in Rome during his sojourn there as ambassador, and his resurrection of the old affair of the murder of Gandia goes some way towards showing the spirit by which he was actuated and his love of sensational matter. It has pleased most writers who have dealt with the matter of the murder of Alfonso of Aragon to follow Capello's statements; consequently these must be examined.

He writes from Rome—as recorded by Sanuto—that on July 16 Alfonso of Biselli was assaulted on the steps of St. Peter's, and received four wounds, "one in the head, one in the arm, one in the shoulder, and one in the back." That was all that was known to Capello at the time he wrote that letter, and you will observe already the discrepancy between his statement, penned upon hearsay, and Burchard's account—which, considering the latter's position at the Vatican, must always be preferred. According to Burchard the wounds were three, and they were in the head, right arm, and knee.

On the 19th Capello writes again, and, having stated that Lucrezia—who was really prostrate with grief at her husband's death—was stricken with fever, adds that "it is not known who has wounded the Duke of Biselli, but it is said that it was the same who killed and threw into Tiber the Duke of Gandia. My Lord of Valentinois has issued an edict that no one shall henceforth bear arms between Sant' Angelo and the Vatican."

On the face of it, that edict of Valentinois' seems to argue vexation at what had happened, and the desire to provide against its repetition—a provision hardly likely to be made by the man who had organized the assault, unless he sought, by this edict, to throw dust into the eyes of the world; and one cannot associate after the event and the fear of criticism with such a nature as Cesare's or with such a character as is given him by those who are satisfied that it was he who murdered Biselli.

The rumour that Alfonso had been assailed by the murderer of Gandia is a reasonable enough rumour, so long as the latter remains unnamed, for it would simply point to some enemy of the House of Borgia who, having slain one of its members, now attempts to slay another. Whether Capello actually meant Cesare when he penned those words on July 19, is not as obvious as may be assumed, for it is to be borne in mind that, at this date, Capello had not yet compiled the "relation" in which he deals with Gandia's murder.

On July 23 he wrote that the duke was very ill, indeed, from the wound in his head, and on the 28th that he was in danger owing to the same wound although the fever had abated.

On August 18 he announces Alfonso's death in the following terms: "The Duke of Biselli, Madonna Lucrezia's husband, died to-day because he was planning the death of the Duke [of Valentinois] by means of an arbalest-bolt when he walked in the garden; and the duke has had him cut to pieces in his room by his archers."

This "cutting-to-pieces" form of death is one very dear to the imagination of Capello, and bears some witness to his sensation-mongering proclivities.

Coming to matters more public, and upon which his evidence is more acceptable, he writes on the 20th that some servants of the prince's have been arrested, and that, upon being put to the question, they confessed to the prince's intent to kill the Duke of Valentinois, adding that a servant of the duke's was implicated. On the 23rd Capello circumstantially confirms this matter of Alfonso's attempt upon Cesare's life, and states that this has been confessed by the master of Alfonso's household, "the brother of his mother, Madonna Drusa."

That is the sum of Capello's reports to the Senate, as recorded by Sanuto. The rest, the full, lurid, richly-coloured, sensational story, is contained in his "relation" of September 20. He prefaces the narrative by informing the Senate that the Pope is on very bad terms with Naples, and proceeds to relate the case of Alfonso of Aragon as follows:

"He was wounded at the third hour of night near the palace of the Duke of Valentinois, his brotherin-law, and the prince ran to the Pope, saying that he had been wounded and that he knew by whom; and his wife Lucrezia, the Pope's daughter, who was in the room, fell into anguish. He was ill for thirty-three days, and his wife and sister, who is the wife of the Prince of Squillace, another son of the Pope's, were with him and cooked for him in a saucepan for fear of his being poisoned, as the Duke of Valentinois so hated him. And the Pope had him guarded by sixteen men for fear that the duke should kill him. And when the Pope went to visit him Valentinois did not accompany him, save on one occasion, when he said that what had not been done at breakfast might be done at supper.... On August 17 he [Valentinois] entered the room where the prince was already risen from his bed, and, driving out the wife and sister, called in his man, named Michieli, and had the prince strangled; and that night he was buried."

Now the following points must arise to shake the student's confidence in this narrative, and in Capello as an authority upon any of the other matters that he relates:

(i) "He was wounded near the palace of the Duke of Valentinois." This looks exceedingly like an attempt to pile up evidence against Cesare, and shows a disposition to resort to the invention of it. Whatever may not have been known about Alfonso's death, it

was known by everybody that he was wounded on the steps of St. Peter's, and Capello himself, in his dispatches, had said so at the time. A suspicion that Capello's whole relation is to serve the purpose of heaping odium upon Cesare at once arises and receives confirmation when we consider that, as we have already said, it is in this same relation that the fiction about Pedro Caldes finds place and that the guilt of the murder of the Duke of Gandia is definitely fixed upon Cesare.

(ii) "He ran to the Pope ['Corse dal Papa'] saying that he had been wounded, and that he knew by whom." A man with a wound in his head which endangered his life for over a week would hardly be conscious on receiving it, nor is it to be supposed that, had he been conscious, his assailants would have departed. It cannot be doubted that they left him for dead. He was carried into the palace, and we know, from Burchard, that the Cardinal of Capua gave him absolution in articulo mortis, which abundantly shows his condition. It is unthinkable that he should have been able to "run to the Pope," doubtful that he should have been able to speak; and, if he did, who was it reported his words to the Venetian ambassador? Capello wisely refrains from saying.

(iii) Lucrezia and Sancia attempt to protect him from poison by cooking his food in his room. This is quite incredible. Even admitting the readiness to do so on the part of these princesses, where was the need, considering the presence of the doctor—admitted by Capello—sent from Naples and his hunchback assistant? (iv) "The Pope had him guarded by sixteen men for fear the duke should kill him." Yet when, according to Capello, the duke comes on his murderous errand, attended only by Michieli (who has been generally assumed by writers to have been Don Michele da Corella, one of Cesare's captains), where were these sixteen guards? Capello mentions the dismissal only of Lucrezia and Sancia.

(v) "Valentinois...said that what had not been done at breakfast might be done at supper." It will be observed that Capello never once considers it necessary to give his authorities for anything that he states. It becomes, perhaps, more particularly noteworthy than usual in the case of this reported speech of Cesare's. He omits to say to whom Cesare addressed those sinister words, and who

reported them to him. The statement is hardly one to be accepted
without that very necessary mention of authorities, nor can we
conceive Capello omitting them had he possessed them.

It will be seen that it is scarcely necessary to go outside of Capello's own relation for the purpose of traversing the statements contained in it, so far as the death of Alfonso of Aragon is concerned.

It is, however, still to be considered that, if Alfonso knew who had attempted his life—as Capello states that he told the Pope—and knew that he was in hourly danger of death from Valentinois, it may surely be taken for granted that he would have imparted the information to the Neapolitan doctor sent him by his uncle, who must have had his confidence.

We know that, after the prince's death, the physician and his hunchback assistant were arrested, but subsequently released. They returned to Naples, and in Naples, if not elsewhere, the truth must have been known—definite and authentic facts from the lips of eye-witnesses, not mere matters of rumour, as was the case in Rome. It is to Neapolitan writings, then, that we must turn for the truth of this affair; and yet from Naples all that we find is a rumour—the echo of the Roman rumour—"They say," writes the Venetian ambassador at the Court of King Federigo, "that he was killed by the Pope's son."

A more mischievous document than Capello's Relazione can seldom have found its way into the pages of history; it is the prime source of several of the unsubstantiated accusations against Cesare Borgia upon which subsequent writers have drawn—accepting without criticism—and from which they have formed their conclusions as to the duke's character. Even in our own times we find the learned Gregorovius following Capello's relation step by step, and dealing out this matter of the murder of the Duke of Biselli in his own paraphrases, as so much substantiated, unquestionable fact. We find in his Lucrezia Borgia the following statement: "The affair was no longer a mystery. Cesare himself publicly declared that he had killed the duke because his life had been attempted by the latter."

To say that Cesare "publicly declared that he had killed the duke" is to say a very daring thing, and is dangerously to improve upon Capello. If it is true that Cesare made this public declaration how does it happen that no one but Capello heard him? for in all other documents there is no more than offered us a rumour of how Alfonso died. Surely it is to be supposed that, had Cesare made any such declaration, the letters from the ambassadors would have rung with it. Yet they will offer you nothing but statements of what is being rumoured!

Nor does Gregorovius confine himself to that in his sedulous following of Capello's Relation. He serves up out of Capello the lying story of the murder of Pedro Caldes. "What," he says of Cesare, to support his view that Cesare murdered Alfonso of Aragon, "could be beyond this terrible man who had poignarded the Spaniard Pedro Caldes...under the Pope's very cloak, so that his blood spurted up into the Pope's face?" This in his History of Rome. In his Lucrezia Borgia he almost improves upon it when he says that "The Venetian ambassador, Paolo Capello, reports how Cesare Borgia stabbed the chamberlain Perotto, etc., but Burchard makes no mention of the fact." Of the fact of the stabbing, Burchard certainly makes no mention; but he does mention that the man was accidentally drowned, as has been considered. It is again—and more flagrantly than ever—a case of proving Cesare guilty of a crime of which there is no conclusive evidence by charging him with another, which—in this instance—there is actually evidence that he did not commit.

But this is by the way.

Burchard's entries in his diary relating to the assault upon Alfonso of Aragon can no more escape the criticism of the thoughtful than can Capello's relation. His forty horsemen, for instance, need explaining. Apart from the fact that this employment of forty horsemen would be an altogether amazing and incredible way to set about the murder of a single man, it is to be considered that such a troop, drawn up in the square before St. Peter's, must of necessity have attracted some attention. It was the first hour of the night, remember—according to Burchard—that is to say, at dusk. Presumably, too, those horsemen were waiting when the prince arrived. How then, did he— and why was he allowed—to pass them, only to be assailed in ascending the steps? Burchard, presumably, did not himself see these horsemen; certainly he cannot have seen them escorting the murderers to the Pertusa Gate. Therefore he must have had the matter reported to him. Naturally enough, had the horsemen existed, they must have been seen. How, then, does it happen that Capello did not hear of them? nor the Florentine ambassador, who says that the murderers were four, nor any one else apparently?

To turn for a moment to the Florentine ambassador's letters upon the subject, we find in this other Capello—Francesco Capello was his name— accounts which differ alike from Paolo Capello's and from Burchard' stories. But he is careful to say that he is simply repeating the rumours that are abroad, and cites several different versions that are current, adding that the truth of the affair is not known to anybody. His conclusions, however, particularly those given in cipher, point to Cesare Borgia as the perpetrator of the deed, and hint at some such motive of retaliation for an attempt upon his own life as that which is given by the ambassador of Venice.

There is much mystery in the matter, despite Gregorovius's assertion to the contrary—mystery which mere assertion will not dissipate. This conclusion, however, it is fair to draw: if, on Capello's evidence, we are to accept it that Cesare Borgia is responsible for the death of Alfonso of Aragon, then, on the same evidence, we must accept the motive as well as the deed. We must accept as equally exact his thrice-repeated statement in letters to the Senate that the prince had planned Cesare's death by posting crossbow-men to shoot him.(1)

> 1 It is extremely significant that Capello's Relazione contains no mention of Alfonso's plot against Cesare's life, a matter which, as we have seen, had figured so repeatedly in that ambassador's dispatches from Rome at the time of the event. This omission is yet another proof of the malicious spirit by which the "relation" was inspired. The suppression of anything that might justify a deed attributed to Cesare reveals how much defamation and detraction were the aims of this Venetian.

Either we must accept all, or we must reject all, that Capello tells us. If we reject all, then we are left utterly without information as to how Alfonso of Aragon died. If we accept all, then we find that it was as a measure of retaliation that Cesare compassed the death of his brother-in-law, which made it not a murder, but a private execution—justifiable under the circumstances of the provocation received and as the adjustment of these affairs was understood in the Cinquecento.

CHAPTER VI
RIMINI AND PESARO

In the autumn of 1500, fretting to take the field again, Cesare was occupied in raising and equipping an army—an occupation which received an added stimulus when, towards the end of August, Louis de Villeneuve, the French ambassador, arrived in Rome with the articles of agreement setting forth the terms upon which Louis XII was prepared further to assist Cesare in the resumption of his campaign. In these it was stipulated that, in return for such assistance, Cesare should engage himself, on his side, to aid the King of France in the conquest of Naples when the time for that expedition should be ripe. Further, Loius XII was induced to make representations to Venice to the end that the Republic should remove her protection from the Manfredi of Faenza and the Malatesta of Rimini.

Venice being at the time in trouble with the Turk, and more anxious than ever to conciliate France and the Pope, was compelled to swallow her reluctance and submit with the best grace she could assume. Accordingly she dispatched her ambassadors to Rome to convey her obedience to the Pope's Holiness, and formally to communicate the news that she withdrew her protection from the proscribed fiefs.

Later in the year—in the month of October—the Senate was to confer upon Cesare Borgia the highest honour in her gift, the honour of which the Venetians were jealous above all else—the honour of Venetian citizenship, inscribing his name in the Golden Book, bestowing upon him a palace in Venice and conferring the other marks of distinction usual to the occasion. One is tempted to ask, Was it in consequence of Paolo Capello's lurid Relation that the proud Republic considered him qualified for such an honour?

To return, however, to the matter of the Republic's removal of her shield from Rimini and Faenza, Alexander received the news of this with open joy and celebrated it with festivities in the Vatican, whilst from being angry with Venice and from declaring that the Republic need never again look to him for favour, he now veered round completely and assured the Venetian envoys, in a burst of gratitude, that he esteemed no Power in the world so highly. Cesare joined in his father's expressions of gratitude and appreciation, and promised that Alexander should be succeeded in St. Peter's Chair by such a Pope as should be pleasing to Venice, and that, if the cardinals but remained united, the Pontificate should go to none but a Venetian.

Thus did Cesare, sincerely or otherwise, attempt to lessen the Republic's chagrin to see him ride lance-on-thigh as conqueror into the dominions which she so long had coveted.

France once more placed Yves d'Allègre at Cesare's disposal, and with him went six hundred lances and six hundred Swiss foot. These swelled the forces which already Cesare had assembled into an army some ten thousand strong. The artillery was under the command of Vitellozzo Vitelli, whilst Bartolomeo da Capranica was appointed camp-master. Cesare's banner was joined by a condotta under Paolo Orsini—besides whom there were several Roman gentlemen in the duke's following, including most of those who had formed his guard of honour on the occasion of his visit to France, and who had since then continued to follow his fortunes. Achille Tiberti came to Rome with a condotta which he had levied in the Romagna of young men who had been moved by Cesare's spreading fame to place their swords at his disposal. A member of the exiled Malvezzi family of Bologna headed a little troop of fellow-exiles which came to take service with the duke, whilst at Perugia a strong body of foot awaited him under Gianpaolo Baglioni.

In addition to these condotte, numerous were the adventurers who came to offer Cesare their swords; indeed he must have possessed much of that personal magnetism which is the prime equipment of every born leader, for he stirred men to the point of wild enthusiasm in those days, and inspired other than warriors to bear arms for him. We see men of letters, such as Justolo, Calmeta, Sperulo, and others throwing down their quills to snatch up swords and follow him. Painters, and sculptors, too, are to be seen abandoning the ideals of art to pursue the ugly realities of war in this young condottiero's train. Among these artists, bulks the great Pietro Torrigiani. The astounding pen of his brother-sculptor, Benvenuto Cellini, has left us a sharp portrait of this man, in which he speaks of his personal beauty and tells us that he had more the air of a great soldier than a sculptor (which must have been, we fancy, Cellini's own case). Torrigiani lives in history chiefly for two pieces of work widely dissimilar in character—the erection of the tomb of Henry VII of England, and the breaking of the nose of Michelangelo Buonarroti in the course of a quarrel which he had with him in Florence when they were fellow-students under Masaccio. Of nothing that he ever did in life was he so proud—as we may gather from Cellini—as of having disfigured Michelangelo, and in that sentiment the naïve spirit of his age again peeps forth.

We shall also see Leonardo da Vinci joining the duke's army as engineer—but that not until some months later.

Meanwhile his forces grew daily in Rome, and his time was consumed in organizing, equipping, and drilling these, to bring about that perfect unity for which his army was to be conspicuous in spite of the variety of French, Italian, Spanish, and Swiss elements of which it was composed. So effectively were his troops armed and so excellent was the discipline prevailing among them, that their like had probably never before been seen in the peninsula, and they were to excite—as much else of Cesare's work—the wonder and admiration of that great critic Macchiavelli.

So much, however, was not to be achieved without money, and still more would be needed for the campaign ahead. For this the Church provided. Never had the coffers of the Holy See been fuller than at this moment. Additional funds accrued from what is almost universally spoken of as "the sale of twelve cardinals' hats."

In that year—in September—twelve new cardinals were appointed, and upon each of those was levied, as a tax, a tithe of the first year's revenues of the benefices upon which they entered. The only justifiable exception that can be taken to this lies in the number of cardinals elected at one time, which lends colour to the assumption that the sole aim of that election was to raise additional funds for Cesare's campaign. Probably it was also Alexander's aim further to strengthen his power with the Sacred College, so that he could depend upon a majority to ensure his will in all matters. But we are at the moment concerned with the matter of the levied tax.

It has been dubbed "an atrocious act of simony;" but the reasoning that so construes it is none so clear. The cardinals' hats carried with them vast benefices. These benefices were the property of the Church; they were in the gift and bestowal of the Pope, and in the bestowing of them the Pope levied a proportionate tax. Setting aside the argument that this tax was not an invention of Alexander's, does such a proceeding really amount to a "sale" of benefices? A sale presupposes bargaining, a making of terms between two parties, an adjusting of a price to be paid. There is evidence of no such marketing of these benefices; indeed one cardinal, vowed to poverty, received his hat without the imposition of a tax, another was Cesare's brother-in-law, Amanieu d'Albret, who had been promised the hat a year ago. It is further to be borne in mind that, four months earlier, the Pope had levied a similar decima, or tax, upon the entire College of Cardinals and every official in the service of the Holy See, for the purposes of the expedition against the

Muslim, who was in arms against Christianity. Naturally that tax was not popular with luxurious, self-seeking, cinquecento prelates, who in the main cared entirely for their own prosperity and not at all for that of Christianity, and you may realize how, by levying it, Alexander laid himself open to harsh criticism.

The only impugnable matter in the deed lies, as has been said, in the number of cardinals so created at a batch. But the ends to be served may be held to justify, if not altogether, at least in some measure, the means adopted. The Romagna war for which the funds were needed was primarily for the advancement of the Church, to expunge those faithless vicars who, appointed by the Holy See and holding their fiefs in trust for her, refused payment of just tribute and otherwise so acted as to alienate from the Church the States which she claimed for her own. Their restoration to the Church—however much it might be a means of founding a Borgia dynasty in the Romagna—made for the greater power and glory of the Holy See. Let us remember this, and that such was the end which that tax, levied upon those newly elected cardinals, went to serve. The aggrandizement of the House of Borgia was certainly one of the results to be expected from the Romagna campaign, but we are not justified in accounting it the sole aim and end of that campaign.

Alexander had this advantage over either Sixtus IV or Innocent VIII— not to go beyond those Popes whom he had served as Vice-Chancellor, for instances of flagrant nepotism—that he at least served two purposes at once, and that, in aggrandizing his own family, he strengthened the temporal power of the Church, whereas those others had done nothing but undermine it that they might enrich their progeny.

And whilst on this subject of the "sale" of cardinals' hats, it may not be amiss to say a word concerning the "sale" of indulgences with which Alexander has been so freely charged. Here again there has been too loud an outcry against Alexander—an outcry whose indignant stridency leads one to suppose that the sale of indulgences was a simony invented by him, or else practised by him to an extent shamefully unprecedented. Such is very far from being the case. The arch-type of indulgence-seller—as of all other simoniacal practices—is Innocent VIII. In his reign we have seen the murderer commonly given to choose between the hangman and the purchase of a pardon, and we have seen the moneys so obtained providing his bastard, the Cardinal Francesco Cibo, with the means for the luxuriously licentious life whose gross disorders prematurely killed him.

To no such flagitious lengths as these can it be shown that Alexander carried the "sale" of the indulgences he dispensed. He had no lack of precedent for the practice, and, so far as the actual practice itself is concerned, it would be difficult to show that it was unjustifiable or simoniacal so long as confined within certain well-defined bounds, and so long as the sums levied by it were properly employed to the benefit of Christianity. It is a practice comparable to the mulcting of a civil offender against magisterial laws. Because our magistrates levy fines, it does not occur to modern critics to say that they sell pardons and immunity from gaol. It is universally recognized as a wise and commendable measure, serving the twofold purpose of punishing the offender and benefiting the temporal State against which he has offended. Need it be less commendable in the case of spiritual offences against a spiritual State? It is more useful than the imposition of the pattering of a dozen prayers at bedtime, and since, no doubt, it falls more heavily upon the offender, it possibly makes to an even greater extent for his spiritual improvement.

Thus considered, this "sale" of indulgences loses a deal of the heinousness with which it has been invested. The funds so realized go into the coffers of the Church, which is fit and proper. What afterwards becomes of them at the hands of Alexander opens up another matter altogether, one in which we cannot close our eyes to the fact that he was as undutiful as many another who wore the Ring of the Fisherman before him. Yet this is to be said for him: that, if he plunged his hands freely into the treasury of the Holy See, at least he had the ability to contrive that this treasury should be well supplied; and the circumstance that, when he died, he left the church far wealthier and more powerful than she had been for centuries, with her dominions which his precursors had wantonly alienated reconsolidated into that powerful State that was to endure for three hundred years, is an argument to the credit of his pontificate not lightly to be set aside.

Imola and Forli had, themselves, applied to the Pontiff to appoint Cesare Borgia their ruler in the place of the deposed Riarii. To these was now added Cesena. In July disturbances occurred there between Guelphs and Ghibellines. Swords were drawn and blood flowed in the streets, until the governor was constrained to summon Ercole Bentivogli and his horse from Forli to quell the rioting. The direct outcome of this was that—the Ghibellines predominating in council—Cesena sent an embassy to Rome to beg his Holiness to give the lordship of the fief to the Duke of Valentinois. To this the Pope acceded, and on August 2 Cesare was duly appointed Lord Vicar of Cesena. He celebrated his investiture by remitting a portion of the taxes, abolishing altogether the duty on flour, and by bringing about a peace between the two prevailing factions.

By the end of September Cesare's preparations for the resumption of the campaign were completed, and early in October (his army fortified in spirit by the Pope's blessing) he set out, and made his first halt at Nepi. Lucrezia was there, with her Court and her child Roderigo, having withdrawn to this her castle to mourn her dead husband Alfonso; and there she abode until recalled to Rome by her father some two months later.

Thence Cesare pushed on, as swiftly as the foul weather would allow him, by way of Viterbo, Assisi, and Nocera to cross the Apennines at Gualdo. Here he paused to demand the release of certain prisoners in the hill fortress of Fossate, and to be answered by a refusal. Angered by this resistance of his wishes and determined to discourage others from following the example of Fossate, he was swift and terrible in his rejoinder. He seized the Citadel, and did by force what had been refused to his request. Setting at liberty the prisoners in durance there, he gave the territory over to devastation by fire and pillage.

That done he resumed his march, but the weather retarded him more and more. The heavy and continuous rains had reduced the roads to such a condition that his artillery fell behind, and he was compelled to call a halt once more, at Deruta, and wait there four days for his guns to overtake him.

In Rimini the great House of Malatesta was represented by Pandolfo— Roberto Malatesta's bastard and successor—a degenerate so detested by his subjects that he was known by the name of Pandolfaccio (a contumelious augmentative, expressing the evil repute in which he was held).

Among his many malpractices and the many abuses to which he resorted for the purposes of extorting money from his long-suffering subjects was that of compelling the richer men of Rimini to purchase from him the estates which he confiscated from the fuorusciti—those who had sought in exile safety from the anger provoked by their just resentment of his oppressive misrule. He was in the same case as other Romagna tyrants, and now that Venice had lifted from him her protecting aegis, he had no illusions as to the fate in store for him. So when once more the tramp of Cesare Borgia's advancing legions rang through the Romagna, Pandolfaccio disposed himself, not for battle, but for surrender on the best terms that he might succeed in making.

He was married to Violante, the daughter of Giovanni Bentivogli of Bologna, and in the first week of October he sent her, with their children, to seek shelter at her father's Court. Himself, he withdrew into his citadel—the famous fortress of his terrible grandfather Sigismondo. The move suggested almost that he was preparing to resist the Duke of Valentinois, and it may have prompted the message sent him by the Council to inquire what might be his intention.

Honour was a thing unknown to this Pandolfaccio—even so much honour as may be required for a dignified retreat. Since all was lost it but remained—by his lights—to make the best bargain that he could and get the highest possible price in gold for what he was abandoning. So he replied that the Council must do whatever it considered to its best advantage, whilst to anticipate its members in any offer of surrender, and thus seek the favour and deserve good terms at the hands of this man who came to hurl him from the throne of his family, he dispatched a confidential servant to Cesare to offer him town and citadel.

In the meantime—as Pandolfo fully expected—the Council also sent proposals of surrender to Cesare, as well as to his lieutenant-general of Romagna, Bishop Olivieri, at Cesena. The communications had the effect of bringing Olivieri immediately to Rimini, and there, on October 10, the articles of capitulation were signed by the bishop, as the duke's representative, and by Pandolfo Malatesta. It was agreed in these that Malatesta should have safe-conduct for himself and his familiars, 3,000 ducats and the value—to be estimated—of the artillery which he left in the citadel. Further, for the price of 5,500 ducats he abandoned also the strongholds of Sarsina and Medola and the castles of the Montagna.

His tyranny thus disposed of, Pandolfaccio took ship to Ravenna, where the price of his dishonour was to be paid him, and in security for which he took with him Gianbattista Baldassare, the son of the ducal commissioner.

On the day of his departure, to celebrate the bloodless conquest of Rimini, solemn High Mass was sung in the Cathedral, and Bishop Olivieri received the city's oath of allegiance to the Holy See, whither very shortly afterwards Rimini sent her ambassadors to express to the Pope her gratitude for her release from the thraldom of Pandolfaccio.

Like Rimini, Pesaro too fell without the striking of a blow, for all that it was by no means as readily relinquished on the part of its ruler. Giovanni Sforza had been exerting himself desperately for the past two months to obtain help that should enable him to hold his tyranny against the Borgia might. But all in vain. His entreaties to the emperor had met with no response, whilst his appeal to Francesco Gonzaga of Mantua—whose sister, it will be remembered, had been his first wife—had resulted in the Marquis's sending him a hundred men under an Albanian, named Giacopo.

What Giovanni was to do with a hundred men it is difficult to conceive, nor are the motives of Gonzaga's action clear. We know that at this time he was eagerly seeking Cesare's friendship, sorely uneasy as to the fate that might lie in store for his own dominions, once the Duke of Valentinois should have disposed of the feudatories of the Church. Early in that year

1500 he had asked Cesare to stand godfather for his child, and Cesare had readily consented, whereby a certain bond of relationship and good feeling had been established between them, which everything shows Gonzaga most anxious to preserve unsevered. The only reasonable conclusion in the matter of that condotta of a hundred men is that Gonzaga desired to show friendliness to the Lord of Pesaro, yet was careful not to do so to any extent that might be hurtful to Valentinois.

As for Giovanni Sforza of whom so many able pens have written so feelingly as the constant, unfortunate victim of Borgia ambition, there is no need to enter into analyses for the purpose of judging him here. His own subjects did so in his own day. When a prince is beloved by all classes of his people, it must follow that he is a good prince and a wise ruler; when his subjects are divided into two factions, one to oppose and the other to support him, he may be good or bad, or good and bad; but when a prince can find none to stand by him in the hour of peril, it is to be concluded that he has deserved little at the hands of those whom he has ruled. The latter is the case of Giovanni Sforza—this prince whom, Yriarte tells us, "rendered sweet the lives of his subjects." The nobility and the proletariate of Pesaro abhorred him; the trader classes stood neutral, anxious to avoid the consequences of partisanship, since it was the class most exposed to those consequences.

On Sunday, October 11—the day after Pandolfo Malatesta had relinquished Rimini—news reached Pesaro that Ercole Bentivogli's horse was marching upon the town, in advance of the main body of Cesare's army. Instantly there was an insurrection against Giovanni, and the people, taking to arms, raised the cry of "Duca!" in acclamation of the Duke of Valentinois, under the very windows of their ruler's palace.

Getting together the three hundred men that constituted his army, Giovanni beat a hasty retreat to Pesaro's magnificent fortress, and that same night he secretly took ship to Ravenna accompanied by the Albanian Giacopo, and leaving his half-brother, Galeazzo Sforza di Cotignola, in command of the citadel. Thence Giovanni repaired to Bologna, and, already repenting his precipitate flight, he appealed for help to Bentivogli, who was himself uneasy, despite the French protection he enjoyed. Similarly, Giovanni addressed fresh appeals to Francesco Gonzaga; but neither of these tyrants could or dared avail him, and, whilst he was still imploring their intervention his fief had fallen into Cesare's power.

Ercole Bentivogli, with a small body of horse, had presented himself at the gates of Pesaro on October 21, and Galeazzo Sforza, having obtained safe-conduct for the garrison, surrendered.

Cesare, meanwhile, was at Fano, where he paused to allow his army to come up with him, for he had outridden it from Fossate, through foul wintry weather, attended only by his light horse. It was said that he hoped that Fano might offer itself to him as other fiefs had done, and—if Pandolfo Collenuccio is correct—he had been counselled by the Pope not to attempt to impose himself upon Fano, but to allow the town a free voice in the matter. If his hopes were as stated, he was disappointed in them, for Fano made no offer to him, and matters remained for the present as they were.

On the 27th, with the banners of the bull unfurled, he rode into Pesaro at the head of two thousand men, making his entrance with his wonted pomp, of whose dramatic values he was so fully aware. He was met at the gates by the Council, which came to offer him the keys of the town, and, despite the pouring rain under which he entered the city, the people of Pesaro thronged the streets to acclaim him as he rode.

He took up his lodgings at the Sforza Palace, so lately vacated by Giovanni—the palace where Lucrezia Borgia had held her Court when, as Giovanni's wife, she had been Countess of Pesaro and Cotignola. Early on the morrow he visited the citadel, which was one of the finest in Italy, rivalling that of Rimini for strength. On his arrival there, a flourish of trumpets imposed silence, while the heralds greeted him formally as Lord of Pesaro. He ordered one of the painters in his train to draw up plans of the fortress to be sent to the Pope, and issued instructions for certain repairs and improvements which he considered desirable.

Here in Pesaro came to him the famous Pandolfo Collenuccio, as envoy from the Duke of Ferrara, to congratulate Cesare upon the victory. In sending Collenuccio at such a time Ercole d'Este paid the Duke of Valentinois a subtle, graceful compliment. This distinguished poet, dramatist, and historian was a native of Pesaro who had been exiled ten years earlier by Giovanni— which was the tyrant's way of showing his gratitude to the man who, more than any other, had contributed to the bastard Sforza's succession to his father as Lord of Pesaro and Cotignola.

Collenuccio was one of the few literary men of his day who was not above using the Italian tongue, treating it seriously as a language and not merely as a debased form of Latin. He was eminent as a jurisconsult, and, being a man of action as well as a man of letters, he had filled the office of Podestá in various cities; he had found employment under Lorenzo dei Medici, and latterly under Ercole d'Este, whom we now see him representing.

Cesare received him with all honour, sending the master of his household, Ramiro de Lorqua, to greet him on his arrival and to bear him the usual gifts of welcome, of barley, wine, capons, candles, sweet-meats, etc., whilst on the morrow the duke gave him audience, treating him in the friendliest manner, as we see from Collenuccio's own report to the Duke of Ferrara. In this he says of Cesare: "He is accounted valiant, joyous, and open-handed, and it is believed that he holds honest men in great esteem. Harsh in his vengeance, according to many, he is great of spirit and of ambition, athirst for eminence and fame."

Collenuccio was reinstated by Cesare in the possessions of which Giovanni had stripped him, a matter which so excited the resentment of the latter that, when ultimately he returned to his dominions, one of his first acts was to avenge it. Collenuccio, fearing that he might not stand well with the tyrant, had withdrawn from Pesaro. But Giovanni, with all semblance of friendliness, treacherously lured him back to cast him into prison and have him strangled—a little matter which those who, to the detriment of the Borgia, seek to make a hero of this Giovanni Sforza, would do well not to suppress.

A proof of the splendid discipline prevailing in Cesare's army is afforded during his brief sojourn in Pesaro. In the town itself, some two thousand of his troops were accommodated, whilst some thousands more swarmed in the surrounding country. Occupation by such an army was, naturally enough, cause for deep anxiety on the part of a people who were but too well acquainted with the ways of the fifteenthcentury men-at-arms. But here was a general who knew how to curb and control his soldiers. Under the pain of death his men were forbidden from indulging any of the predations or violences usual to their kind; and, as a consequence, the inhabitants of Pesaro had little to complain of.

Justolo gives us a picture of the Duke of Valentinois on the banks of the River Montone, which again throws into relief the discipline which his very presence—such was the force of his personality—was able to enforce. A disturbance arose among his soldiers at the crossing of this river, which was swollen with rains and the bridge of which had been destroyed. It became necessary to effect the crossing in one small boat—the only craft available—and the men, crowding to the bank, stormed and fought for precedence until the affair grew threatening. Cesare rode down to the river, and no more than his presence was necessary to restore peace. Under that calm, cold eye of his the men instantly became orderly, and, whilst he sat his horse and watched them, the crossing was soberly effected, and as swiftly as the single craft would permit.

The duke remained but two days in Pesaro. On the 29th, having appointed a lieutenant to represent him, and a captain to the garrison, he marched out again, to lie that night at Cattolica and enter Rimini on the morrow.

There again he was received with open arms, and he justified the people's welcome of him by an immediate organization of affairs which gave universal satisfaction. He made ample provision for the proper administration of justice and the preservation of the peace; he recalled the fuorusciti exiled by the unscrupulous Pandolfaccio, and he saw them reinstated in the property of which that tyrant had dispossessed them. As his lieutenant in Rimini, with strict injunctions to preserve law and order, he left Ramiro de Lorqua, when, on November 2, he departed to march upon Faenza, which had prepared for resistance.

What Cesare did in Rimini was no more than he was doing throughout the Romagna, as its various archives bear witness. They bear witness no less to his vast ability as an administrator, showing how he resolved the prevailing chaos into form and order by his admirable organization and suppression of injustice. The same archives show us also that he found time for deeds of beneficence which endeared him to the people, who everywhere hailed him as their deliverer from thraldom. It would not be wise to join in the chorus of those who appear to have taken Cesare's altruism for granted. The rejection of the wild stories that picture him as a corrupt and murderous monster, utterly inhuman, and lay a dozen ghastly crimes to his account need not entail our viewing Cesare as an angel of deliverance, a divine agent almost, rescuing a suffering people from oppression out of sheer humanitarianism.

He is the one as little as the other. He is just—as Collenuccio wrote to Ercole d'Este—"great of spirit and of ambition, athirst for eminence and fame." He was consumed by the desire for power and worldly greatness, a colossus of egotism to whom men and women were pieces to be handled by him on the chess-board of his ambition, to be sacrificed ruthlessly where necessary to his ends, but to be husbanded and guarded carefully where they could serve him.

With his eyes upon the career of Cesare Borgia, Macchiavelli was anon to write of principalities newly-acquired, that "however great may be the military resources of a prince, he will discover that, to obtain firm footing in a province, he must engage the favour and interest of the inhabitants."

That was a principle self-evident to Cesare—the principle upon which he acted throughout in his conquest of the Romagna. By causing his new subjects to realize at once that they had exchanged an oppressive for a generous rule, he attached them to himself.

CHAPTER VII
THE SIEGE OF FAENZA

The second campaign of the Romagna had opened for Cesare as easily as had the first. So far his conquest had been achieved by little more than a processional display of his armed legions. Like another Joshua, he reduced cities by the mere blare of his trumpets. At last, however, he was to receive a check. Where grown men had fled cravenly at his approach, it remained for a child to resist him at Faenza, as a woman had resisted him at Forli.

His progress north from Pesaro was of necessity slow. He paused, as we have seen, at Rimini, and he paused again, and for a rather longer spell, at Forli, so that it was not until the second week of November that Astorre Manfredi—the boy of sixteen who was to hold Faenza—caught in the distance the flash of arms and the banners with the bull device borne by the host which the Duke of Valentinois led against him.

At first it had been Astorre's intent to follow the examples set him by Malatesta and Sforza, and he had already gone so far as to remove his valuables to Ravenna, whither he, too, meant to seek refuge. But he was in better case than any of the tyrants so far deposed inasmuch as his family, which had ruled Faenza for two hundred years, had not provoked the hatred of its subjects, and these were now ready and willing to stand loyally by their young lord. But loyalty alone can do little, unless backed by the might of arms, against such a force as Cesare was prepared to hurl upon Faenza. This Astorre realized, and for his own and his subjects' sake was preparing to depart, when, to his undoing, support reached him from an unexpected quarter.

Bologna—whose ruler, Giovanni Bentivogli, was Astorre's grandfather—in common with Florence and Urbino, grew daily more and more alarmed at the continual tramp of armed multitudes about her frontiers, and at the steady growth in numbers and in capacity of this splendid army which followed Casare—an army captained by such enemies of the Bentivogli as the Baglioni, the Orsini, and the exiled Malvezzi.

Bentivogli had good grounds for his anxiety, not knowing how long he might depend upon the protection of France, and well aware that, once that protection was removed, there would be no barrier between Bologna and Cesare's manifest intentions concerning her.

Next to Cesare's utter annihilation, to check his progress was the desire dearest just then to the heart of Bentivogli, and with this end in view he dispatched Count Guido Torella to Faenza, in mid-October, with an offer to assist Astorre with men and money.

Astorre, who had succeeded Galeotto Manfredi in the tyranny of Faenza at the age of three, had been and still continued under the tutelage of the Council which really governed his territories. To this Council came Count Torella with Bentivogli's offer, adding the proposal that young Astorre should be sent to Venice for his personal safety. But to this the Council replied that it would be useless, if that course were adopted, to attempt resistance, as the people could only be urged to it by their affection for their young lord, and that, if he were removed from their midst, they would insist upon surrender.

News of these negotiations reached Rome, and on October 24 Alexander sent Bentivogli his commands to refrain, under pain of excommunication, from interfering in the affairs of Faenza. Bentivogli made a feeble attempt to mask his disobedience. The troops with which he intended to assist his grandson were sent ostensibly to Castel Bolognese, but with instructions to desert thence and make for Faenza. This they did, and thus was Astorre strengthened by a thousand men, whilst the work of preparing his city for resistance went briskly forward.

Meanwhile, ahead of Cesare Borgia, swept Vitellozzo Vitelli with his horse into Astorre's dominions. He descended upon the valley of the Lamone, and commenced hostilities by the capture and occupation of Brisghella on November 7. The other lesser strongholds and townships offered no resistance to Cesare's arms. Indeed they were induced into ready rebellion against their lord by Dionigio di Naldo—the sometime defender of Imola, who had now taken service with Cesare.

On November 10 Cesare himself halted his host beneath the walls of Faenza and called upon the town to surrender. Being denied, he encamped his army for the siege. He chose the eastern side of the town, between the rivers Lamone and Marzano, and, that his artillery might have free play, he caused several houses to be demolished.

In Faenza itself, meanwhile, the easy conquest of the valley had not produced a good effect. Moreover, the defenders had cause to fear treachery within their gates, for a paper had been picked up out of the moat containing an offer of terms of surrender. It had been shot into the castle attached to an arbalestbolt, and was intended for the castellan Castagnini. This Castagnini was arrested, thrown into prison, and his possessions confiscated, whilst the Council placed the citadel in the hands of four of its own members together with Gianevangelista Manfredi—Astorre's half-brother, and a bastard of Galeotto's. These set about defending it against Cesare, who had now opened fire. The duke caused the guns to be trained upon a certain bastion through which he judged that a good assault might be delivered and an entrance gained. Night and day was the bombardment of that bastion kept up, yet without producing visible effect until the morning of the 20th, when suddenly one of its towers collapsed thunderously into the moat.

Instantly, and without orders, the soldiers, all eager to be among the first to enter, flung themselves forward in utter and fierce disorder to storm the breach. Cesare, at breakfast—as he himself wrote to the Duke of Urbino—sprang up at the great noise, and, surmising what was taking place, dashed out to restrain his men. But the task was no easy one, for, gathering excitement and the frenzy of combat as they ran, they had already gained the edge of the ditch, and thither Cesare was forced to follow them, using voice and hands to beat back again.

At last he succeeded in regaining control of them, and in compelling them to make an orderly retreat, and curb their impatience until the time for storming should have come, which was not yet. In the affair Cesare had a narrow escape from a stone-shot fired from the castle, whilst one of his officers—Onorio Savelli—was killed by a cannon-ball from the duke's own guns, whose men, unaware of what was taking place, were continuing the bombardment.

Hitherto the army had been forced to endure foul weather—rain, fogs, and wind; but there was worse come. Snow began to fall on the morning of the 22nd. It grew to a storm, and the blizzard continued all that day, which was a Sunday, all night, and all the following day, and lashed the men pitilessly and blindingly. The army, already reduced by shortness of victuals, was now in a miserable plight in its unsheltered camp, and the defenders of Faenza, as if realizing this, made a sortie on the 23rd, from which a fierce fight ensued, with severe loss to both sides. On the 25th the snow began again, whereupon the hitherto unconquerable Cesare, defeated at last by the elements and seeing that his men could not possibly continue to endure the situation, was compelled to strike camp on the 26th and go into winter quarters, no doubt with immense chagrin at leaving so much work unaccomplished.

So he converted the siege into a blockade, closing all roads that lead to Faenza, with a view to shutting out supplies from the town; and he distributed troops throughout the villages of the territory with orders constantly to harass the garrison and allow it no rest.

He also sent an envoy with an offer of terms of surrender, but the Council rejected it with the proud answer that its members "had agreed, in general assembly, to defend the dominions of Manfredi to the death."

Thereupon Cesare withdrew to Forli with 150 lances and 2,500 foot, and here he affords a proof of his considerateness. The town had already endured several occupations and the severities of being the seat of war during the siege of the citadel. Cesare was determined that it should feel the present occupation as little as possible; so he issued an order to the inhabitants upon whom his soldiers were billeted to supply the men only with bed, light, and fire. What more they required must be paid for, and, to avoid disputes as to prices of victuals and other necessaries, he ordered the Council to draw up a tariff, and issued an edict forbidding his soldiers, under pain of death, from touching any property of the townsfolk. Lest they should doubt his earnestness, he hanged two of his soldiers on December 7—a Piedmontese and a Gascon—and on the 13th a third, all from the windows of his own palace, and all with a label hanging from their feet proclaiming that they had been hanged for taking goods of others in spite of the ban of the Lord Duke, etc.

He remained in Forli until the 23rd, when he departed to Cesena, which was really his capital in Roomagna, and in the huge citadel of which there was ample accommodation for the troops that accompanied him. In Forli he left, as his lieutenants, the Bishop of Trani and Don Michele da Corella—the "Michieli" of Capello's Relation and the "Michelotto" of so many Borgia fables. That this officer ruled the soldiers left with him in Forli in accordance with the stern example set him by his master we know from the chronicles of Bernardi.

In Cesena the duke occupied the splendid palace of Malatesta Novello, which had been magnificently equipped for him, and there, on Christmas Eve, he entertained the Council of the town and other important citizens to a banquet worthy of the repuation for lavishness which he enjoyed. He was very different in this from his father, whose table habits were of the most sparing—to which, no doubt, his Holiness owed the wonderful, almost youthful vigour which he still enjoyed in this his seventieth year. It was notorious that ambassadors cared little for invitations to the Pope's table, where the meal never consisted of more than one dish.

On Christmas Day the duke attended Mass at the Church of San Giovanni Evangelista with great pomp, arrayed in the ducal chlamys and followed by his gentlemen. With these young patricians Cesare made merry during the days that followed. The time was spent in games and joustings, in all of which the duke showed himself freely, making display of his physical perfections, fully aware, no doubt, of what a short cut these afforded him to the hearts of the people, ever ready to worship physical beauty, prowess, and address.

Yet business was not altogether neglected, for on January 4 he went to Porto Cesenatico, and there published an edict against all who had practised with the fuorusciti from his States, forbidding the offence under pain of death and forfeiture of possessions.

He remained in winter quarters until the following April, from which, however, it is not to be concluded that Faenza was allowed to be at peace for that spell. The orders which he had left behind him, that the town was constantly to be harassed, were by no means neglected. On the night of January 21, by arrangement with some of the inhabitants of the beleaguered city, the foot surrounding Faenza attempted to surprise the garrison by a secret escalade. They were, however, discovered betimes in the attempt and repulsed, some who had the mischance—as it happened—to gain the battlements before the alarm was raised being taken and hanged. The duke's troops, however, consoled themselves by capturing Russi and Solarolo, the last two strongholds in the valley that had held for Astorre.

Meanwhile, Cesare and his merry young patricians spent the time as agreeably as might be in Cesena during that carnival. The author of the Diario Cesenate is moved by the duke's pastimes to criticize him severely as indulging in amusements unbecoming the dignity of his station. He is particularly shocked to know that the duke should have gone forth in disguise with a few companions to repair to carnival festivities in the surrounding villages and there to wrestle with the rustics. It is not difficult to imagine the discomfiture suffered by many a village Hercules at the hands of this lithe young man, who could behead a bull at a single stroke of a spadoon and break a horseshoe in his fingers. The diary in question, you will have gathered, is that of a pedant, prim and easily scandalized. So much being obvious, it is noteworthy that Cesare's conduct should have afforded him no subject for graver strictures than these, Cesare being such a man as has been represented, and the time being that of carnival when licence was allowed full play.

The Pope accounted that the check endured by Cesare before Faenza was due not so much to the foul weather by which his army had been beset as to the assistance which Giovanni Bentivogli had rendered his grandson Astorre, and bitter were the complaints of it which he addressed to the King of France. Alarmed by this, and fearing that he might have compromised himself and jeopardized the French protection by his action in the matter, Bentivogli made haste to recall his troops, and did in fact withdraw them from Faenza early in December, shortly after Cesare had gone into winter quarters. Nevertheless, the Pope's complaints continued, Alexander in his secret, crafty heart no doubt rejoicing that Bentivogli should have afforded him so sound a grievance. As Louis XII desired, for several reasons, to stand well with Rome, he sent an embassy to Bentivogli to express his regret and censure of the latter's intervention in the affairs of Faenza. He informed Bentivogli that the Pope was demanding the return of Bologna to the States of the Church, and, without expressing himself clearly as to his own view of the matter, he advised Bentivogli to refrain from alliances with the enemies of the Holy See and to secure Bologna to himself by some sound arrangement. This showed Bentivogli in what danger he stood, and his uneasiness was increased by the arrival at Modena of Yves d'Allègre, sent by the King of France with a condotta of 500 horse for purposes which were not avowed but which Bentivogli sorely feared might prove to be hostile to himself.

At the beginning of February Cesare moved his quarters from Cesena to Imola, and thence he sent his envoys to demand winter quarters for his troops in Castel Bolognese. This flung Bentivogli into positive terror, as he interpreted the request as a threat of invasion. Castel Bolognese was too valuable a stronghold to be so lightly placed in the duke's hands. Thence Bentivogli might, in case of need, hold the duke in check, the fortress commanding, as it did, the road from Imola to Faenza. He had the good sense, however, to compromise the matter by returning Cesare an offer of accommodation for his men with victuals, artillery, etc., but without the concession of Castel Bolognese. With this Cesare was forced to be content, there being no reasonable grounds upon which he could decline so generous an offer. It was a cunning concession on Bentivogli's part, for, without strengthening the duke's position, it yet gave the latter what he ostensibly required, and left no cause for grievance and no grounds upon which to molest Bologna. So much was this the case that on February 26 the Pope wrote to Bentivogli expressing his thanks at the assistance which he had thus given Cesare in the Faenza emprise.

It was during this sojourn of Cesare's at Imola that the abduction took place of Dorotea Caracciolo, the young wife of Gianbattista Caracciolo, a captain of foot in the Venetian service. The lady, who was attached to the Duchess of Urbino, had been residing at the latter's Court, and in the previous December Caracciolo had begged leave of the Council of Ten that he might himself go to Urbino for the purpose of escorting her to Venice. The Council, however, had replied that he should send for her, and this the captain had done. Near Cervia, on the confines of the Venetian territory, towards evening of February 14, the lady's escort was set upon by ten wellarmed men, and rudely handled by them, some being wounded and one at least killed, whilst the lady and a woman who was with her were carried off.

The Podestá of Cervia reported to the Venetian Senate that the abductors were Spaniards of the army of the Duke of Valentinois, and it was feared in Venice—according to Sanuto—that the deed might be the work of Cesare.

The matter contained in that Relation of Capello's to the Senate must by now have been widespread, and of a man who could perpetrate the wickednesses therein divulged anything could be believed. Indeed, it seems to have followed that, where any act of wickedness was brought to light, at once men looked to see if Cesare might not be responsible, nor looked close enough to make quite sure. To no other cause can it be assigned that, in the stir which the Senate made, the name of Cesare was at once suggested as that of the abductor, and this so broadly that letters poured in upon him on all sides begging him to right this cruel wrong. So much do you see assumed, upon no more evidence than was contained in that letter from the Podestá of Cervia, which went no further than to say that the abductors were "Spaniards of the Duke of Valentinois' army." The envoy Manenti was dispatched at once to Cesare by the Senate, and he went persuaded, it is clear, that Cesare Borgia was the guilty person. He enlisted the support of Monsieur de Trans (the French ambassador then on his way to Rome) and that of Yves d'Allègre, and he took them with him to the Duke at Imola.

There, acting upon his strong suspicions, Manenti appears to have taken a high tone, representing to the duke that he had done an unworthy thing, and imploring him to restore the lady to her husband. Cesare's patience under the insolent assumption in justification of which Manenti had not a single grain of evidence to advance, is—guilty or innocent—a rare instance of self-control. He condescended to take oath that he had not done this thing which they imputed to him. He admitted that he had heard of the outrage, and he expressed the belief that it was the work of one Diego Ramires—a captain of foot in his service. This Ramires, he explained, had been in the employ of the Duke of Urbino, and in Urbino had made the acquaintance and fallen enamoured of the lady; and he added that the fellow had lately disappeared, but that already he had set on foot a search for him, and that, once taken, he would make an example of him.

In conclusion he begged that the Republic should not believe this thing against him, assuring the envoy that he had not found the ladies of the

Romagna so difficult that he should be driven to employ such rude and violent measures.

The French ambassador certainly appears to have attached implicit faith to Cesare's statement, and he privately informed Manenti that Ramires was believed to be at Medola, and that the Republic might rest assured that, if he were taken, exemplary justice would be done.

All this you will find recorded in Sanuto. After that his diary entertains us with rumours which were reaching Venice, now that the deed was the duke's, now that the lady was with Ramires. Later the two rumours are consolidated into one, in a report of the Podestá of Cervia to the effect that "the lady is in the Castle of Forli with Ramires, and that he took her there by order of the duke." The Podestá says that a man whom he sent to gather news had this story from one Benfaremo. But he omits to say who and what is this Benfaremo, and what the source of his information.

Matters remaining thus, and the affair appearing in danger of being forgotten, Caracciolo goes before the Senate on March 16 and implores permission to deal with it himself. This permission is denied him, the Doge conceiving that the matter will best be dealt with by the Senate, and Caracciolo is ordered back to his post at Gradisca. Thence he writes to the Senate on March 30 that he is certain his wife is in the citadel of Forli.

After this Sanuto does not mention the matter again until December of 1503—nearly three years later—when we gather that, under pressure of constant letters from the husband, the Venetian ambassador at the Vatican makes so vigorous a stir that the lady is at last delivered up, and goes for the time being into a convent. But we are not told where or how she is found, nor where the convent in which she seeks shelter. That is Sanuto's first important omission.

And now an odd light is thrown suddenly upon the whole affair, and it begins to look as if the lady had been no unwilling victim of an abduction, but, rather, a party to an elopement. She displays a positive reluctance to return to her husband; she is afraid to do so—"in fear for her very life"—and she implores the Senate to obtain from Caracciolo some security for her, or else to grant her permission to withdraw permanently to a convent.

The Senate summons the husband, and represents the case to him. He assures the Senate that he has forgiven his wife, believing her to be innocent. This, however, does not suffice to allay her uneasiness—or her reluctance—for on January 4, 1504, Sanuto tells us that the Senate has received a letter of thanks from her in which she relates her misfortunes, and in which again she begs that her husband be compelled to pledge security to treat her well ("darli buona vita") or else that she should be allowed to return to her mother. Of the nature of the misfortunes which he tells us she related in her letter, Sanuto says nothing. That is his second important omission.

The last mention of the subject in Sanuto relates to her restoration to her husband. He tells us that Caracciolo received her with great joy; but he is silent on the score of the lady's emotions on that occasion.

There you have all that is known of Dorotea Caracciolo's abduction, which later writers—including Bembo in his Historiae—have positively assigned to Cesare Borgia, drawing upon their imagination to fill up the lacunae in the story so as to support their point of view.

Those lacunae, however, are invested with a certain eloquence which it is well not to disregard. Admitting that the construing of silence into evidence is a dangerous course, all fraught with pitfalls, yet it seems permissible to pose the following questions:

If the revelation of the circumstances under which she was found, the revelations contained in her letters to the Senate, and the revelations which one imagines must have followed her return to her husband, confirm past rumours and convict Cesare of the outrage, how does it happen that Sanuto—who has never failed to record anything that could tell against Cesare—should be silent on the matter? And how does it happen that so many pens that busied themselves greedily with scandal that touched the Borgias should be similarly silent? Is it unreasonable to infer that those revelations did not incriminate him—that they gave the lie to all the rumours that had been current? If that is not the inference, then what is?

It is further noteworthy that on January 16—after Dorotea's letter to the Senate giving the details of her misfortunes, which details Sanuto has suppressed—Diego Ramires, the real and known abductor, is still the object of a hunt set afoot by some Venetians. Would that be the case had her revelations shown Ramires to be no more than the duke's instrument? Possibly; but not probably. In such a case he would not have been worth the trouble of pursuing.

Reasonably may it be objected: How, if Cesare was not guilty, does it happen that he did not carry out his threat of doing exemplary justice upon Ramires when taken—since Ramires obviously lay in his power for years after the event? The answer to that you will find in the lady's reluctance to return to Caracciolo, and the tale it tells. It is not in the least illogical to assume that, when Cesare threatened that vengeance upon Ramires for the outrage which it was alleged had been committed, he fully intended to execute it; but that, upon taking Ramires, and upon discovering that here was no such outrage as had been represented, but just the elopement of a couple of lovers, he found there was nothing for him to avenge. Was it for Cesare Borgia to set up as a protector and avenger of cuckolds? Rather would it be in keeping with the feelings of his age and race to befriend the fugitive pair who had planted the antlers upon the brow of the Venetian captain.

Lastly, Cesare's attitude towards women may be worth considering, that we may judge whether such an act as was imputed to him is consistent with it. Women play no part whatever in his history. Not once shall you find a woman's influence swaying him; not once shall you see him permitting dalliance to retard his advancement or jeopardize his chances. With him, as with egotists of his type, governed by cold will and cold intellect, the sentimental side of the relation of the sexes has no place. With him one woman was as another woman; as he craved women, so he took women, but with an almost contemptuous undiscrimination. For all his needs concerning them the lupanaria sufficed.

Is this mere speculation, think you? Is there no evidence to support it, do you say? Consider, pray, in all its bearings the treatise on pudendagra dedicated to a man of Cesare Borgia's rank by the physician Torella, written to meet his needs, and see what inference you draw from that. Surely such an inference as will invest with the ring of truth—expressing as it does his intimate nature, and confirming further what has here been said—that answer of his to the Venetian envoy, "that he had not found the ladies of Romagna so difficult that he should be driven to such rude and violent measures."

CHAPTER VIII
ASTORRE MANFREDI

On March 29 Cesare Borgia departed from Cesena — whither, meanwhile, he had returned — to march upon Faenza, resume the attack, and make an end of the city's stubborn resistance.

During the past months, however, and notwithstanding the presence of the Borgia troops in the territory, the people of Faenza had been able to increase their fortifications by the erection of out-works and a stout bastion in the neighbourhood of the Osservanza Hospital, well beyond the walls. This bastion claimed Cesare's first attention, and it was carried by assault on April 12. Thither he now fetched his guns, mounted them, and proceeded to a steady bombardment of the citadel. But the resistance continued with unabated determination — a determination amounting to heroism, considering the hopelessness of their case and the straits to which the Faentini were reduced by now. Victuals and other necessaries of life had long since been running low. Still the men of Faenza tightened their belts, looked to their defences, and flung defiance at the Borgia. The wealthier inhabitants distributed wine and flour at prices purely nominal, and lent Astorre money for the payment of his troops. It is written that to the same end the very priests, their patriotism surmounting their duty to the Holy Father in whose name this war was waged, consented to the despoiling of the churches and the melting down of the sacred vessels.

Even the women of Faenza bore their share of the burden of defence, carrying to the ramparts the heavy stones that were to be hurled down upon the besiegers, or actually donning casque and body-armour and doing sentry duty on the walls while the men rested.

But the end was approaching. On April 18 the Borgia cannon opened at last a breach in the walls, and Cesare delivered a terrible assault upon the citadel. The fight upon the smoking ruins was fierce and determined on both sides, the duke's men pressing forward gallantly under showers of scalding pitch and a storm of boulders, launched upon them by the defenders, who used the very ruins of the wall for ammunition. For four hours was that assault maintained; nor did it cease until the deepening dusk compelled

Cesare to order the retreat, since to continue in the failing light was but to sacrifice men to no purpose.

Cesare's appreciation of the valour of the garrison ran high. It inspired him with a respect which shows his dispassionate breadth of mind, and he is reported to have declared that with an army of such men as those who held Faenza against him he would have conquered all Italy. He did not attempt a second assault, but confined himself during the three days that followed to continuing the bombardment.

Within Faenza men were by now in desperate case. Weariness and hunger were so exhausting their endurance, so sapping their high valour that nightly there were desertions to the duke's camp of men who could bear no more. The fugitives from the town were well received, all save one—a man named Grammante, a dyer by trade—who, in deserting to the duke, came in to inform him that at a certain point of the citadel the defences were so weak that an assault delivered there could not fail to carry it.

This man afforded Cesare an opportunity of marking his contempt for traitors and his respect for the gallant defenders of Faenza. The duke hanged him for his pains under the very walls of the town he had betrayed.

On the 21st the bombardment was kept up almost without interruption for eight hours, and so shattered was the citadel by that pitiless cannonade that the end was in sight at last. But the duke's satisfaction was tempered by his chagrin at the loss of Achille Tiberti, one of the most valiant of his captains, and one who had followed his fortunes from the first with conspicuous devotion. He was killed by the bursting of a gun. A great funeral at Cesena bore witness to the extent to which Cesare esteemed and honoured him.

Astorre, now seeing the citadel in ruins and the possibility of further resistance utterly exhausted, assembled the Council of Faenza to determine upon their course of action, and, as a result of their deliberations, the young tyrant sent his ambassadors to the duke to propose terms of surrender. It was a belated proposal, for there was no longer on Cesare's part the necessity to make terms. The city's defences were destroyed, and to talk of surrender now was to talk of giving something that no longer existed. Yet Cesare met the ambassadors in a spirit of splendid generosity.

The terms proposed were that the people of Faenza should have immunity for themselves and their property; that Astorre should have freedom to depart and to take with him his moveable possessions, his immoveables remaining at the mercy of the Pope. By all the laws of war Cesare was entitled to a heavy indemnity for the losses he had sustained through the resistance opposed to him. Considering those same laws and the application they were wont to receive in his day, no one could have censured him had he rejected all terms and given the city over to pillage. Yet not only does he grant the terms submitted to him, but in addition he actually lends an ear to the Council's prayer that out of consideration for the great suffering of the city in the siege he should refrain from exacting any indemnity. This was to be forbearing indeed; but he was to carry his forbearance even further. In answer to the Council's expressed fears of further harm at the hands of his troopers once these should be in Faenza, he actually consented to effect no entrance into the town.

We are not for a moment to consider Cesare as actuated in all this by any lofty humanitarianism. He was simply pursuing that wise policy of his, in refraining from punishing conquered States which were to be subject henceforth to his rule, and which, therefore, must be conciliated that they might be loyal to him. But it is well that you should at least appreciate this policy and the fruit it bore when you read that Cesare Borgia was a blood-glutted monster of carnage who ravaged the Romagna, rending and devouring it like some beast of prey.

On the 26th the Council waited upon Cesare at the Hospital of the Osservanza—where he was lodged—to tender the oath of fealty. That same evening Astorre himself, attended by a few of his gentlemen, came to the duke.

To this rather sickly and melancholy lad, who had behind him a terrible family history of violence, and to his bastard brother, Gianevangelista, the duke accorded the most gracious welcome. Indeed, so amiable did Astorre find the duke that, although the terms of surrender afforded him perfect liberty to go whither he listed, he chose to accept the invitation Cesare extended to him to remain in the duke's train.

It is eminently probable, however, that the duke's object in keeping the young man about him was prompted by another phase of that policy of his which Macchiavelli was later to formulate into rules of conduct, expedient in a prince:

"In order to preserve a newly acquired State particular attention should be given to two points. In the first place care should be taken entirely to extinguish the family of the ancient sovereign; in the second, laws should not be changed, nor taxes increased."

Thus Macchiavelli. The second point is all that is excellent; the first is all that is wise—cold, horrible, and revolting though it be to our twentieth-century notions.

Cesare Borgia, as a matter of fact, hardly went so far as Macchiavelli advises. He practised discrimination. He did not, for instance, seek the lives of Pandolfaccio Malatesta, or of Caterina Sforza-Riario. He saw no danger in their living, no future trouble to apprehend from them. The hatred borne them by their subjects was to Cesare a sufficient guarantee that they would not be likely to attempt a return to their dominions, and so he permitted them to keep their lives. But to have allowed Astorre Manfredi, or even his bastard brother, to live would have been bad policy from the appallingly egotistical point of view which was Cesare's—a point of view, remember, which receives Macchiavelli's horribly intellectual, utterly unsentimental, revoltingly practical approval.

So—to anticipate a little—we see Cesare taking Astorre and Gianevangelista Manfredi to Rome when he returned thither in the following June. A fortnight later—on June 26—the formidable amazon of Forli, the Countess Sforza-Riario, was liberated, as we know, from the Castle of Sant' Angelo, and permitted to withdraw to Florence. But the gates of that grim fortress, in opening to allow her to pass out, opened also for the purpose of admitting Astorre and Gianevangelista, upon whom they closed.

All that is known positively of the fate of these unfortunate young men is that they never came forth again alive.

The record in Burchard (June 9, 1502) of Astorre's body having been found in the Tiber with a stone round his neck, suffers in probability from the addition that, "together with it were found the bodies of two young men with their arms tied, a certain woman, and many others."

The dispatch of Giustiniani to the effect that: "It is said that this night were thrown into Tiber and drowned the two lords of Faenza together with their seneschal," was never followed up by any other dispatch confirming the rumour, nor is it confirmed by any dispatch so far discovered from any other ambassador, nor yet does the matter find place in the Chronicles of Faenza.

But that is of secondary importance. The ugliest feature of the case is not the actual assassination of the young men, but the fact that Cesare had pledged himself that Astorre should go free, and yet had kept him by him— at first, it would seem, in his train, and later as a prisoner—until he put an end to his life. It was an ugly, unscrupulous deed; but there is no need to exaggerate its heinousness, as is constantly done, upon no better authority than Guicciardini's, who wrote that the murder had been committed "saziata prima la libidine di qualcuno."

Of all the unspeakable calumnies of which the Borgias have been the subject, none is more utterly wanton than this foul exhalation of

Guicciardini's lewd invention. Let the shame that must eternally attach to him for it brand also those subsequent writers who repeated and retailed that abominable and utterly unsupported accusation, and more particularly those who have not hesitated to assume that Guicciardini's "qualcuno" was an old man in his seventy-second year—Pope Alexander VI.

Others a little more merciful, a little more careful of physical possibilities (but no whit less salacious) have taken it that Cesare was intended by the Florentine historian.

But, under one form or another, the lie has spread as only such foulness can spread. It has become woven into the warp of history; it has grown to be one of those "facts" which are unquestioningly accepted, but it stands upon no better foundation than the frequent repetition which a charge so monstrous could not escape. Its source is not a contemporary one. It is first mentioned by Guicciardini; and there is no logical conclusion to be formed other than that Guicciardini invented it. Another story which owes its existence mainly, and its particulars almost entirely, to Guicciardini's libellous pen—the story of the death of Alexander VI, which in its place shall be examined—provoked the righteous anger of Voltaire. Atheist and violent anti-clerical though he was, the story's obvious falseness so revolted him that he penned his formidable indictment in which he branded Guicciardini as a liar who had deceived posterity that he might vent his hatred of the Borgias. Better cause still was there in this matter of Astorre Manfredi for Voltaire's indignation, as there is for the indignation of all conscientious seekers after truth.

CHAPTER IX
CASTEL BOLOGNESE AND PIOMBINO

To return to the surrender of Faenza on April 26, 1501, we see Cesare on the morrow of that event, striking camp with such amazing suddenness that he does not even pause to provide for the government of the conquered tyranny, but appoints a vicar four days later to attend to it.

He makes his abrupt departure from Faenza, and is off like a whirlwind to sweep unexpectedly into the Bolognese territory, and, by striking swiftly, to terrify Bentivogli into submission in the matter of Castel Bolognese.

This fortress, standing in the duke's dominions, on the road between Faenza and Imola, must be a menace to him whilst in the hands of a power that might become actively hostile.

Ahead of him Cesare sent an envoy to Bentivogli, to demand its surrender.

The alarmed Lord of Bologna, having convened his Council (the Reggimento), replied that they must deliberate in the matter; and two days later they dispatched their ambassador to lay before Cesare the fruits of these deliberations. They were to seek the duke at Imola; but they got no farther than Castel S. Pietro, which to their dismay they found already in the hands of Vitellozzo Vitelli's men-atarms. For, what time Bentivogli had been deliberating, Cesare Borgia had been acting with that promptness which was one of his most salient characteristics, and, in addition to Castel S. Pietro he had already captured Casalfiuminense, Castel Guelfo, and Medecina, which were now invested by his troops.

When the alarming news of this swift action reached Bologna it caused Bentivogli to bethink him at last of Louis XII's advice, that he should come to terms with Cesare Borgia, and he realized that the time to do so could no longer be put off. He made haste, therefore, to agree to the surrender of Castel Bolognese to the duke, to concede him stipend for one hundred lances of three men each, and to enter into an undertaking to lend him every assistance for one year against any power with which he might be at war, the King of France excepted. In return, Cesare was to relinquish the captured strongholds and undertake that the Pope should confirm Bentivogli in his ancient privileges. On April 29 Paolo Orsini went as Cesare's plenipotentiary to Bologna to sign this treaty.

It was a crafty arrangement on Bentivogli's part, for, over and above the pacification of Cesare and the advantage of an alliance with him, he gained as a result the alliance also of those famous condottieri Vitelli and Orsini, both bitter enemies of Florence—the latter intent upon the restoration of the Medici, the former impatient to avenge upon the Signory the execution of his brother Paolo. As an instalment, on account of that debt, Vitelli had already put to death Pietro da Marciano—the brother of Count Rinuccio da Marciano—when this gentleman fell into his hands at Medicina.

Two days before the treaty was signed, Bentivogli had seized four members of the powerful House of Marescotti. This family was related to the exiled Malvezzi, who were in arms with Cesare, and Bentivogli feared that communications might be passing between the two to his undoing. On that suspicion he kept them prisoners for the present, nor did be release them when the treaty was signed, nor yet when, amid public rejoicings expressing the relief of the Bolognese, it was published on May 2.

Hermes Bentivogli—Giovanni's youngest son—was on guard at the palace with several other young Bolognese patricians, and he incited these to go with him to make an end of the traitors who had sought to destroy the peace by their alleged plottings with Bentivogli's enemies in Cesare's camp. He led his companions to the chamber where the Marescotti were confined, and there, more or less in cold blood, those four gentlemen were murdered for no better reason—ostensibly—than because it was suspected they had been in communication with their relatives in the Duke of Valentinois's army. That was the way of the Cinquecento, which appears to have held few things of less account than human life.

In passing, it may be mentioned that Guicciardini, of course, does his ludicrous best to make this murder appear—at least indirectly, since directly it would be impossible—the work of Cesare Borgia.

As for Castel Bolognese itself, Cesare Borgia sent a thousand demolishers in the following July to raze it to the ground. It is said to have been the most beautiful castle in the Romagna; but Cesare had other qualities than beauty to consider in the matter of a stronghold. Its commanding position rendered it almost in the nature of a gateway controlling, as we know, the road from Faenza to Imola, and its occupation by the Bolognese or other enemies in time of disturbance might be of serious consequence to Cesare. Therefore he ruthlessly ordered Ramiro de Lorqua to set about its demolition.

The Council of Castel Bolognese made great protest, and implored Ramiro to stay his hand until they should have communicated with the duke petitioning for the castle's preservation; but Ramiro—a hard, stern man, and Cesare's most active officer in the Romagna—told them bluntly that to petition the duke in such a matter would be no better than a waste of time. He was no more than right; for Cesare, being resolved upon the expediency of the castle's destruction, would hardly be likely to listen to sentimental reasonings for its preservation. Confident of this, Ramiro without more ado set about the execution of the orders he had received. He pulled down the walls and filled up the moat, until nothing remained so much as to show the place where the fortress had stood.

Another fortress which shared the fate of Castel Bolognese was the Castle of Sant' Arcangelo, and similarly would Cesare have disposed of Solarolo, but that, being of lesser importance and the inhabitants offering, in their petition for its preservation, to undertake, themselves, the payment of the Castellan, he allowed it to remain.

Scarcely was the treaty with Bologna signed than Cesare received letters from the Pope recalling him to Rome, and recommending that he should not molest the Florentines in his passage—a recommendation which Alexander deemed very necessary considering the disposition towards Florence of Vitelli and Orsini. He foresaw that they would employ arguments to induce Valentinois into an enterprise of which all the cost would be his, and all the possible profit their own.

The duke would certainly have obeyed and avoided Tuscany, but that—precisely as the shrewd Pope had feared—Vitelli and Orsini implored him to march through Florentine territory. Vitelli, indeed, flung himself on his knees before Cesare in the vehemence of his supplications, urging that his only motive was to effect the deliverance from his unjust imprisonment of Cerbone, who had been his executed brother's chancellor. Beyond that, he swore he would make no demands upon Florence, that he would not attempt to mix himself in the affairs of the Medici, and that he would do no violence to town or country.

Thus implored, Cesare gave way. Probably he remembered the very circumstances under which Vitelli had joined his banner, and considered that he could not now oppose a request backed by a promise of so much moderation; so on May 7 he sent his envoys to the Signory to crave leave of passage for his troops through Florentine territory.

Whilst still in the Bolognese he was sought out by Giuliano de'Medici, who begged to be allowed to accompany him, a request which Cesare instantly refused, as being contrary to that to which he had engaged himself, and he caused Giuliano to fall behind at Lojano. Nor would he so much as receive in audience Piero de'Medici, who likewise sought to join him in Siennese territory, as soon as he perceived what was toward. Yet, however much the duke protested that he had no intention to make any change in the State of Florence, there were few who believed him. Florence, weary and sorely reduced by the long struggle of the Pisan war, was an easy prey. Conscious of this, great was her anxiety and alarm at Cesare's request for passage. The Signory replied granting him the permission sought, but imposing the condition that he should keep to the country, refraining from entering any town, nor bring with him into Florentine territory Vitelli, Orsini, or any other enemy of the existing government. It happened, however, that when the Florentine ambassador reached him with this reply the duke was already over the frontier of Tuscany with the excluded condottieri in his train.

It was incumbent upon him, as a consequence, to vindicate this high-handed anticipation of the unqualified Florentine permission which had not arrived. So he declared that he had been offended last year by Florence in the matter of Forli, and again this year in the matter of Faenza, both of which cities he charged the Signory with having assisted to resist him, and he announced that, to justify his intentions so far as Florence was concerned, he would explain himself at Barberino.

There, on May 12, he gave audience to the ambassador. He declared to him that he desired a good understanding with Florence, and that she should offer no hindrance to the conquest of Piombino, upon which he was now bound; adding that since he placed no trust in the present government, which already had broken faith with him, he would require some good security for the treaty to be made. Of reinstating the Medici he said nothing; but he demanded that some satisfaction be given Vitelli and Orsini, and, to quicken Florence in coming to a decision, he pushed forward with his army as far as Forno dei Campi—almost under her very walls.

The Republic was thrown into consternation. Instantly she got together what forces she disposed of, and proceeded to fling her artillery into the Arno, to the end that she should be constrained neither to refuse it to Cesare upon his demand, nor yet to deliver it.

Macchiavelli censures the Signory's conduct of this affair as impolitic. He contends that the duke, being in great strength of arms, and Florence not armed at all, and therefore in no case to hinder his passage, it would have been wiser and the Signory would better have saved its face and dignity, had it accorded Cesare the permission to pass which he demanded, rather than have been subjected to behold him enforce that passage by weight of arms. But all that now concerned the Florentines was to be rid of an army whose presence in their territory was a constant menace. And to gain that end they were ready to give any undertakings, just as they were resolved to fulfil none.

Similarly, it chanced that Cesare was in no less a hurry to be gone; for he had received another letter from the Pope commanding his withdrawal, and in addition, he was being plagued by Vitelli and Orsini—grown restive—with entreaties for permission to go into either Florence or Pistoja, where they did not lack for friends. To resist them Cesare had need of all the severity and resolution he could command; and he even went so far as to back his refusal by a threat himself to take up arms against them if they insisted.

On the 15th, at last, the treaty—which amounted to an offensive and defensive alliance—was signed. By the terms of this, Florence undertook to give Cesare a condotta of 300 lances for three years, to be used in Florentine service, with a stipend of 36,000 ducats yearly. How much this really meant the duke was to discover two days later, when he sent to ask the Signory to lend him some cannon for the emprise against Piombino, and to pay him the first instalment of one quarter of the yearly stipend before he left Florentine territory. The Signory replied that, by the terms of the agreement, there was no obligation for the immediate payment of the instalment, whilst in the matter of the artillery they put him off from day to day, until Cesare understood that their only aim in signing the treaty had been the immediate one of being rid of his army.

The risk Florence incurred in so playing fast-and-loose with such a man, particularly in a moment of such utter unfitness to resist him, is, notwithstanding the French protection enjoyed by the Signory, amazing in its reckless audacity. It was fortunate for Florence that the Pope's orders tied the duke's hands—and it may be that of this the Signory had knowledge, and that it was upon such knowledge, in conjunction with France's protection, that it was presuming. Cesare took the matter in the spirit of an excellent loser.

Not a hint of his chagrin and resentment did he betray; instead, he set about furnishing his needs elsewhere, sending Vitelli to Pisa with a request for artillery, a request to which Pisa very readily responded, as much on Vitelli's account as on the duke's. As for Florence, if Cesare Borgia could be terribly swift in punishing, he could also be formidably slow. If he could strike upon the instant where the opening for a blow appeared, he could also wait for months until the opening should be found. He waited now.

It would be at about this time that young Loenardo da Vinci sought employment in Cesare Borgia's service. Leonardo had been in Milan until the summer of 1500, when he repaired to Florence in quest of better fortune;

but, finding little or no work to engage him there, he took the chance of the duke of Valentinois's passage to offer his service to one whose liberal patronage of the arts was become proverbial. Cesare took him into his employ as engineer and architect, leaving him in the Romagna for the present. Leonardo may have superintended the repairs of the Castle of Forli, whilst he certainly built the canal from Cesena to the Porto Cesenatico, before rejoining the duke in Rome.

On May 25 Cesare moved by the way of the valley of Cecina to try conclusions with Giacomo d'Appiano, Tyrant of Piombino, who with some Genoese and some Florentine aid, was disposed to offer resistance to the duke. The first strategic movement in this affair must be the capture of the Isle of Elba, whence aid might reach Piombino on its promontory thrusting out into the sea. For this purpose the Pope sent from Civita Vecchia six galleys, three brigantines, and two galleons under the command of Lodovico Mosca, captain of the papal navy, whilst Cesare was further reinforced by some vessels sent him from Pisa together with eight pieces of cannon. With these he made an easy capture of Elba and Pianosa. That done, he proceeded to lay siege to Piombino, which, after making a gallant resistance enduring for two months, was finally pressed to capitulate.

Long before that happened, however, Cesare had taken his departure. Being awaited in Rome, he was unable to conduct the siege operations in person. So he quitted Piombino in June to join the French under d'Aubigny, bound at last upon the conquest of Naples, and claiming—as their treaty with him provided—Cesare's collaboration.

CHAPTER X
THE END OF THE HOUSE OF ARAGON

Cesare arrived in Rome on June 13. There was none of the usual pomp on this occasion. He made his entrance quietly, attended only by a small body of men-at-arms, and he was followed, on the morrow, by Yves d'Allègre with the army—considerably reduced by the detachments which had been left to garrison the Romagna, and to lay siege to Piombino.

Repairing to his quarters in the Vatican, the duke remained so close there for the few weeks that he abode in Rome on this occasion(1) that, from now onward, it became a matter of the utmost difficulty to obtain audience from him. This may have been due to his habit of turning night into day and day into night, whether at work or at play, which in fact was the excuse offered by the Pope to certain envoys sent to Cesare from Rimini, who were left to cool their heels about the Vatican ante-chambers for a fortnight without succeeding in obtaining an audience.

1 *"Mansit in Palatio secrete,"* says Burchard.

Cesare Borgia was now Lord of Imola, Forli, Rimini, Faenza and Piombino, warranting his assumption of the inclusive title of Duke of Romagna which he had taken immediately after the fall of Faenza.

As his State grew, so naturally did the affairs of government; and, during those four weeks in Rome, business claimed his attention and an enormous amount of it was dispatched. Chiefly was he engaged upon the administration of the affairs of Faenza, which he had so hurriedly quitted. In this his shrewd policy of generosity is again apparent. As his representative and lieutenant he appointed a prominent citizen of Faenza named Pasi, one of the very members of that Council which had been engaged in defending the city and resisting Cesare. The duke gave it as his motive for the choice that the man was obviously worthy of trust in view of his fidelity to Astorre.

And there you have not only the shrewdness of the man who knows how to choose his servants—which is one of the most important factors of success—but a breadth of mind very unusual indeed in the Cinquecento.

In addition to the immunity from indemnity provided for by the terms of the city's capitulation, Cesare actually went so far as to grant the peasantry of the valley 2,000 ducats as compensation for damage done in the war. Further, he supported the intercessions of the Council to the Pope for the erection of a new convent to replace the one that had been destroyed in the bombardment. In giving his consent to this—in a brief dated July 12, 1501—the Pope announces that he does so in response to the prayers of the Council and of the duke.

Giovanni Vera, Cesare's erstwhile preceptor—and still affectionately accorded this title by the duke—was now Archbiship of Salerno, Cardinal of Santa Balbina, and papal legate in Macerata, and he was chosen by the Pope to go to Pesaro and Fano for the purpose of receiving the oath of fealty. With him Cesare sent, as his own personal representative, his secretary, Agabito Gherardi, who had been in his employ in that capacity since the duke's journey into France, and who was to follow his fortunes to the end.

However the people of Fano may have refrained from offering themselves to the duke's dominion when, in the previous October, he had afforded them by his presence the opportunity of doing so, their conduct now hardly indicated that the earlier abstention had been born of reluctance, or else their minds had undergone, in the meanwhile, a considerable change. For, when they received the brief appointing him their lord, they celebrated the event by public rejoicings and illuminations; whilst on July 21 the Council, representing the people, in the presence of Vera and Gherardi, took oath upon the Gospels of allegiance to Cesare and his descendants for ever.

In the Consistory of June 25 of that year the French and Spanish ambassadors came formally to notify the Holy Father of the treaty of Granada, entered into in the previous November by Louis XII of the one part, and Ferdinand and Isabella of the other, concerning the conquest and division of the Kingdom of Naples. The rival claimants had come to a compromise by virtue of which they were to undertake together the conquest and thereafter share the spoil—Naples and the Abruzzi going to France, and Calabria and Puglia to Spain.

Alexander immediately published his Bull declaring Federigo of Naples deposed for disobedience to the Church, and for having called the Turk to his aid, either of which charges it would have taxed Alexander's ingenuity—vast though it was—convincingly to have established; or, being established, to censure when all the facts were considered. The charges were no better than pretexts for the spoliation of the unfortunate king who, in the matter of his daughter's alliance with Cesare, had conceived that he might flout the Borgias with impunity.

On June 28 d'Aubigny left Rome with the French troops, accompanied by the bulk of the considerable army with which Cesare supported his French ally, besides 1,000 foot raised by the Pope and a condotta of 100 lances under Morgante Baglioni. As the troops defiled before the Castle of Sant' Angelo they received the apostolic benediction from the Pope, who stood on the lower ramparts of the fortress.

Cesare himself cannot have followed to join the army until after July 10, for as late as that date there is an edict indited by him against all who should offer injury to his Romagna officers. At about the same time that he quitted Rome to ride after the French, Gonsalo de Cordoba landed a Spanish army in Calabria, and the days of the Aragon dominion in Naples were numbered.

King Federigo prepared to face the foe. Whilst himself remaining in Naples with Prospero Colonna, he sent the bulk of his forces to Capua under Fabrizio Colonna and Count Rinuccio Marciano—the brother of that Marciano whom Vitelli had put to death in Tuscany.

Ravaging the territory and forcing its strongholds as they came, the allies were under the walls of Capua within three weeks of setting out; but on July 17, when within two miles of the town, they were met by six hundred lances under Colonna, who attempted to dispute their passage. It was Cesare Borgia himself who led the charge against them. Jean d'Auton— in his Chronicles of Louis XII—speaks in warm terms of the duke's valour and of the manner in which, by words and by example, he encouraged his followers to charge the Colonna forces, with such good effect that they utterly routed the Neapolitans, and drove them headlong back to the shelter of Capua's walls.

The allies brought up their cannon, and opened the bombardment. This lasted incessantly from July 17—which was a Monday—until the following Friday, when two bastions were so shattered that the French were able to gain possession of them, putting to the sword some two hundred Neapolitan soldiers who had been left to defend those outworks. Thence admittance to the town itself was gained four days later—on the 25th— through a breach, according to some, through the treacherous opening of a gate, according to others. Through gate or breach the besiegers stormed to meet a fierce resistance, and the most horrible carnage followed. Back and back they drove the defenders, fighting their way through the streets and sparing none in the awful fury that beset them. The defence was shattered; resistance was at an end; yet still the bloody work went on. The combat had imperceptibly merged into a slaughter; demoralized and panic-stricken in the reaction from their late gallantry, the soldiers of Naples flung down their weapons and fled, shrieking for quarter. But none was given. The invader butchered every human thing he came upon, indiscriminant of age or sex, and the blood of some four thousand victims flowed through the streets of Capua like water after a thundershower. That sack of Capua is one of the most horrid pages in the horrid history of sacks. You will find full details in d'Auton's chronicle, if you have a mind for such horrors. There is a brief summary of the event in Burchard's diary under date of July 26, 1501, which runs as follows:

"At about the fourth hour last night the Pope had news of the capture of Capua by the Duke of Valentinois. The capture was due to the treason of one Fabrizio—a citizen of Capua—who secretly introduced the besiegers and was the first to be killed by them. After him the same fate was met by some three thousand foot and some two hundred horse-soldiers, by citizens, priests, conventuals of both sexes, even in the very churches and monasteries, and all the women taken were given in prey to the greatest cruelty. The total number of the slain is estimated at four thousand."

D'Auton, too, bears witness to this wholesale violation of the women, "which," he adds, "is the very worst of all war's excesses." He informs us further that "the foot-soldiers of the Duke of Valentinois acquitted themselves so well in this, that thirty of the most beautiful women went captive to Rome," a figure which is confirmed by Burchard.

"What an opportunity was not this for Guicciardini! The foot-soldiers of the Duke of Valentinois acquitted themselves so well in this, that thirty of the most beautiful women went captive to Rome."

Under his nimble, malicious, unscrupulous pen that statement is re-edited until not thirty but forty is the number of the captured victims taken to Rome, and not Valentinois's foot, but Valentinois himself the ravisher of the entire forty! But hear the elegant Florentine's own words:

"It was spread about [divulgossi]" he writes, "that, besides other wickednesses worthy of eternal infamy, many women who had taken refuge in a tower, and thus escaped the first fury of the assault, were found by the Duke of Valentinois, who, with the title of King's Lieutenant, followed the army with no more people than his gentlemen and his guards.(1) He desired to see them all, and, after carefully examining them [consideratele diligentemente] he retained forty of the most beautiful."

> 1 This, incidentally, is another misstatement. Valentinois had with him, besides the thousand foot levied by the Pope and the hundred lances under Morgante Baglioni, an army some thousands strong led for him by Yves d'Allègre.

Guicciardini's aim is, of course, to shock you; he considers it necessary to maintain in Cesare the character of ravenous wolf which he had bestowed upon him. The marvel is not that Guicciardini should have penned that utterly ludicrous accusation, but that more or less serious subsequent writers—and writers of our own time even—instead of being moved to contemptuous laughter at the wild foolishness of the story, instead of seeking in the available records the germ of true fact from which it was sprung, should sedulously and unblushingly have carried forward its dissemination.

Yriarte not only repeats the tale with all the sober calm of one utterly destitute of a sense of the ridiculous, but he improves upon it by a delicious touch, worthy of Guicciardini himself, when he assures us that Cesare took these forty women for his harem!

It is a nice instance of how Borgia history has grown, and is still growing.

If verisimilitude itself does not repudiate Guicciardini's story, there are the Capuan chronicles to do it—particularly that of Pellegrini, who witnessed the pillage. In those chronicles from which Guicciardini drew the matter for this portion of his history of Italy, you will seek in vain for any confirmation of that fiction with which the Florentine historian—he who had a pen of gold for his friends and one of iron for his foes—thought well to adorn his facts.

If the grotesque in history-building is of interest to you, you may turn the pages of the Storia Civile di Capua, by F. Granata, published in 1752. This writer has carefully followed the Capuan chroniclers in their relation of the siege; but when it comes to these details of the forty ladies in the tower (in which those chroniclers fail him) he actually gives Guicciardini as his authority, setting a fashion which has not lacked for unconscious, and no less egregious, imitators.

To return from the criticism of fiction to the consideration of fact, Fabrizio Colonna and Rinuccio da Marciano were among the many captains of the Neapolitan army that were taken prisoners. Rinuccio was the head of the Florentine faction which had caused the execution of Paolo Vitelli, and Giovio has it that Vitellozzo Vitelli, who had already taken an instalment of vengeance by putting Pietro da Marciano to death in Tuscany, caused Rinuccio's wounds to be poisoned, so that he died two days later.

The fall of Capua was very shortly followed by that of Gaeta, and, within a week, by that of Naples, which was entered on August 3 by Cesare Borgia in command of the vanguard of the army. "He who had come as a cardinal to crown King Federigo, came now as a condottiero to depose him."

Federigo offered to surrender to the French all the fortresses that still held for him, on condition that he should have safe-conduct to Ischia and liberty to remain there for six months. This was agreed, and Federigo was further permitted to take with him his moveable possessions and his artillery, which latter, however, he afterwards sold to the Pope.

Thus the last member of the House of Aragon to sit upon the throne of Naples took his departure, accompanied by the few faithful ones who loved him well enough to follow him into exile; amongst these was that poet Sanazzaro, who, to avenge the wrong suffered by the master whom he loved, was to launch his terrible epigrams against Alexander, Cesare, and Lucrezia, and by means of those surviving verses enable the enemies of the House of Borgia to vilify their memories through centuries to follow.

Federigo's captains Prospero and Fabrizio Colonna, upon being ransomed, took their swords to Gonzalo de Cordoba, hoping for the day when they might avenge upon the Borgia the ruin which, even in this Neapolitan conquest they attributed to the Pope and his son.

And here, so far as Naples is concerned, closes the history of the House of Aragon. In Italy it was extinct; and it was to become so, too, in Spain within the century.

CHAPTER XI
THE LETTER TO SILVIO SAVELLI

By September 15 Cesare was back in Rome, the richer in renown, in French favour, and in a matter of 40,000 ducats, which is estimated as the total of the sums paid him by France and Spain for the support which his condotta had afforded them.

During his absence two important events had taken place: the betrothal of his widowed sister Lucrezia to Alfonso d'Este, son of Duke Ercole of Ferrara, and the publication of the Bull of excommunication (of August 20) against the Savelli and Colonna in consideration of all that they had wrought against the Holy See from the pontificate of Sixtus IV to the present time. By virtue of that Bull the Pope ordered the confiscation of the possessions of the excommunicated families, whilst the Caetani suffered in like manner at the same time.

These possessions were divided into two parts, and by the Bull of September 17 they were bestowed, one upon Lucrezia's boy Roderigo, and with them the title of Duke of Sermoneta; the other to a child, Giovanni Borgia (who is made something of a mystery) with the title of Duke of Nepi and Palestrina.

The entire proceeding is undoubtedly open to grave censure, since the distribution of the confiscated fiefs subjects to impeachment the purity of the motives that prompted this confiscation. It was on the part of Alexander a gross act of nepotism, a gross abuse of his pontifical authority; but there is, at least, this to be said, that in perpetrating it he was doing no more than in his epoch it was customary for Popes to do. Alexander, it may be said again in this connection, was part of a corrupt system, not the corrupter of a pure one.

Touching the boy Giovanni Borgia, the mystery attaching to him concerns his parentage, and arises out of the singular circumstance that there are two papal Bulls, both dated September 1, 1501, in each of which a different father is assigned to him, the second appearing to supplement and correct the first.

The first of these Bulls, addressed to "Dilecto Filio Nobili Joanni de Borgia, Infanti Romano," declares him to be a child of three years of age, the illegitimate son of Cesare Borgia, unmarried (as Cesare was at the time of the child's birth) and of a woman (unnamed, as was usual in such cases) also unmarried.

The second declares him, instead, to be the son of Alexander, and runs: "Since you bear this deficiency not from the said duke, but from us and the said woman, which we for good reasons did not desire to express in the preceding writing."

That the second Bull undoubtedly contains the truth of the matter is the only possible explanation of its existence, and the "good reasons" that existed for the first one are, no doubt, as Gregorovius says, that officially and by canon law the Pope was inhibited from recognizing children. (His other children, be it remembered, were recognized by him during his cardinalate and before his elevation to St. Peter's throne.) Hence the attempt by these Bulls to circumvent the law to the end that the child should not suffer in the matter of his inheritance.

Burchard, under date of November 3 of that year, freely mentions this Giovanni Borgia as the son of the Pope and "a certain Roman woman" ("quadam Romana").

On the same date borne by those two Bulls a third one was issued confirming the House of Este perpetually in the dominion of Ferrara and its other Romagna possessions, and reducing by one-third the tribute of 4,000 ducats yearly imposed upon that family by Sixtus IV; and it was explicitly added that these concessions were made for Lucrezia and her descendants.

Three days later a courier from Duke Ercole brought the news that the marriage contract had been signed in Ferrara, and it was in salvoes of artillery that day and illuminations after dark that the Pope gave expression to the satisfaction afforded him by the prospect of his daughter's entering one of the most ancient families and ascending one of the noblest thrones in Italy.

It would be idle to pretend that the marriage was other than one of convenience. Love between the contracting parties played no part in this transaction, and Ercole d'Este was urged to it under suasion of the King of France, out of fear of the growing might of Cesare, and out of consideration for the splendid dowry which he demanded and in the matter of which he displayed a spirit which Alexander contemptuously described as that of a tradesman. Nor would Ercole send the escort to Rome for the bride until he had in his hands the Bull of investiture in the fiefs of Cento and

Pieve, which, with 100,000 ducats, constituted Lucrezia's dowry. Altogether a most unromantic affair.

The following letter from the Ferrarese ambassador in Rome, dated September 23, is of interest in connection with this marriage:

"MOST ILLUSTRIOUS PRINCE AND MOST NOBLE LORD,

"His Holiness the Pope, taking into consideration such matters as might occasion displeasure not only to your Excellency and to the Most Illustrious Don Alfonso, but also to the duchess and even to himself, has charged us to write to your Excellency to urge you so to contrive that the Lord Giovanni of Pesaro, who, as your Excellency is aware, is in Mantua, shall not be in Ferrara at the time of the nuptials. Notwithstanding that his divorce from the said duchess is absolutely legitimate and accomplished in accordance with pure truth, as is publicly known not only from the proceedings of the trial but also from the free confession of the said Don Giovanni, it is possible that he may still be actuated by some lingering ill-will; wherefore, should he find himself in any place where the said lady might be seen by him, her Excellency might, in consequence, be compelled to withdraw into privacy, to be spared the memory of the past. Wherefore, his Holiness exhorts your Excellency to provide with your habitual prudence against such a contingency."

Meanwhile, the festivities wherewith her betrothal was celebrated went merrily amain, and into the midst of them, to bear his share, came Cesare crowned with fresh laurels gained in the Neapolitan war. No merry-makings ever held under the auspices of Pope Alexander VI at the Vatican had escaped being the source of much scandalous rumour, but none had been so scandalous and disgraceful as the stories put abroad on this occasion. These found a fitting climax in that anonymous Letter to Silvio Savelli, published in Germany—which at the time, be it borne in mind, was extremely inimical to the Pope, viewing with jaundiced eyes his ever-growing power, and stirred perhaps to this unspeakable burst of venomous fury by the noble Este alliance, so valuable to Cesare in that it gave him a friend upon the frontier of his Romagna possessions.

The appalling publication, which is given in full in Burchard, was fictitiously dated from Gonzola de Cordoba's Spanish camp at Taranto on November 25. A copy of this anonymous pamphlet, which is the most violent attack on the Borgias ever penned, perhaps the most terrible indictment against any family ever published—a pamphlet which Gregorovius does not hesitate to call "an authentic document of the state of Rome under the Borgias"—fell into the hands of the Cardinal of Modena, who on the last day of the year carried it to the Pope.

Before considering that letter it is well to turn to the entries in Burchard's diary under the dates of October 27 and November 11 of that same year. You will find two statements which have no parallel in the rest of the entire diary, few parallels in any sober narrative of facts. The sane mind must recoil and close up before them, so impossible does it seem to accept them.

The first of these is the relation of the supper given by Cesare in the Vatican to fifty courtesans—a relation which possibly suggested to the debauched Regent d'Orléans his fêtes d'Adam, a couple of centuries later.

Burchard tells us how, for the amusement of Cesare, of the Pope, and of Lucrezia, these fifty courtesans were set to dance after supper with the servants and some others who were present, dressed at first and afterwards not so. He draws for us a picture of those fifty women on all fours, in all their plastic nudity, striving for the chestnuts flung to them in that chamber of the Apostolic Palace by Christ's Vicar—an old man of seventy—by his son and his daughter. Nor is that all by any means. There is much worse to follow—matter which we dare not translate, but must leave more or less discreetly veiled in the decadent Latin of the Caerimoniarius:

"Tandem exposita dona ultima, diploides de serico, paria caligarum, bireta ed alia pro illis qui pluries dictas meretrices carnaliter agnoscerent; que fuerunt ibidem in aula publice carnaliter tractate arbitrio presentium, dona distributa victoribus."

Such is the monstrous story!

Gregorovius, in his defence of Lucrezia Borgia, refuses to believe that she was present; but he is reluctant to carry his incredulity any further.

"Some orgy of that nature," he writes, "or something similar may very well have taken place. But who will believe that Lucrezia, already the legal wife of Alfonso d'Este and on the eve of departure for Ferrara, can have been present as a smiling spectator?"

Quite so. Gregorovius puts his finger at once upon one of the obvious weaknesses of the story. But where there is one falsehood there are usually others; and if we are not to believe that Lucrezia was present, why should we be asked to believe in the presence of the Pope? If Burchard was mistaken in the one, why might he not be mistaken in the other? But the question is not really one of whom you will believe to have been present at that unspeakable performance, but rather whether you can possibly bring yourself to believe that it ever took place as it is related in the Diarium.

Gregorovius says, you will observe, "Some orgy of that nature, or something similar, may very well have taken place." We could credit that Cesare held "some orgy of that nature." He had apartments in the Vatican, and if it shock you to think that it pleased him, with his gentlemen, to make merry by feasting a parcel of Roman harlots, you are—if you value justice—to be shocked at the times rather than the man. The sense of humour of the Cinquecento was primitive, and in primitive humour prurience plays ever an important part, as is discernible in the literature and comedies of that age. If you would appreciate this to the full, consider Burchard's details of the masks worn at Carnival by some merry-makers ("Venerunt ad plateam St. Petri larvati...habentes nasos lungos et grossos in forma priaporum") and you must realize that in Cesare's conduct in this matter there would have been nothing so very abnormal considered from the point of view of the Cinquecento, even though it were to approach the details given by Burchard.

But even so, you will hesitate before you accept the story of that saturnalia in its entirety, and before you believe that an old man of seventy, a priest and Christ's Vicar, was present with Cesare and his friends. Burchard does not say that he himself was a witness of what he relates. But the matter shall presently be further considered.

Meanwhile, let us pass to the second of these entries in the diary, and (a not unimportant detail) on the very next page of it, under the date of November 11. In this it is related that certain peasants entered Rome by the Viridarian Gate, driving two mares laden with timber; that, in crossing the Square of St. Peter's, some servants of the Pope's ran out and cut the cords so that the timber was loosened and the beasts relieved of their burden; they were then led to a courtyard within the precincts of the palace, where four stallions were loosed upon them. "Ascenderunt equas et coierunt cum eis et eas graviter pistarunt et leserunt," whilst the Pope at a window above the doorway of the Palace, with Madonna Lucrezia, witnessed with great laughter and delight, the show which it is suggested was specially provided for their amusement.

The improbabilities of the saturnalia of the fifty courtesans pale before the almost utter impossibility of this narrative. To render it possible in the case of two chance animals as these must have been under the related circumstances, a biological coincidence is demanded so utterly unlikely and incredible that we are at once moved to treat the story with scorn, and reject it as a fiction. Yet not one of those many writers who have retailed that story from Burchard's Diarium as a truth incontestable as the Gospels, has paused to consider this—so blinded are we when it is a case of accepting that which we desire to accept.

The narrative, too, is oddly—suspiciously—circumstantial, even to the unimportant detail of the particular gate by which the peasants entered

Rome. In a piece of fiction it is perfectly natural to fill in such minor details to the end that the picture shall be complete; but they are rare in narratives of fact. And one may be permitted to wonder how came the Master of Ceremonies at the Vatican to know the precise gate by which those peasants came. It is not—as we have seen—the only occasion on which an excess of detail in the matter of a gate renders suspicious the accuracy of a story of Burchard's.

Both these affairs find a prominent place in the Letter to Silvio Savelli. Indeed Gregorovius cites the pamphlet as one of the authorities to support Burchard, and to show that what Burchard wrote must have been true; the other authority he cites is Matarazzo, disregarding not only the remarkable discrepancy between Matarazzo's relation and that of Burchard, but the circumstance that the matter of that pamphlet became current throughout Italy, and that it was thus—and only thus—that Matarazzo came to hear of the scandal.(1)

> 1 *The frequency with which the German historian cites Matarazzo as an authority is oddly inconsistent, considering that when he finds Matarazzo's story of the murder of the Duke of Gandia upsetting the theory which Gregorovius himself prefers, by fastening the guilt upon Giovanni Sforza, he devotes some space to showing—with perfect justice—that Matarazzo is no authority at all.*

The Letter to Silvio Savelli opens by congratulating him upon his escape from the hands of the robbers who had stripped him of his possessions, and upon his having found a refuge in Germany at the Emperor's Court. It proceeds to marvel that thence he should have written letters to the Pope begging for justice and reinstatement, his wonder being at the credulity of Savelli in supposing that the Pope—"betrayer of the human race, who has spent his life in betrayals"—will ever do any just thing other than through fear or force. Rather does the writer suggest the adoption of other methods; he urges Savelli to make known to the Emperor and all princes of the Empire the atrocious crimes of that "infamous wild beasts" which have been perpetrated in contempt of God and religion. He then proceeds to relate these crimes. Alexander, Cesare, and Lucrezia, among others of the Borgia family, bear their share of the formidable accusations. Of the Pope are related perfidies, simonies, and ravishments; against Lucrezia are urged the matter of her incest, the supper of the fifty courtesans, and the scene of the stallions; against Cesare there are the death of Biselli, the murder of Pedro Caldes, the ruin of the Romagna, whence he has driven out the legitimate lords, and the universal fear in which he is held.

It is, indeed, a compendium of all the stories which from Milan, Naples, and Venice—the three States where the Borgias for obvious reasons are best hated—have been disseminated by their enemies, and a more violent work of rage and political malice was never uttered. This malice becomes particularly evident in the indictment of Cesare for the ruin of the Romagna. Whatever Cesare might have done, he had not done that—his bitterest detractor could not (without deliberately lying) say that the Romagna was other than benefiting under his sway. That is not a matter of opinion, not a matter of inference or deduction. It is a matter of absolute fact and irrefutable knowledge.

To return now to the two entries in Burchard's Diarium when considered in conjunction with the Letter to Silvio Savelli (which Burchard quotes in full), it is remarkable that nowhere else in the discovered writings of absolute contemporaries is there the least mention of either of those scandalous stories. The affair of the stallions, for instance, must have been of a fairly public character. Scandal-mongering Rome could not have resisted the dissemination of it. Yet, apart from the Savelli letter, no single record of it has been discovered to confirm Burchard.

At this time, moreover, it is to be remembered, Lucrezia's betrothal to Alfonso d'Este was already accomplished; preparations for her departure and wedding were going forward, and the escort from Ferrara was daily expected in Rome. If Lucrezia had never been circumspect, she must be circumspect now, when the eyes of Italy were upon her, and there were not wanting those who would have been glad to have thwarted the marriage— the object, no doubt, of the pamphlet we are considering. Yet all that was written to Ferrara was in praise of her—in praise of her goodness and her modesty, her prudence, her devoutness, and her discretion, as presently we shall see.

If from this we are to conclude—as seems reasonable—that there was no gossip current in Rome of the courtesans' supper and the rest, we may assume that there was no knowledge in Rome of such matters; for with knowledge silence would have been impossible. So much being admitted, it becomes a matter of determining whether the author of the Letter to Silvio Savelli had access to the diary of Burchard for his facts, or whether Burchard availed himself of the Letter to Silvio Savelli to compile these particular entries. The former alternative being out of the question, there but remains the latter—unless it is possible that the said entries have crept into the copies of the "Diarium" and are not present in the original, which is not available.

This theory of interpolation, tentatively put forward, is justified, to some extent at least, by the following remarkable circumstances: that two such entries, having—as we have said—absolutely no parallel in the whole of the Diarium, should follow almost immediately the one upon the other; and that Burchard should relate them coldly, without reproof or comment of any kind—a most unnatural reticence in a writer who loosed his indignation one Easter-tide to see Lucrezia and her ladies occupying the choir of St. Peter's, where women never sat.

The Pope read the anonymous libel when it was submitted to him by the Cardinal of Modena—read it, laughed it to scorn, and treated it with the contempt which it deserved, yet a contempt which, considering its nature, asks a certain greatness of mind.

If the libel was true it is almost incredible that he should not have sought to avenge it, for an ugly truth is notoriously hurtful and provocative of resentment, far more so than is a lie. Cesare, however, was not of a temper quite as long-suffering as his father. Enough and more of libels and lampoons had he endured already. Early in December a masked man—a Neapolitan of the name of Mancioni—who had been going through Rome uttering infamies against him was seized and so dealt with that he should in future neither speak nor write anything in any man's defamation. His tongue was cut out and his right hand chopped off, and the hand, with the tongue attached to its little finger, was hung in sight of all and as a warning from a window of the Church of Holy Cross.

And towards the end of January, whilst Cesare's fury at that pamphlet out of Germany was still unappeased, a Venetian was seized in Rome for having translated from Greek into Latin another libel against the Pope and his son. The Venetian ambassador intervened to save the wretch, but his intervention was vain. The libeller was executed that same night.

Costabili—the Ferrara ambassador—who spoke to the Pope on the matter of this execution, reported that his Holiness said that more than once had he told the duke that Rome was a free city, in which any one was at liberty to say or write what he pleased; that of himself, too, much evil was being spoken, but that he paid no heed to it.

"The duke," proceeded Alexander, "is good-natured, but he has not yet learnt to bear insult." And he added that, irritated, Cesare had protested that, "However much Rome may be in the habit of speaking and writing, for my own part I shall give these libellers a lesson in good manners."

The lesson he intended was not one they should live to practise.

CHAPTER XII
LUCREZIA'S THIRD MARRIAGE

At about the same time that Burchard was making in his Diarium those entries which reflect so grossly upon the Pope and Lucrezia, Gianluca Pozzi, the ambassador of Ferrara at the Vatican, was writing the following letter to his master, Duke Ercole, Lucrezia's father-in-law elect:

"This evening, after supper, I accompanied Messer Gerardo Saraceni to visit the Most Illustrious Madonna Lucrezia in your Excellency's name and that of the Most Illustrious Don Alfonso. We entered into a long discussion touching various matters. In truth she showed herself a prudent, discreet, and good-natured lady."(1)

> 1 See Gregorovius's *Lucrezia Borgia.*

The handsome, athletic Cardinal Ippolito d'Este, with his brothers Sigismondo and Fernando, had arrived in Rome on December 23 with the imposing escort that was to accompany their brother Alfonso's bride back to Ferrara.

Cesare was prominent in the welcome given them. Never, perhaps, had he made greater display than on the occasion of his riding out to meet the Ferrarese, accompanied by no fewer than 4,000 men-at-arms, and mounted on a great war-horse whose trappings of cloth of gold and jewels were estimated at 10,000 ducats.

The days and nights that followed, until Lucrezia's departure a fortnight later, were days and nights of gaiety and merry-making at the Vatican; in banquets, dancing, the performance of comedies, masques, etc., was the time made to pass as agreeably as might be for the guests from Ferrara, and in all Cesare was conspicuous, either for the grace and zest with which he nightly danced, or for the skill and daring which he displayed in the daily joustings and entertainments, and more particularly in the bull-fight that was included in them.

Lucrezia was splendidly endowed, to the extent, it was estimated, of 300,000 ducats, made up by 100,000 ducats in gold, her jewels and equipage, and the value of the Castles of Pieve and Cento. Her departure from Rome took place on January 6, and so she passes out of this chronicle, which, after all, has been little concerned with her.

Of the honour done her everywhere on that journey to Ferrara, the details are given elsewhere, particularly in the book devoted to her history and rehabilitation by Herr Gregorovius. After all, the real Lucrezia Borgia fills a comparatively small place in the actual history of her house. It is in the fictions concerning her family that she is given such unenviable importance, and presented as a Maenad, a poisoner, and worse. In reality she appears to us, during her life in Rome, as a rather childish, naïve, and entirely passive figure, important only in so far as she found employment at her father's or brother's hands for the advancement of their high ambitions and unscrupulous aims.

In the popular imagination she lives chiefly as a terrific poisoner, an appalling artist in venenation. It is remarkable that this should be the case, for not even the scandal of her day so much as suggests that she was connected—directly or even indirectly—with a single case of poisoning. No doubt that popular conception owes its being entirely to Victor Hugo's drama.

Away from Rome and settled in Ferrara from the twenty-second year of her age, to become anon its duchess, her life is well known and admits of no argument. The archives of the State she ruled show her devout, god-fearing, and beloved in life, and deeply mourned in death by a sorrowing husband and a sorrowing people. Not a breath of scandal touches her from the moment that she quits the scandalous environment of the Papal Court.

Cesare continued at the Vatican after her departure. His duchess was to have come to Rome in that Easter of 1502, and it had been disposed that the ladies and gentlemen who had gone as escort of honour with Lucrezia should proceed—after leaving her in Ferrara—to Lombardy, to do the like office by Charlotte d'Albret, and, meeting her there, accompany her to Rome. She was coming with her brother, the Cardinal Amanieu d'Albret, and bringing with her Cesare's little daughter, Louise de Valentinois, now two years of age. But the duchess fell ill at the last moment, and was unable to undertake the journey, of which Cardinal d'Albret brought word to Rome, where he arrived on February 7.

Ten days later Cesare set out with his father for Piombino, for which purpose six galleons awaited them at Civita Vecchia under the command of Lodovico Mosca, the captain of the Pontifical navy. On these the Pope and his son embarked, upon their visit to the scene of the latest addition to Cesare's ever-growing dominions.

They landed at Piombino on February 21, and made a solemn entrance into the town, the Pope carried in state in the Sedia Gestatoria, under a canopy, attended by six cardinals and six singers from the Sixtine Chapel, whilst Cesare was accompanied by a number of his gentlemen.

They abode four days in Piombino, whence they crossed to Elba, for the purpose of disposing for the erection there of two fortresses—a matter most probably entrusted to Leonardo da Vinci, who continued in the ducal train as architect and engineer.

On March 1 they took ship to return to Rome; but they were detained at sea for five days by a tempest which seems to have imperilled the vessels. The Pope was on board the captain's galley with his cardinals-in-waiting and servants, and when these were reduced by the storm and the imminent danger to a state of abject terror, the Pope—this old man of seventy-one— sat calm and intrepid, occasionally crossing himself and pronouncing the name of Jesus, and encouraging the very sailors by his example as much as by his words.

In Piombino Cesare had left Michele da Corella as his governor. This Corella was a captain of foot, a soldier of fortune, who from the earliest days of Cesare's military career had followed the duke's fortunes—the very man who is alleged to have strangled Alfonso of Aragon by Cesare's orders. He is generally assumed to have been a Spaniard, and is commonly designated as Michelotto, or Don Miguel; but Alvisi supposes him, from his name of Corella, to have been a Venetian, and he tells us that by his fidelity to Cesare and the implicit manner in which he executed his master's orders, he earned—as is notorious—considerable hatred. He has been spoken of, indeed, as the âme damnée of Cesare Borgia; but that is a purely romantic touch akin to that which gave the same designation to Richelieu's Father Joseph.

The Romagna was at this time administered for Cesare Borgia by Ramiro de Lorqua, who, since the previous November, had held the office of Governor in addition to that of Lieutenant-General in which he had been earlier invested. His power in the Romagna was now absolute, all Cesare's other officers, even the very treasurers, being subject to him.

He was a man of some fifty years of age, violent and domineering, feared by all, and the dispenser of a harsh justice which had at least the merit of an impartiality that took no account of persons.

Bernardi gives us an instance of the man's stern, uncompromising, pitiless nature. On January 29, 1502, two malefactors were hanged in Faenza. The rope suspending one of them broke while the fellow was alive, and the crowd into which he tumbled begged for mercy for him at first, then, swayed by pity, the people resolved to save him in spite of the officers of justice who demanded his surrender. Preventing his recapture, the mob bore him off to the Church of the Cerviti. The Lieutenant of Faenza came to demand the person of the criminal, but he was denied by the Prior, who claimed to extend him sanctuary.

But the days of sanctuary were overpast, and the laws of the time held that any church or consecrated place in which a criminal took refuge should ipso facto be deemed unconsecrated by his pursuers, and further, that any ecclesiastic sheltering such a fugitive did so under peril of excommunication from his bishop. This law Ramiro accounted it his duty to enforce when news was carried to him at Imola of what had happened.

He came at once to Faenza, and, compelling the Prior by actual force to yield up the man he sheltered, he hanged the wretch, for the second time, from a window of the Palace of the Podestá. At the same time he seized several who were alleged to have been ringleaders of the fellow's rescue from the hands of the officers, and made the citizens of Faenza compromise for the lives of these by payment of a fine of 10,000 ducats, giving them a month in which to find the money.

The Faentini sent their envoys to Ramiro to intercede with him; but that harsh man refused so much as to grant them audience—which was well for them, for, as a consequence, the Council sent ambassadors to Rome to submit the case to the Pope's Holiness and to the Duke of Valentinois, together with a petition that the fine should be remitted—a petition that was readily granted.

Harsh as it was, however, Ramiro's rule was salutary, its very harshness necessary in a province where lawlessness had become a habit through generations of misgovernment. Under Cesare's dominion the change already was remarkable. During his two years of administration—to count from its commencement—the Romagna was already converted from a seething hell of dissensions, disorders and crimes—chartered brigandage and murder—into a powerful State, law-abiding and orderly, where human life and personal possessions found zealous protection, and where those who disturbed the peace met with a justice that was never tempered by mercy.

A strong hand was wanted there, and the duke, supreme judge of the tools to do his work, ruled the Romagna and crushed its turbulence by means of the iron hand of Ramiro de Lorqua.

It was also under the patronage of Valentinois that the first printing-press of any consequence came to be established in Italy. This was set up at Fano by Girolamo Sancino in 1501, and began the issue of worthy books. One of the earliest works undertaken (says Alvisi) was the printing of the Statutes of Fano for the first time in January of 1502. And it was approved by the Council, civil and ecclesiastical, that Sancino should undertake this printing of the Statutes "Ad perpetuam memoriam Illmi. Domini nostri Ducis."

CHAPTER XIII
URBINO AND CAMERINO

It may well be that it was about this time that Cesare, his ambition spreading—as men's ambition will spread with being gratified—was considering the consolidation of Central Italy into a kingdom of which he would assume the crown.

It was a scheme in the contemplation of which he was encouraged by Vitellozzo Vitelli, who no doubt conceived that in its fulfilment the ruin of Florence would be entailed—which was all that Vitelli cared about. What to Cesare would have been no more than the means, would have been to Vitelli a most satisfactory end.

Before, however, going so far there was still the work of subjugating the States of the Church to be completed, as this could not be so considered until Urbino, Camerino, and Sinigaglia should be under the Borgia dominion.

For this, no doubt, Cesare was disposing during that Easter of 1502 which he spent in Rome, and during which there were heard from the south the first rumblings of the storm of war whereof ill-starred Naples was once more—for the third time within ten years—to be the scene. The allies of yesterday were become the antagonists of to-day, and France and Spain were ready to fly at each other's throats over the division of the spoil, as a consequence of certain ill-definitions of the matter in the treaty of Granada. The French Viceroy, Louis d'Armagnac, and the great Spanish Captain, Gonzalo de Cordoba, were on the point of coming to blows.

Nor was the menace of disturbance confined to Naples. In Florence, too, the torch of war was alight, and if—as he afterwards swore—Cesare Borgia had no hand in kindling it, it is at least undeniable that he complacently watched the conflagration, conscious that it would make for the fulfilment of his own ends. Besides, there was still that little matter of the treaty of Forno dei Campi between Cesare and Florence, a treaty which the Signory had never fulfilled and never intended to fulfil, and Cesare was not the man to forget how he had been fooled.

But for the protection of France which she enjoyed, Florence must long ere this have been called to account by him, and crushed out of all shape under the weight of his mailed hand. As it was she was to experience the hurt of his passive resentment, and find this rather more than she could bear.

Vitellozzo Vitelli, that vindictive firebrand whose original motive in allying himself with Cesare had been the hope that the duke might help him to make Florence expiate his brother's blood, finding that Cesare withheld the expected help, was bent at last upon dealing, himself, with Florence. He entered into plots with the exiled Piero de'Medici to restore the latter to his dominion; he set intrigues afoot in Pisa, where his influence was vast, and in Siena, whose tyrant, Pandolfo Petrucci, was ready and willing to forward his designs, and generally made so disturbing a stir in Tuscany that the Signory became gravely alarmed.

Cesare certainly took no apparent active part in the affair. He lent Vitelli no aid; but neither did he attempt to restrain him or any other of the Borgia condottieri who were allied with him.

The unrest, spreading and growing sullenly a while, burst suddenly forth in Arezzo on June 4, when the cries of "Medici!" and "Marzocco!" rang in its streets, to announce that the city was in arms against the government of Florence. Arezzo followed this up by summoning Vitelli, and the waiting, watchful condottiero was quick to answer the desired call. He entered the town three days later at the head of a small body of foot, and was very shortly afterwards followed by his brother Giulio Vitelli, Bishop of Città di Castello, with the artillery, and, presently, by Gianpaolo Baglioni with a condotta of horse.

A few days later Vitelli was in possession of all the strongholds of the Val di Chiana, and panic-stricken Florence was speeding ambassadors hot-foot to Rome to lay her complaints of these matters before the Pope.

Alexander was able to reply that, far from supporting the belligerents, he had launched a Bull against them, provoked by the poisoning of the Bishop de'Pazzi.

Cesare looked on with the inscrutable calm for which Macchiavelli was presently to find him so remarkable. Aware as he was of the French protection which Florence enjoyed and could invoke, he perceived how vain must ultimately prove Vitelli's efforts, saw, perhaps, in all this the grave danger of ultimate ruin which Vitelli was incurring. Yet Vitelli's action served Cesare's own purposes, and, so that his purposes were served, there were no other considerations likely to weigh with that cold egotist. Let Vitelli be caught in the toils he was spinning, and be choked in them. Meanwhile, Florence was being harrowed, and that was all to Cesare's satisfaction and advantage. When sufficiently humbled, it might well befall that the Republic should come on her knees to implore his intervention, and his pardon for having flouted him.

While matters stood so in Arezzo, Pisa declared spontaneously for Cesare, and sent (on June 10) to offer herself to his dominion and to announce to him that his banner was already flying from her turrets—and the growth of Florence's alarm at this is readily conceived.

To Cesare it must have been a sore temptation. To accept such a pied-à-terre in Tuscany as was now offered him would have been the first great step towards founding that kingdom of his dreams. An impulsive man had surely gulped the bait. But Cesare, boundless in audacity, most swift to determine and to act, was not impulsive. Cold reason, foresight and calculation were the ministers of his indomitable will. He looked ahead and beyond in the matter of Pisa's offer, and he perceived the danger that might await him in the acceptance. The time for that was not yet. To take what Pisa offered might entail offending France, and although Cesare was now in case to dispense with French support, he was in no case to resist her opposition.

And so, the matter being considered and determined, Cesare quitted Rome on the 12th and left it for the Pope to give answer to the Pisan envoys in the Consistory of June 14—that neither his Holiness nor the Duke of Valentinois could assent to the proposals which Pisa made.

From Rome Cesare travelled swiftly to Spoleto, where his army, some ten thousand strong, was encamped. He was bent at last upon the conquest of Camerino, and, ever an opportunist, he had seized the moment when Florence, which might have been disposed to befriend Varano, Tyrant of Camerino, was over-busy with her own affairs.

In addition to the powerful army awaiting him at Spoleto, the duke had a further 2,000 men in the Romagna; another 1,000 men held themselves at his orders between Sinigaglia and Urbino, and Dionigio di Naldo was arming yet another 1,000 men at Verucchio for his service. Yet further to increase this force, Cesare issued an edict during his brief sojourn at Spoleto ordering every house in the Romagna to supply him with one man-at-arms.

It was whilst here—as he afterwards wrote to the Pope—that news reached him that Guidobaldo da Montefeltre, Duke of Urbino, was arming men and raising funds for the assistance of Camerino. He wrote that he could not at first believe it, but that shortly afterwards—at Foligni—he took a chancellor of Camerino who admitted that the hopes of this State were all founded upon Urbino's assistance; and later, a messenger from Urbino falling into his hands, he discovered that there was a plot afoot to seize the Borgia artillery as it passed through Ugubio, it being known that, as Cesare had no suspicions, the guns would be guarded only by a small force. Of this treachery the duke strongly expressed his indignation in his letter to the Pope.

Whether the matter was true—or whether Cesare believed it to be true—it is impossible to ascertain with absolute conviction. But it is in the highest degree unlikely that Cesare would have written such a letter to his father solely by way of setting up a pretext. Had that been his only aim, letters expressing his simulated indignation would have been in better case to serve his ends had they been addressed to others.

If Guidobaldo did engage in such an act, amounting to a betrayal, he was certainly paid by Cesare in kind and with interest. If the duke had been short of a pretext for carrying a drawn sword into the dominions of Guidobaldo, he had that pretext now in this act of enmity against himself and the Holy See.

First, however, he disposed for the attack upon Camerino. This State, lying on the Eastern spurs of the Apennines, midway between Spoleto and Urbino, was ruled by Giulio Cesare Varano, an old war-dog of seventy years of age, ruthless and bloodthirsty, who owed his throne to his murder of his own brother.

He was aided in the government of his tyranny by his four sons, Venanzio, Annibale, Pietro, and Gianmaria.

Several times already had he been menaced by Cesare Borgia, for he was one of the Vicars proscribed for the non-payment of tribute due to the Holy See, and at last his hour was come. Against him Cesare now dispatched an army under the command of Francesco Orsini, Duke of Gravina, and Oliverotto Eufreducci, another murderous, bloody gentleman who had hitherto served the duke in Vitelli's condotta, and who, by an atrocious act of infamy and brigandage, had made himself Lord of Fermo, which he pretended—being as sly as he was bloody—to hold as Vicar for the Holy See.

This Oliverotto Eufreducci—hereafter known as Oliverotto da Fermo—was a nephew of Giovanni Fogliano, Lord of Fermo. He had returned home to his uncle's Court in the early part of that year, and was there received with great honour and affection by Fogliano and his other relatives. To celebrate his home-coming, Oliverotto invited his uncle and the principal citizens of Fermo to a banquet, and at table contrived to turn the conversation upon the Pope and the Duke of Valentinois; whereupon, saying that these were matters to be discussed more in private, he rose from table and begged them to withdraw with him into another room.

All unsuspecting—what should old Fogliano suspect from one so loved and so deeply in his debt?—they followed him to the chamber where he had secretly posted a body of his men-at-arms. There, no sooner had the door closed upon this uncle, and those others who had shown him so much affection, than he gave the signal for the slaughter that had been concerted. His soldiers fell upon those poor, surprised victims of his greed, and made a speedy and bloody end of all.

That first and chief step being taken, Oliverotto flung himself on his horse, and, gathering his men-at-arms about him, rode through Fermo on the business of butchering what other relatives and friends of Fogliano might remain. Among these were Raffaele della Rovere and two of his children, one of whom was inhumanly slaughtered in its mother's lap.

Thereafter he confiscated to his own uses the property of those whom he had murdered, and of those who, more fortunate, had fled his butcher's hands. He dismissed the existing Council and replaced it by a government of his own. Which done—to shelter himself from the consequences—he sent word to the Pope that he held Fermo as Vicar of the Church.

Whilst a portion of his army marched on Camerino, Cesare, armed with his pretext for the overthrow of Guidobaldo, set himself deliberately and by an elaborate stratagem to the capture of Urbino. Of this there can be little doubt. The cunning of the scheme is of an unsavoury sort, when considered by the notions that obtain to-day, for the stratagem was no better than an act of base treachery. Yet, lest even in this you should be in danger of judging Cesare Borgia by standards which cannot apply to his age, you will do well to consider that there is no lack of evidence that the fifteenth century applauded the business as a clever coup.

Guidobaldo da Montefeltre was a good prince. None in all Italy was more beloved by his people, towards whom he bore himself with a kindly, paternal bonhomie. He was a cultured, scholarly man, a patron of the arts, happiest in the splendid library of the Palace of Urbino. It happened, unfortunately, that he had no heir, which laid his dominions open to the danger of division amongst the neighbouring greedy tyrants after his death. To avoid this he had adopted Francesco Maria della Rovere, hereditary Prefect of Sinigaglia, his sister's child and a nephew of Cardinal Giuliano della Rovere's. There was wisdom and foresight in the adoption, considering the favour enjoyed in Rome and in France by the powerful cardinal.

From Nocera Cesare sent Guidobaldo a message calculated to allay whatever uneasiness he may have been feeling, and to throw him completely off his guard. The duke notified him that he was marching upon Camerino—which was at once true and untrue—and begged Guidobaldo to assist him in this enterprise by sending him provisions to Gubbio, which he should reach on the morrow—since he was marching by way of Cagli and Sassoferrato. Further—and obviously with intent that the Duke of Urbino should reduce the forces at his disposal—he desired Guidobaldo to send Vitelli the support of a thousand men, which the latter had earlier solicited, but which Guidobaldo had refused to supply without orders from the Pope. Cesare concluded his letter with protestations of brotherly love—the Judas' kiss which makes him hateful to us in this affair.

It all proved very reassuring to Guidobaldo who set his mind at ease and never bethought him of looking to his defences, when, from Nocera, Cesare made one of those sudden movements, terrible in their swiftness as the spring of a tiger—enabling him to drive home his claws where least expected. Leaving all baggage behind him, and with provisions for only three days, he brought his troops by forced marches to Cagli, within the Urbino State, and possessed himself of it almost before the town had come to realize his presence.

Not until the citadel, taken entirely by surprise, was in Cesare's hands did a messenger speed to Guidobaldo with the unwelcome tidings that the Duke of Valentinois was in arms, as an enemy, within the territory. Together with that message came others into the garden of the Zoccolanti monastery—that favourite resort of Guidobaldo's—where he was indulging his not unusual custom of supping in the cool of that summer evening. They brought him word that, while Valentinois was advancing upon him from the south, a force of 1,000 men were marching upon Urbino from Isola di Fano in the east, and twice that number through the passes of Sant' Angelo and Verucchio in the north—all converging upon his capital.

The attack had been shrewdly planned and timed, and if anything can condone the treachery by which Guidobaldo was lulled into his false security, it is the circumstance that this conduct of the matter avoided bloodshed—a circumstance not wholly negligible, and one that was ever a part of Cesare Borgia's policy, save where punishment had to be inflicted or reprisals taken.

Guidobaldo, seeing himself thus beset upon all sides at once, and being all unprepared for resistance, perceived that nothing but flight remained him; and that very night he left Urbino hurriedly, taking with him the boy Francesco Maria, and intending at first to seek shelter in his Castle of S. Leo—a fortress that was practically impregnable. But already it was too late. The passes leading thither were by now in the hands of the enemy, as Guidobaldo discovered at dawn. Thereupon, changing his plans, he sent the boy and his few attendants to Bagno, and, himself, disguised as a peasant, took to the hills, despite the gout by which he was tormented. Thus he won to Ravenna, which was fast becoming a home for dethroned princes.

Urbino, meanwhile, in no case to resist, sent its castellan to meet Cesare and to make surrender to him—whereof Cesare, in the letter already mentioned, gives news to the Pope, excusing himself for having undertaken this thing without the Pope's knowledge, but that "the treachery employed against me by Guidobaldo was so enormous that I could not suffer it."

Within a few hours of poor Guidobaldo's flight Cesare was housed in Urbino's splendid palace, whose stupendous library was the marvel of all scholars of that day. Much of this, together with many of the art-treasures collected by the Montefeltri, Cesare began shortly afterwards to transfer to Cesena.

In addition to publishing an edict against pillage and violence in the City of Urbino, Cesare made doubly sure that none should take place by sending his soldiers to encamp at Fermignano, retaining near him in Urbino no more than his gentlemen-at-arms. The capital being taken, the remainder of the duchy made ready surrender, all the strongholds announcing their submission to Cesare with the exception of that almost inaccessible Castle of S. Leo, which capitulated only after a considerable resistance.

From Urbino Cesare now entered into communication with the Florentines, and asked that a representative should be sent to come to an agreement with him. In response to this request, the Republic sent him Bishop Soderini as her ambassador. The latter arrived in Urbino on June 25 and was immediately and very cordially received by the duke. With him, in the subordinate capacity of secretary, came a lean, small-headed, tight-lipped man, with wide-set, intelligent eyes and prominent cheek-bones—one Niccolò Macchiavelli, who, in needy circumstances at present, and comparatively obscure, was destined to immortal fame. Thus did Macchiavelli meet Cesare Borgia for the first time, and, for all that we have no records of it, it is not to be doubted that his study of that remarkable man began then in Urbino, to be continued presently, as we shall see, when Macchiavelli returns to him in the quality of an ambassador himself.

To Soderini the duke expounded his just grievance, founded upon the Florentines' unobservance of the treaty of Forno dei Campi; he demanded that a fresh treaty should be drawn up to replace the broken one, and that, for the purpose, Florence should change her government, as in the ruling one, after what had passed, he could repose no faith. He disclaimed all associations with the affair of Vitelli, but frankly declared himself glad of it, as it had, no doubt, led Florence to perceive what came of not keeping faith with him. He concluded by assuring Soderini that, with himself for their friend, the Florentines need fear no molestation from any one; but he begged that the Republic should declare herself in the matter, since, if she did not care to have him for her friend, she was, of course, at liberty to make of him her enemy.

So impressed was Soderini by Cesare Borgia that on that same night he wrote to the Signory:

"This lord is very magnificent and splendid, and so spirited in feats of arms that there is nothing so great but that it must seem small to him. In the pursuit of glory and in the acquisition of dominions he never rests, and he knows neither danger nor fatigue. He moves so swiftly that he arrives at a place before it is known that he has set out for it. He knows how to make himself beloved of his soldiers, and he has in his service the best men of Italy. These things render him victorious and formidable, and to these is yet to be added his perpetual good fortune. He argues," the Florentine envoy proceeds, "with such sound reason that to dispute with him would be a long affair, for his wit and eloquence never fail him" ("dello ingegno e della lingua si vale quanto vuole").

You are to remember that this homage is one of the few surviving impressions of one who came into personal contact with Cesare, and of one, moreover, representing a Government more or less inimical to him, who would therefore have no reason to draw a favourable portrait of him for that Government's benefit. One single page of such testimony is worth a dozen volumes of speculation and inference drawn afterwards by men who never knew him—in many cases by men who never began to know his epoch.

The envoy concludes by informing the Signory that he has the duke's assurances that the latter has no thought of attempting to deprive Florence of any of her possessions, as "the object of his campaign has not been to tyrannize, but to extirpate tyrants."

Whilst Cesare awaited the Florentines' reply to their ambassador's communication, he withdrew to the camp at Fermignano, where he was sought on July 6 by a herald from Louis XII. This messenger came to exhort Cesare to embark upon no enterprise against the Florentine Republic, because to offend Florence would be to offend the Majesty of France. Simultaneously, however, Florence received messages from the Cardinal d'Amboise, suggesting that they should come to terms with Valentinois by conceding him at least a part of what had been agreed in the Treaty of Forno dei Campi.

As a consequence, Soderini was able to inform Cesare that the Republic was ready to treat with him, but that first he must withdraw Vitelli from Arezzo, and compel him to yield up the captured fortresses. The duke, not trusting—as he had frankly avowed—a Government which once already had broken faith with him, and perceiving that, if he whistled his war-dogs to heel as requested, he would have lost the advantages of his position, refused to take any such steps until the treaty should be concluded. He consented, however, to enforce meanwhile an armistice.

But now it happened that news reached Florence of the advance of Louis XII with an army of 20,000 men, bound for Naples to settle the dispute with Spain. So the Republic—sly and treacherous as any other Italian Government of the Cinquecento—instructed Soderini to temporize with the duke; to spend the days in amiable, inconclusive interviews and discussions of terms which the Signory did not mean to make. Thus they counted upon gaining time, until the arrival of the French should put an end to the trouble caused by Vitelli, and to the need for any compromise.

But Cesare, though forced to submit, was not fooled by Soderini's smooth, evasive methods. He too—having private sources of information in France—was advised of the French advance and of the imminence of danger to himself in consequence of the affairs of Florence. And it occasioned him no surprise to see Soderini come on July 19 to take his leave of him, advised by the Signory that the French vanguard was at hand, and that, consequently, the negotiations might now with safety be abandoned.

To console him, he had news on the morrow of the conquest of Camerino.

The septuagenarian Giulio Cesare Varano had opposed to the Borgia forces a stout resistance, what time he sent his two sons Pietro and Gianmaria to Venice for help. It was in the hope of this solicited assistance that he determined to defend his tyranny, and the war opened by a cavalry skirmish in which Venanzio Varano routed the Borgia horse under the command of the Duke of Gravina. Thereafter, however, the Varani had to endure a siege; and the old story of the Romagna sieges was repeated. Varano had given his subjects too much offence in the past, and it was for his subjects now to call the reckoning.

A strong faction, led by a patrician youth of Camerino, demanded the surrender of the State, and, upon being resisted, took arms and opened the gates to the troops of Valentinois. The three Varani were taken prisoners. Old Giulio Cesare was shut up in the Castle of Pergola, where he shortly afterwards died—which was not wonderful or unnatural at his time of life, and does not warrant Guicciardini for stating, without authority, that he was strangled. Venanzio and Annibale were imprisoned in the fortress of Cattolica.

In connection with this surrender of Camerino, Cesare wrote the following affectionate letter to his sister Lucrezia—who was dangerously ill at Ferrara in consequence of her delivery of a still-born child:

"Most Illustrious and most Excellent Lady, our very dear Sister,—Confident of the circumstance that there can be no more efficacious and salutary medicine for the indisposition from which you are at present suffering than the announcement of good and happy news, we advise you that at this very moment we have received sure tidings of the capture of Camerino. We beg that you will do honour to this message by an immediate improvement, and inform us of it, because, tormented as we are to know you so ill, nothing, not even this felicitous event, can suffice to afford us pleasure. We beg you also kindly to convey the present to the Illustrious Lord Don Alfonso, your husband and our beloved Brother-in-law, to whom we are not writing to-day."

CHAPTER XIV
THE REVOLT OF THE CONDOTTIERI

The coincidence of the arrival of the French army with the conquest of Urbino and Camerino and the Tuscan troubles caused one more to be added to that ceaseless stream of rumours that flowed through Italy concerning the Borgias. This time the envy and malice that are ever provoked by success and power gave voice in that rumour to the thing it hoped, and there ensued as pretty a comedy as you shall find in the pages of history.

The rumour had it that Louis XII, resentful and mistrustful of the growth of Cesare's might, which tended to weaken France in Italy and became a menace to the French dominions, was come to make an end of him. Instantly Louis's Court in Milan was thronged by all whom Cesare had offended—and they made up by now a goodly crowd, for a man may not rise so swiftly to such eminence without raising a rich crop of enemies.

Meanwhile, however, Valentinois in the Montefeltre Palace at Urbino remained extremely at ease. He was not the man to be without intelligences. In the train of Louis was Francesco Troche, the Pope's confidential chamberlain and Cesare's devoted servant, who, possessed of information, was able to advise Valentinois precisely what were the intentions of the King of France. Gathering from these advices that it was Louis's wish that the Florentines should not be molested further, and naturally anxious not to run counter to the king's intentions, Cesare perceived that the time to take action had arrived, the time for passivity in the affairs of Florence was at an end.

So he dispatched an envoy to Vitelli, ordering his instant evacuation of Arezzo and his withdrawal with his troops from Tuscany, and he backed the command by a threat to compel Vitelli by force of arms, and to punish disobedience by depriving him of his state of Città di Castello—"a matter," Cesare informed him, "which would be easily accomplished, as the best men of that State have already offered themselves to me."

It was a command which Vitelli had no choice but to obey, not being in sufficient force to oppose the duke. So on July 29, with Gianpaolo Baglioni, he relinquished the possession of Arezzo and departed out of Tuscany, as he had been bidden. But so incensed was he against the duke for this intervention between himself and his revenge, and so freely did he express himself in the matter, that it was put about at once that he intended to go against Cesare.

And that is the first hint of the revolt of the condottieri.

Having launched that interdict of his, Cesare, on July 25, in the garb of a knight of St. John of Jerusalem, and with only four attendants, departed secretly from Urbino to repair to Milan and King Louis. He paused for fresh horses at Forli on the morrow, and on the 28th reached Ferrara, where he remained for a couple of hours to visit Lucrezia, who was now in convalescence. Ahead of him he dispatched, thence, a courier to Milan to announce his coming, and, accompanied by Alfonso d'Este, resumed his journey.

Meanwhile, the assembly of Cesare's enemies had been increasing daily in Milan, whither they repaired to support Louis and to vent their hatred of Cesare and their grievances against him. There, amongst others, might be seen the Duke of Urbino, Pietro Varano (one of the sons of the deposed Lord of Camerino), Giovanni Sforza of Pesaro, and Francesco Gonzaga of Mantua—which latter was ever ready to turn whichever way the wind was blowing, and was now loudest in his denunciations of Cesare and eagerly advocating the formation of a league against him.

Louis received the news of Cesare's coming, and—endowed, it is clear, with a nice sense of humour-kept the matter secret until within a few hours of the duke's actual arrival. On the morning of August 5, according to Bernardi,(1) he whispered the information in Trivulzio's ear-and whispered it loudly enough to be overheard by those courtiers who stood nearest.

1 *Cronache Forlivesi.*

Whatever check their satisfaction at the supposed state of things may have received then was as nothing to their feelings a few hours later when they witnessed the greeting that passed between king and duke. Under their uneasy eyes Louis rode forth to meet his visitor, and gave him a glad and friendly welcome, addressing him as "cousin" and "dear relative," and so, no doubt, striking dismay into the hearts of those courtiers, who may well have deemed that perhaps they had expressed themselves too freely.

Louis, in person, accompanied Valentinois to the apartments prepared for him in the Castle of Milan, and on the morrow gave a banquet and commanded merry-makings in his visitor's honour.

Conceive the feelings of those deposed tyrants and their friends, and the sudden collapse of the hopes which they had imagined the king to be encouraging. They did, of course, the only thing there was to do. They took their leave precipitately and went their ways—all save Gonzaga, whom the king retained that he might make his peace with Cesare, and engage in friendship with him, a friendship consolidated there and then by the betrothal of their infant children: little Francesco Gonzaga and Louise de Valentinois, aged two, the daughter whom Cesare had never beheld and was never to behold.

Two factors were at work in the interests of Valentinois—the coming war in Naples with the Spaniard, which caused Louis to desire to stand well with the Pope; and the ambition of Louis's friend and counsellor, the Cardinal d'Amboise, to wear the tiara, which caused this prelate to desire to stand well with Cesare himself, since the latter's will in the matter of a Pope to succeed his father should be omnipotent with the Sacred College.

Therefore, that they might serve their interests in the end, both king and cardinal served Cesare's in the meantime.

The Duke of Valentinois's visit to Milan had served to increase the choler of Vitelli, who accounted that by this action Cesare had put him in disgrace with the King of France; and Vitelli cried out that thus was he repaid for having sought to make Cesare King of Tuscany. In such high dudgeon was the fierce Tyrant of Città di Castello that he would not go to pay his court to Louis, and was still the more angry to hear of the warm welcome accorded in Milan to the Cardinal Orsini. In this he read approval of the Orsini for having stood neutral in the Florentine business, and, by inference from that, disapproval of himself.

Before accusing Valentinois of treachery to his condottieri, before saying that he shifted the blame of the Tuscan affair on to the shoulders of his captains, it would be well to ascertain that there was any blame to shift—that is to say, any blame that must originally have fallen upon Cesare. Certainly he made no effort to restrain Vitelli until the King of France had arrived and he had secret information which caused him to deem it politic to intervene. But of what avail until that moment, would any but an armed intervention have been with so vindictive and one-idea'd a man, and what manner of fool would not Cesare have been to have spent his strength in battle with his condottieri for the purpose of befriending a people who had never shown themselves other than his own enemies?

Like the perfect egotist he was, he sat on the fence, and took pleasure in the spectacle of the harassing of his enemies by his friends, prepared to reap any advantages there might be, but equally prepared to avoid any disadvantages.

It was not heroic, it was not noble; but it was extremely human.

Cesare was with the King of France in Genoa at the end of August, and remained in his train until September 2, when finally he took his leave of him. When they heard of his departure from the Court of Louis, his numerous enemies experienced almost as much chagrin as that which had been occasioned them by his going thither. For they had been consoling themselves of late with a fresh rumour; and again they were believing what it pleased them to believe. Rumours, you perceive, were never wanting where the Borgias were concerned, and it may be that you are beginning to rate these voces populi at their proper value, and to apprehend the worth of many of those that have been embalmed as truths in the abiding records.

This last one had it that Louis was purposely keeping Cesare by him, and intended ultimately to carry him off to France, and so put an end to the disturbances the duke was creating in Italy. What a consolation would not that have been to those Italian princelings to whose undoing he had warred! And can you marvel that they believed and circulated so readily the thing for which they hoped so fondly? By your appreciation of that may you measure the fresh disappointment that was theirs.

So mistaken were they, indeed, as it now transpired, that Louis had actually, at last, removed his protection from Bologna, under the persuasion of Cesare and the Pope. Before the duke took his departure from King Louis's Court, the latter entered into a treaty with him in that connection to supply him with three hundred lances: "De bailler au Valentinois trois cents lances pour l'aider à conquérir Bologne au nome de l'Eglise, et opprimer les Ursins, Baillons et Vitelozze."

It was a double-dealing age, and Louis's attitude in this affair sorted well with it. Feeling that he owed Bologna some explanation, he presently sent a singularly lame one by Claude de Seyssel. He put it that the Bentivogli personally were none the less under his protection than they had been hitherto, but that the terms of the protection provided that it was granted exclusively of the rights and authority of the Holy Roman See over Bologna, and that the king could not embroil himself with the Pope. With such a shifty message went M. de Seyssel to make it quite clear to Bentivogli what his position was. And on the heels of it came, on September 2, a papal brief citing Bentivogli and his two sons to appear before the Pontiff within fifteen days for the purpose of considering with his Holiness the matter of the pacification and better government of Bologna, which for so many years had been so disorderly and turbulent. Thus the Pope's summons, with a menace that was all too thinly veiled.

But Bentivogli was not taken unawares. He was not even astonished. Ever since Cesare's departure from Rome in the previous spring he had been disposing against such a possibility as this—fortifying Bologna, throwing up outworks and erecting bastions beyond the city, and levying and arming men, in all of which he depended largely upon the citizens and particularly upon the art-guild, which was devoted to the House of Bentivogli.

Stronger than the affection for their lord—which, when all is said, was none too great in Bologna—was the deep-seated hatred of the clergy entertained by the Bolognese. This it was that rallied to Bentivogli such men as Fileno della Tuate, who actually hated him. But it was a choice of evils with Fileno and many of his kidney. Detesting the ruling house, and indignant at the injustices it practised, they detested the priests still more— so much that they would have taken sides with Satan himself against the Pontificals. In this spirit did they carry their swords to Bentivogli.

Upon the nobles Bentivogli could not count—less than ever since the cold-blooded murder of the Marescotti; but in the burghers' adherence he deemed himself secure, and indeed on September 17 he had some testimony of it.

On that date—the fortnight's grace expiring—the brief was again read to the Reggimento; but it was impossible to adopt any resolution. The people were in arms, and, with enormous uproar, protested that they would not allow Giovanni Bentivogli or his sons to go to Rome, lest they should be in danger once they had left their own State.

Italy was full of rumours at the time of Cesare's proposed emprise against Bologna, and it was added that he intended, further, to make himself master of Città di Castello and Perugia, and thus, by depriving them of their tyrannies, punish Vitelli and Baglioni for their defection.

This was the natural result of the terms of Cesare's treaty with France having become known; but the part of it which regarded the Orsini, Vitelli, and Baglioni was purely provisional. Considering that these condottieri were now at odds with Cesare, they might see fit to consider themselves bound to

Bentivogli by the Treaty of Villafontana, signed by Vitelli and Orsini on the duke's behalf at the time of the capitulation of Castel Bolognese. They might choose to disregard the fact that this treaty had already been violated by Bentivogli himself, through the non-fulfilment of the terms of it, and refuse to proceed against him upon being so bidden by Valentinois.

It was for such a contingency as this that provision was made by the clause concerning them in Cesare's treaty with Louis.

The Orsini were still in the duke's service, in command of troops levied for him and paid by him, and considering that with them Cesare had no quarrel, it is by no means clear why they should have gone over to the alliance of the condottieri that was now forming against the duke. Join it, however, they did. They, too, were in the Treaty of Villafontana; but that they should consider themselves bound by it, would have been—had they urged it—more in the nature of a pretext than a reason. But they chose a pretext even more slender. They gave out that in Milan Louis XII had told Cardinal Orsini that the Pope's intention was to destroy the Orsini.

To accept such a statement as true, we should have to believe in a disloyalty and a double-dealing on the part of Louis XII altogether incredible. To what end should he, on the one side, engage to assist Cesare with 300 lances to "oppress" the Orsini—if necessary, and among others— whilst, on the other, he goes to Orsini with the story which they attribute to him? What a mean, treacherous, unkingly figure must he not cut as a consequence! He may have been—we know, indeed, that he was—no more averse to doubledealing than any other Cinquecentist; but he was probably as averse to being found out in a meanness and made to look contemptible as any double-dealer of our own times. It is a consideration worth digesting.

When word of the story put about by the Orsini was carried to the Pope he strenuously denied the imputation, and informed the Venetian ambassador that he had written to complain of this to the King of France, and that, far from such a thing being true, Cesare was so devoted to the Orsini as to be "more Orsini than Borgian."

It is further worth considering that the defection of the Orsini was neither immediate nor spontaneous, as must surely have been the case had the story been true. It was the Baglioni and Vitelli only who first met to plot at Todi, to declare that they would not move against their ally of Bologna, and to express the hope that they might bring the Orsini to the same mind. They succeeded so well that the second meeting was held at Magione—a place belonging to the powerful Cardinal Orsini, situated near the Baglioni's stronghold of Perugia. Vitellozzo was carried thither on his bed, so stricken with the morbo gallico—which in Italy was besetting most princes, temporal and ecclesiastical—that he was unable to walk.

Gentile and Gianpaolo Baglioni, Cardinal Gianbattista Orsini, Francesco Orsini, Duke of Gravina, Paolo Orsini, the bastard son of the Archbishop of Trani, Pandolfo Petrucci—Lord of Siena—and Hermes Bentivogli were all present. The last-named, prone to the direct methods of murder by which he had rid Bologna of the Marescotti, is said to have declared that he would kill Cesare Borgia if he but had the opportunity, whilst Vitelli swore solemnly that within a year he would slay or capture the duke, or else drive him out of Italy.

From this it will be seen that the Diet of Magione was no mere defensive alliance, but actually an offensive one, with the annihilation of Cesare Borgia for its objective.

They certainly had the power to carry out their resolutions, for whilst Cesare disposed at that moment of not more than 2,500 foot, 300 men-at-arms, and the 100 lances of his Caesarean guard of patricians, the confederates had in arms some 9,000 foot and 1,000 horse. Conscious of their superior strength, they determined to strike at once, before Cesare should be further supported by the French lances, and to make sure of him by assailing him on every side at once. To this end it was resolved that Bentivogli should instantly march upon Imola, where Cesare lay, whilst the others should possess themselves of Urbino and Pesaro simultaneously.

They even approached Florence and Venice in the matter, inviting the Republics to come into the league against Valentinois.

The Florentines, however, could not trust such enemies of their own as Vitelli and the Orsini, nor dared they join in an enterprise which had for scope to make war upon an ally of France; and they sent word to Cesare of their resolve to enter into no schemes against him.

The Venetians would gladly have moved to crush a man who had snatched the Romagna from under their covetous eyes; but in view of the league with France they dared not. What they dared, they did. They wrote to Louis at length of the evils that were befalling Italy at the hands of the Duke of Valentinois, and of the dishonour to the French crown which lay for

Louis in his alliance with Cesare Borgia. They even went so far—and most treacherously, considering the league—as to allow their famous captain, Bartolomeo d'Alviano, to reconduct Guidobaldo to Urbino, as we shall presently see.

Had the confederates but kept faith with one another Cesare's knell had soon been tolled. But they were a weak-kneed pack of traitors, irresolute in their enmity as in their friendships. The Orsini hung back. They urged that they did not trust themselves to attack Cesare with men actually in his pay; whilst Bentivogli—treacherous by nature to the back-bone of him—actually went so far as to attempt to open secret negotiations with Cesare through Ercole d'Este of Ferrara.

CHAPTER XV
MACCHIAVELLI'S LEGATION

On October 2 news of the revolt of the condottieri and the diet of Magione had reached the Vatican and rendered the Pope uneasy. Cesare, however, had been informed of it some time before at Imola, where he was awaiting the French lances that should enable him to raid the Bolognese and drive out the Bentivogli.

Where another might have been paralyzed by a defection which left him almost without an army, and would have taken the course of sending envoys to the rebels to attempt to make terms and by concessions to patch up a treaty, Cesare, with characteristic courage, assurance, and promptitude of action, flung out officers on every side to levy him fresh troops.

His great reputation as a condottiero, the fame of his wealth and his notorious liberality, stood him now in excellent stead. The response to his call was instantaneous. Soldiers of fortune and mercenaries showed the trust they had in him, and flocked to his standard from every quarter. One of the first to arrive was Gasparo Sanseverino, known as Fracassa, a condottiero of great renown, who had been in the Pontifical service since the election of Pope Alexander. He was a valuable acquisition to Cesare, who placed him in command of the horse. Another was Lodovico Pico della Mirandola, who brought a small condotta of 60 lances and 60 light horse. Ranieri della Sassetta rode in at the head of 100 mounted arbalisters, and Francesco de Luna with a body of 50 arquebusiers.(1)

> 1 The arquebus, although it had existed in Italy for nearly a century, was only just coming into general use.

Valentinois sent out Raffaele dei Pazzi and Galeotto Pallavicini, the one into Lombardy to recruit 1,000 Gascons, the other to raise a body of Swiss mercenaries. Yet, when all is said, these were but supplementary forces; the main strength of Cesare's new army lay in the troops raised in the Romagna, which, faithful to him and confident of his power and success, rallied to him now in the hour of his need. Than this there can be no more eloquent testimony to the quality of his rule. In command of these Romagnuoli troops he placed such Romagnuoli captains as Dionigio di Naldo and Marcantonio da Fano, thereby again affording proof of his wisdom, by giving these soldiers their own compatriots and men with whom they were in sympathy for their leaders.

With such speed had he acted, and such was the influence of his name, that already, by October 14, he had assembled an army of upwards of 6,000 men, which his officers were diligently drilling at Imola, whilst daily now were the French lances expected, and the Swiss and Gascon mercenaries he had sent to levy.

It may well be that this gave the confederates pause, and suggested to them that they should reconsider their position and ask themselves whether the opportunity for crushing Cesare had not slipped by whilst they had stood undecided.

It was Pandolfo Petrucci who took the first step towards a reconciliation, by sending word to Valentinois that it was not his intention to take any measures that might displease his Excellency. His Excellency will no doubt have smiled at that belated assurance from the sparrow to the hawk. Then, a few days later, came news that Giulio Orsini had entered into an agreement with the Pope. This appeared to give the confederacy its death-blow, and Paolo Orsini was on the point of setting out to seek Cesare at Imola for the purpose of treating with him—which would definitely have given burial to the revolt—when suddenly there befell an event which threw the scales the other way.

Cesare's people were carrying out some work in the Castle of S. Leo, in the interior of which a new wall was in course of erection. For the purposes of this, great baulks of timber were being brought into the castle from the surrounding country. Some peasants, headed by one Brizio, who had been a squire of Guidobaldo's, availed themselves of the circumstance to capture the castle by a stratagem. Bringing forward some great masses of timber and felled trees, they set them down along the drawbridge in such a manner as to prevent its being hoisted. That done, an attack in force was directed against the fortress. The place, whose natural defences rendered it practically impregnable, was but slightly manned; being thus surprised, and unable to raise the bridge, it was powerless to offer any resistance, so that the Montefeltre peasants, having killed every Borgia soldier of the garrison, took possession of it and held it for Duke Guidobaldo.

This capture of S. Leo was as a spark that fired a train. Instantly the hardy hillmen of Urbino were in arms to reconquer Guidobaldo's duchy for him. Stronghold after stronghold fell into their hands, until they were in Urbino itself. They made short work of the capital's scanty defenders, flung Cesare's governor into prison, and finally obtained possession of the citadel.

It was the news of this that caused the confederates once more to pause. Before declaring themselves, they waited to see what action Venice would take, whilst in the meantime they sought shelter behind a declaration that they were soldiers of the Church and would do nothing against the will of the Pontiff. They were confidently assured that Venice would befriend Guidobaldo, and help him back to his throne now that his own people had done so much towards that end. It remained, however, to be seen whether Venice would at the same time befriend Pesaro and Rimini.

Instantly Cesare Borgia—who was assailed by grave doubts concerning the Venetians—took his measures. He ordered Bartolomeo da Capranica, who was chief in command of his troops in Urbino, to fall back upon Rimini with all his companies, whilst to Pesaro the duke dispatched Michele da Corella and Ramiro de Lorqua.

It was a busy time of action with the duke at Imola, and yet, amid all the occupation which this equipment of a new army must have given him, he still found time for diplomatic measures, and, taking advantage of the expressed friendliness of Florence, he had replied by desiring the Signory to send an envoy to confer with him. Florence responded by sending, as her representative, that same Niccolò Macchiavelli who had earlier accompanied Soderini on a similar mission to Valentinois, and who had meanwhile been advanced to the dignity of Secretary of State.

Macchiavelli has left us, in his dispatches to his Government, the most precious and valuable information concerning that period of Cesare Borgia's history during which he was with the duke on the business of his legation. Not only is it the rare evidence of an eye-witness that Macchiavelli affords us, but the evidence, as we have said, of one endowed with singular acumen and an extraordinary gift of psychological analysis. The one clear and certain inference to be drawn, not only from those dispatches, but from the Florentine secretary's later writings, is that, at close quarters with Cesare Borgia, a critical witness of his methods, he conceived for him a transcending admiration which was later to find its fullest expression in his immortal book The Prince—a book, remember, compiled to serve as a guide in government to Giuliano de'Medici, the feeble brother of Pope Leo X, a book inspired by Cesare Borgia, who is the model prince held up by Macchiavelli for emulation.

Does it serve any purpose, in the face of this work from the pen of the acknowledged inventor of state-craft, to describe Cesare's conquest of the Romagna by opprobrious epithets and sweeping statements of condemnation and censure—statements kept carefully general, and never permitted to enter into detail which must destroy their own ends and expose their falsehood?

> Gregorovius, in this connection, is as full of contradictions as any man must be who does not sift out the truth and rigidly follow it in his writings. Consider the following scrupulously translated extracts from his Geschichte der Stadt Rom:
>
> (a) "Cesare departed from Rome to resume his bloody work in the Romagna."
>
> (b) "...the frightful deeds performed by Cesare on both sides of the Apennines. He assumes the semblance of an exterminating angel, and performs such hellish iniquities that we can only shudder at the contemplation of the evil of which human nature is capable."

And now, pray, consider and compare with those the following excerpt from the very next page of that same monumental work:

"Before him [Cesare] cities trembled; the magistrates prostrated themselves in the dust; sycophantic courtiers praised him to the stars. Yet it is undeniable that his government was energetic and good; for the first time Romagna enjoyed peace and was rid of her vampires. In the name of Cesare justice was administered by Antonio di Monte Sansovino, President of the Ruota of Cesena, a man universally beloved."

It is almost as if the truth had slipped out unawares, for the first period hardly seems a logical prelude to the second, by which it is largely contradicted. If Cesare's government was so good that Romagna knew peace at last and was rid of her vampires, why did cities tremble before him? There is, by the way, no evidence of such trepidations in any of the chronicles of the conquered States, one and all of which hail Cesare as their deliverer. Why, if he was held in such terror, did city after city—as we have seen—spontaneously offer itself to Cesare's dominion?

But to rebut those statements of Gregorovius's there is scarce the need to pose these questions; sufficiently does Gregorovius himself rebut them. The men who praised Cesare, the historian tells us, were sycophantic courtiers. But where is the wonder of his being praised if his government was as good as Gregorovius admits it to have been? What was unnatural in that praise? What so untruthful as to deserve to be branded sycophantic? And by what right is an historian to reject as sycophants the writers who praise a man, whilst accepting every word of his detractors as the words of inspired evangelists, even when their falsehoods are so transparent as to provoke the derision of the thoughtful and analytic?

As l'Espinois points out in his masterly essay in the Revue des Questions Historiques, Gregorovius refuses to recognize in Cesare Borgia the Messiah of a united Central Italy, but considers him merely as a high-flying adventurer; whilst Villari, in his Life and Times of Macchiavelli, tells you bluntly that Cesare Borgia was neither a statesman nor a soldier but a brigand-chief.

These are mere words; and to utter words is easier than to make them good.

"High-flying adventurer," or "brigand-chief," by all means, if it please you. What but a high-flying adventurer was the wood-cutter, Muzio Attendolo, founder of the ducal House of Sforza? What but a high-flying adventurer was that Count Henry of Burgundy who founded the kingdom of Portugal? What else was the Norman bastard William, who conquered England? What else the artillery officer, Napoleon Bonaparte, who became Emperor of the French? What else was the founder of any dynasty but a high-flying adventurer—or a brigand-chief, if the melodramatic term is more captivating to your fancy?

These terms are used to belittle Cesare. They achieve no more, however, than to belittle those who penned them; for, even as they are true, the marvel is that the admirable matter in these truths appears to have escaped those authors.

What else Gregorovius opines—that Cesare was no Messiah of United Italy—is true enough. Cesare was the Messiah of Cesare. The well-being of Italy for its own sake exercised his mind not so much as the well-being of the horse he rode. He wrought for his own aggrandisement—but he wrought wisely; and, whilst the end in view is no more to be censured than the ambition of any man, the means employed are in the highest degree to be commended, since the well-being of the Romagna, which was not an aim, was, nevertheless, an essential and praiseworthy incident.

When it can be shown that every other of those conquerors who cut heroic figures in history were purest altruists, it will be time to damn Cesare Borgia for his egotism.

What Villari says, for the purpose of adding rhetorical force to his "brigand-chief"—that Cesare was no statesman and no soldier—is entirely of a piece with the rest of the chapter in which it occurs(1)—a chapter rich in sweeping inaccuracies concerning Cesare. But it is staggering to find the statement in such a place, amid Macchiavelli's letters on Cesare, breathing an obvious and profound admiration of the duke's talents as a politician and a soldier—an admiration which later is to go perilously near to worship. To Macchiavelli, Cesare is the incarnation of a hazy ideal, as is abundantly shown in The Prince. For Villari to reconcile all this with his own views must seem impossible. And impossible it is; yet Villari achieves it, with an audacity that leaves you breathless.

1 In his Niccolò Macchiavelli.

No—he practically tells you—this Macchiavelli, who daily saw and spoke with Cesare for two months (and during a critical time, which is when men best reveal their natures), this acute Florentine—the acutest man of his age, perhaps—who studied and analysed Cesare, and sent his Government the results of his analyses, and was inspired by them later to write The Prince—this man did not know Cesare Borgia. He wrote, not about Cesare himself, but about a creation of his own intellect.

That is what Villari pretends. Macchiavelli, the representative of a power unfriendly at heart under the mask of the expedient friendliness, his mind already poisoned by all the rumours current throughout Italy, comes on this mission to Valentinois. Florence, fearing and hating Valentinois as she does, would doubtless take pleasure in detractory advices. Other ambassadors—particularly those of Venice—pander to their Governments' wishes in this respect, conscious that there is a sycophancy in slander contrasted with which the ordinary sycophancy of flattery is as water to wine; they diligently send home every scrap of indecent or scandalous rumour they can pick up in the Roman ante-chambers, however unlikely, uncorroborated, or unconcerning the business of an ambassador.

But Macchiavelli, in Cesare Borgia's presence, is overawed by his greatness, his force and his intellect, and these attributes engage him in his dispatches. These same dispatches are a stumbling-block to all who prefer to tread the beaten, sensational track, and to see in Cesare Borgia a villain of melodrama, a monster of crime, brutal, and, consequently, of no intellectual force. But Villari contrives to step more or less neatly, if fatuously, over that formidable obstacle, by telling you that Macchiavelli presents to you not really Cesare Borgia, but a creation of his own intellect, which he had come to admire. It is a simple, elementary expedient by means of which every piece of historical evidence ever penned may be destroyed—including all that which defames the House of Borgia.

Macchiavelli arrived at Imola on the evening of October 7, 1502, and, all travel-stained as he was, repaired straight to the duke, as if the message with which he was charged was one that would not brook a moment's delay in its deliverance. Actually, however, he had nothing to offer Cesare but the empty expressions of Florence's friendship and the hopes she founded upon Cesare's reciprocation. The crafty young Florentine—he was thirty-three at the time—was sent to temporize and to avoid committing himself or his Government.

Valentinois listened to the specious compliments, and replied by similar protestations and by reminding Florence how he had curbed the hand of those very condottieri who had now rebelled against him as a consequence. He showed himself calm and tranquil at the loss of Urbino, telling Macchiavelli that he "had not forgotten the way to reconquer it," when it should suit him. Of the revolted condottieri he contemptuously said that he accounted them fools for not having known how to choose a more favourable moment in which to harm him, and that they would presently find such a fire burning under their feet as would call for more water to quench it than such men as these disposed of.

Meanwhile, the success of those rustics of Urbino who had risen, and the ease of their victories, had fired others of the territory to follow their example. Fossombrone and Pergola were the next to rebel and to put the Borgia garrisons to the sword; but, in their reckless audacity, they chose their moment ill, for Michele da Corella was at hand with his lances, and, although his orders had been to repair straight to Pesaro, he ventured to depart from them to the extent of turning aside to punish the insurgence of those towns by launching his men-at-arms upon them and subjecting them to an appalling and pitiless sack.

When Cesare heard the news of it and the details of the horrors that had been perpetrated, he turned, smiling cruelly, to Macchiavelli, who was with him, and, "The constellations this year seem unfavourable to rebels," he observed.

A battle of wits was toward between the Florentines' Secretary of State and the Duke of Valentinois, each mistrustful of the other. In the end Cesare, a little out of patience at so much inconclusiveness, though outwardly preserving his immutable serenity, sought to come to grips by demanding that Florence should declare whether he was to account her his friend or not. But this was precisely what Macchiavelli's instructions forbade him from declaring. He answered that he must first write to the Signory, and begged the duke to tell him what terms he proposed should form the treaty. But there it was the duke's turn to fence and to avoid a direct answer, desiring that Florence should open the negotiations and that from her should come the first proposal.

He reminded Macchiavelli that Florence would do well to come to a decision before the Orsini sought to patch up a peace with him, since, once that was done, there would be fresh difficulties, owing, of course, to Orsini's enmity to the existing Florentine Government. And of such a peace there was now every indication, Paolo Orsini having at last sent Cesare proposals for rejoining him, subject to his abandoning the Bologna enterprise (in which, the Orsini argued, they could not bear a hand without breaking faith with Bentivogli) and turning against Florence. Vitelli, at the same time, announced himself ready to return to Cesare's service, but first he required some "honest security."

Well might it have pleased Cesare to oblige the Orsini to the letter, and to give a lesson in straight-dealing to these shuffling Florentine pedlars who sent a nimble-witted Secretary of State to hold him in play with sweet words of barren meaning. But there was France and her wishes to be considered, and he could not commit himself. So his answer was peremptory and condescending. He told them that, if they desired to show themselves his friends, they could set about reconquering and holding Urbino for him.

It looked as if the condottieri agreed to this, for on October 11 Vitelli seized Castel Durante, and on the next day Baglioni was in possession of Cagli.

In view of this, Cesare bade the troops which he had withdrawn to advance again upon the city of Urbino and take possession of it. But suddenly, on the 12th, a messenger from Guidobaldo rode into Urbino to announce their duke's return within a few days to defend the subjects who had shown themselves so loyal to him. This, the shifty confederates accounted, must be done with the support of Venice, whence they concluded that Venice must have declared against Valentinois, and again they treacherously changed sides.

The Orsini proceeded to prompt action. Assured of their return to himself, and counting upon their support in Urbino, Cesare had contented himself with sending thither a small force of 100 lances and 200 light horse. Upon these fell the Orsini, and put them to utter rout at Calmazzo, near Fossombrone, capturing Ugo di Moncada, who commanded one of the companies, but missing Michele da Corella, who contrived to escape to Fossombrone.

The conquerors entered Urbino that evening, and, as if to put it on record that they burnt their boats with Valentinois, Paolo Orsini wrote that same night to the Venetian Senate advices of the victory won. Three days later—on October 18—Guidobaldo, accompanied by his nephews Ottaviano Fregioso and Gianmaria Varano, re-entered his capital amid the cheers and enthusiasm of his loyal and loving people.

Vitelli made haste to place his artillery at Guidobaldo's disposal for the reduction of Cagli, Pergola, and Fossombrone, which were still held for Valentinois, whilst Oliverotto da Fermo went with Gianmaria Varano to attempt the reconquest of Camerino, and Gianpaolo Baglioni to Fano, which, however, he did not attempt to enter as an enemy—an idle course, seeing how loyally the town held for Cesare—but as a ducal condottiero.

Fired by Orsini's example, Bentivogli also took the offensive, and began by ordering the canonists of Bologna University to go to the churches and encourage the people to disregard the excommunications launched against the city. He wrote to the King of France to complain that Cesare had broken the Treaty of Villafontana by which he had undertaken never again to molest Bologna—naïvely ignoring the circumstance that he himself had been the first to violate the terms of that same treaty, and that it was precisely upon such grounds that Cesare was threatening him.

Thus matters stood, the confederates turning anxious eyes towards Venice, and, haply, beginning to wonder whether the Republic was indeed going to move to their support as they had so confidently expected, and realizing perhaps by now their rashness, and the ruin that awaited them should Venice fail them. And fail them Venice did. The Venetians had received a reply from Louis XII to that letter in which they had heaped odium upon the Borgia and shown the king what dishonour to himself dwelt in his alliance with Valentinois. Their criticisms and accusations were ignored in that reply, which resolved itself into nothing more than a threat that "if they opposed themselves to the enterprise of the Church they would be treated by him as enemies," and of this letter he sent Cesare a copy, as Cesare himself told Macchiavelli.

So, whilst Valentinois in Imola was able to breathe more freely, the condottieri in Urbino may well have been overcome with horror at their position and at having been thus left in the lurch by Venice. None was better aware than Pandolfo Petrucci of the folly of their action and of the danger that now impended, and he sent his secretary to Valentinois to say that if the duke would but reassure them on the score of his intentions they would return to him and aid him in recovering what had been lost.

Following upon this message came Paolo Orsini himself to Imola on the 25th, disguised as a courier, and having first taken the precaution of obtaining a safe-conduct. He left again on the 29th, bearing with him a treaty the terms of which had been agreed between himself and Cesare during that visit. These were that Cesare should engage to protect the States of all his allied condottieri, and they to serve him and the Church in return. A special convention was to follow, to decide the matter of the Bentivogli, which should be resolved by Cesare, Cardinal Orsini, and Pandolfo Petrucci in consultation, their judgment to be binding upon all.

Cesare's contempt for the Orsini and the rest of the shifty men who formed that confederacy—that "diet of bankrupts," as he had termed it—was expressed plainly enough to Macchiavelli.

"To-day," said he, "Messer Paolo is to visit me, and to-morrow there will be the cardinal; and thus they think to befool me, at their pleasure. But I, on my side, am only dallying with them. I listen to all they have to say and bide my own time."

Later, Macchiavelli was to remember those words, which meanwhile afforded him matter for reflection.

As Paolo Orsini rode away from Imola, the duke's secretary, Gherardi, followed and overtook him to say that Cesare desired to add to the treaty another clause—one relating to the King of France. To this Paolo Orsini refused to consent, but, upon being pressed in the matter by Gherardi, went so far as to promise to submit the clause to the others.

On October 30 Cesare published a notice in the Romagna, intimating the return to obedience on the part of his captains.

Macchiavelli was mystified by this, and apprehensive—as men will be of the things they cannot fathom—of what might be reserved in it for Florence. It was Gherardi who reassured him, laughing in the face of the crafty Florentine, as he informed him that even children should come to smile at such a treaty as this. He added that he had gone after Paolo Orsini to beg the addition of another clause, intentionally omitted by the duke.

"If they accept that clause," concluded Messer Agabito, "it will open a window; if they refuse it, a door, by which the duke can issue from the treaty."

Macchiavelli's wonder increased. But the subject of it now was that the condottieri should be hoodwinked by a document in such terms, and well may he have bethought him then of those words which Cesare had used to him a few days earlier.

CHAPTER XVI
RAMIRO DE LORQUA

It really seemed as if the condottieri were determined to make their score as heavy as possible. For even whilst Paolo Orsini had been on his mission of peace to Cesare, and whilst they awaited his return, they had continued in arms against the duke. The Vitelli had aided Guidobaldo to reconquer his territory, and had killed, in the course of doing so, Bartolomeo da Capranica, Cesare's most valued captain and Vitelli's brotherin-arms of yesterday. The Baglioni were pressing Michele da Corella in Pesaro, but to little purpose; whilst the butcher Oliverotto da Fermo in Camerino—of which he had taken possession with Gianmaria Varano—was slaughtering every Spaniard he could find.

On the other side, Corella in Pesaro hanged five men whom he caught practising against the duke's government, and, having taken young Pietro Varano—who was on his way to join his brother in Camerino in view of the revolt there—he had him strangled in the market-place. There is a story that, with life not yet extinct, the poor youth was carried into church by the pitiful crowd. But here a friar, discovering that he still lived, called in the soldiers and bade them finish him. This friar, going later through Cagli, was recognized, set upon by a mob, and torn to pieces—in which, if the rest of the tale be true, he was richly served.

Into the theatre of bloodshed came Paolo Orsini from his mission to Valentinois, bringing with him the treaty for signature by the condottieri. Accustomed as they were to playing fast and loose, they opined that, so far as Urbino was concerned, enough changes of government had they contrived there already. Vitelli pointed out the unseemliness of once again deposing Guidobaldo, whom they had just reseated upon his throne. Besides, he perceived in the treaty the end of his hopes of a descent upon Florence, which was the cause of all his labours. So he rejected it.

But Valentinois had already got the Orsini and Pandolfo Petrucci on his side, and so the confederacy was divided. Another factor came to befriend the duke. On November 2 he was visited by Antonio Galeazzo Bentivogli, sent by his father Giovanni to propose a treaty with him—this state of affairs having been brought about by the mediation of Ercole d'Este. From the negotiations that followed it resulted that, on the 13th, the Orsini had word from Cesare that he had entered into an alliance with the Bentivogli— which definitely removed their main objection to bearing arms with him.

It was resigning much on Cesare's part, but the treaty, after all, was only for two years, and might, of course, be broken before then, as they understood these matters. This treaty was signed at the Vatican on the 23rd, between Borgia and Bentivogli, to guarantee the States of both. The King of France, the Signory of Florence, and the Duke of Ferrara guaranteed the alliance.

Inter alia, it was agreed between them that Bologna should supply Cesare with 100 lances and 200 light horse for one or two enterprises within the year, and that the condotta of 100 lances which Cesare held from Bologna by the last treaty should be renewed. The terms of the treaty were to be kept utterly secret for the next three months, so that the affairs of Urbino and Camerino should not be prejudiced by their publication.

The result was instantaneous. On November 27 Paolo Orsini was back at Imola with the other treaty, which bore now the signatures of all the confederates. Vitelli, finding himself isolated, had swallowed his chagrin in the matter of Florence, and his scruples in the matter of Urbino, abandoning the unfortunate Guidobaldo to his fate. This came swiftly. From Imola, Paolo Orsini rode to Fano on the 29th, and ordered his men to advance upon Urbino and seize the city in the Duke of Valentinois's name, proclaiming a pardon for all rebels who would be submissive.

Guidobaldo and the ill-starred Lord of Faenza were the two exceptions in Romagna—the only two who had known how to win the affections of their subjects. For Guidobaldo there was nothing that the men of Urbino would not have done. They rallied to him now, and the women of Valbone— like the ladies of England to save Coeur-de-Lion—came with their jewels and trinkets, offering them that he might have the means to levy troops and resist. But this gentle, kindly Guidobaldo could not subject his country to further ravages of war; and so he determined, in his subjects' interests as much as in his own, to depart for the second time.

Early in December the Orsini troops are in his territory, and Paolo, halting them a few miles out of Urbino, sends to beg Guidobaldo's attendance in his camp. Guidobaldo, crippled by gout and unable at the time to walk a step, sends Paolo his excuses and begs that he will come to Urbino, where he awaits him. There Guidobaldo makes formal surrender to him, takes leave of his faithful friends, enjoins fidelity to Valentinois and trust in God, and so on December 19 he departs into exile, the one pathetic noble figure amid so many ignoble ones. Paolo, taking possession of the duchy, assumes the title of governor.

The Florentines had had their chance of an alliance with Cesare, and had deliberately neglected it. Early in November they had received letters from the King of France urging them to come to an accord with Cesare, and they had made known to the duke that they desired to reoccupy Pisa and to assure themselves of Vitelli; but, when he pressed that Florence should give him a condotta, Macchiavelli—following his instructions not to commit the Republic in any way—had answered "that his Excellency must not be considered as other lords, but as a new potentate in Italy, with whom it is more seemly to make an alliance or a friendship than to grant him a condotta; and, as alliances are maintained by arms, and that is the only power to compel their observance, the Signory could not perceive what security they would have when three-quarters or three-fifths of their arms would be in the duke's hands." Macchiavelli added diplomatically that "he did not say this to impugn the duke's good faith, but to show him that princes should be circumspect and never enter into anything that leaves a possibility of their being put at a disadvantage."(1)

1 See the twenty-first letter from Macchiavelli on this legation.

Cesare answered him calmly ("senza segno d'alterazione alcuna") that without a condotta, he didn't know what to make of a private friendship whose first principles were denied him. And there the matter hung, for Macchiavelli's legation had for only aim to ensure the immunity of Tuscany and to safeguard Florentine interests without conceding any advantages to Cesare—as the latter had perceived from the first.

On December 10 Cesare moved from Imola with his entire army, intent now upon the conquest of Sinigaglia, which State Giuliano della Rovere had been unable to save for his nephew, as king and Pope had alike turned a deaf ear upon the excuses he had sought to make for the Prefetessa, Giovanna da Montefeltre—the mother of the young prefect—who had aided her brother Guidobaldo in the late war in Urbino.

On the morrow Valentinois arrived in Cesena and encamped his army there for Christmas, as in the previous year. The country was beginning to feel the effects of this prolonged vast military occupation, and although the duke, with intent to relieve the people, had done all that was possible to provision the troops, and had purchased from Venice 30,000 bushels of wheat for the purpose, yet all had been consumed. "The very stones have been eaten," says Macchiavelli.

To account for this state of things—and possibly for certain other matters—Messer Ramiro de Lorqua, the Governor-General, was summoned from Pesaro; whilst to avert the threatened famine Cesare ordered that the cereals in the private granaries of Cesena should be sold at reduced prices, and he further proceeded, at heavy expense, to procure grain from without. Another, less far-seeing than Valentinois, might have made capital out of Urbino's late rebellion, and pillaged the country to provide for pressing needs. But that would have been opposed to Cesare's policy, of fostering the goodwill of the people he subjected.

On December 20 three of the companies of French lances that had been with Cesare took their leave of him and returned to Lombardy, so that Cesare was left with only one company. There appears to be some confusion as to the reasons for this, and it is stated by some that those companies were recalled to Milan by the French governor. Macchiavelli, ever inquisitive and inquiring, questioned one of the French officers in the matter, to be told that the lances were returning because the duke no longer needed them, the inference being that this was in consequence of the return of the condottieri to their allegiance. But the astute secretary did not at the time account this convincing, arguing that the duke could not yet be said to be secure, nor could he know for certain how far he might trust Vitelli and the Orsini. Presumably, however, he afterwards obtained more certain information, for he says later that Valentinois himself dismissed the French, and that the dismissal was part of the stratagem he was preparing, and had for object to reassure Vitelli and the other confederates, and to throw them off their guard, by causing them to suppose him indifferently supported.

But the departure of the French did not take place without much discussion being provoked, and rumour making extremely busy, whilst it was generally assumed that it would retard the Sinigaglia conquest. Nevertheless, the duke calmly pursued his preparations, and proceeded now to send forward his artillery. There was no real ground upon which to assume that he would adopt any other course. Cesare was now in considerable strength, apart from French lances, and even as these left him he was joined by a thousand Swiss, and another six hundred Romagnuoli from the Val di Lamone. Moreover, as far as the reduction of Sinigaglia was concerned, no resistance was to be expected, for Cardinal Giuliano della Rovere had written enjoining the people to surrender peacefully to the duke.

What matters Cesare may have found in Cesena to justify the arrest of his Governor-General we do not know to the full with absolute certainty. On December 22 Ramiro de Lorqua, coming from Pesaro in response to his master's summons, was arrested on his arrival and flung into prison. His examination was to follow.

Macchiavelli, reporting the arrest, says: "It is thought he [Cesare] may sacrifice him to the people, who have a very great desire of it."

Ramiro had made himself detested in Romagna by the ruthlessness of his rule, and a ruthless servant reflects upon his master, a matter which could nowise suit Borgia. To all who have read The Prince it will be clear that upon that ground alone—of having brought Valentinois's justice into disrepute by the harshness which in Valentinois's name he practised—Macchiavelli would have approved the execution of Ramiro. He would have accounted it perfectly justifiable that Ramiro should be sacrificed to the people for no better reason than because he had provoked their hatred, since this sacrifice made for the duke's welfare. He does, as a matter of fact, justify this execution, but upon much fuller grounds than these. Still, had the reasons been no better than are mentioned, he would still have justified it upon those. So much is clear; and, when so much is clear, much more will be clear to you touching this strange epoch.

There was, however, more than a matter of sacrificing the Governor-General to the hatred of the people. There was, for one thing, the matter of that wheat which had disappeared. Ramiro was charged with having fraudulently sold it to his own dishonest profit, putting the duke to the heavy expense of importing fresh supplies for the nourishment of the people. The seriousness of the charge will be appreciated when it is considered that, had a famine resulted from this peculation, grave disorder might have ensued and perhaps even a rebellion against a government which could provide no better.

The duke published the news of the governor's arrest throughout Romagna. He announced his displeasure and regret at the harshnesses and corrupt practices of Ramiro de Lorqua, in spite of the most urgent admonishings that he should refrain from all undue exactions and the threat of grave punishment should he disobey. These frauds, corruption, extortion, and rapine practised by the governor were so grave, continuous and general, stated the duke in his manifesto, that "there is no city, country-side, or castle, nor any place in all Romagna, nor officer or minister of the duke's, who does not know of these abuses; and, amongst others, the famine of wheat occasioned by the traffic which he held against our express prohibition, sending out such quantities as would abundantly have sufficed for the people and the army."

He concludes with assurances of his intention that, in the future, they shall be ruled with justice and integrity, and he urges all who may have charges to prefer against the said governor to bring them forward immediately.

It was freely rumoured that the charges against Ramiro by no means ended there, and in Bologna—and from Bologna the truth of such a matter might well transpire, all things considered—it was openly said that Ramiro had been in secret treaty with the Bentivogli, Orsini, and Vitelli, against the Duke of Valentinois: "Aveva provixione da Messer Zoane Bentivogli e da Orsini e Vitelozo contro el duca," writes Fileno della Tuate, who, it will be borne in mind, was no friend of the Borgia, and would be at no pains to find justification for the duke's deeds.

But of that secret treaty there was, for the moment, no official mention. Later the rumour of it was to receive the fullest confirmation, and, together with that, we shall give, in the next chapter, the duke's obvious reasons for having kept the matter secret at first. Matter enough and to spare was there already upon which to dispose of Messer Ramiro de Lorqua and disposed of he was, with the most summary justice.

On the morning of December 26 the first folk to be astir in Cesena beheld, in the grey light of that wintry dawn, the body of Ramiro lying headless in the square. It was richly dressed, with all his ornaments upon it, a scarlet cloak about it, and the hands were gloved. On a pike beside the body the black-bearded head was set up to view, and so remained throughout that day, a terrible display of the swift and pitiless justice of the duke.

Macchiavelli wrote: "The reason of his death is not properly known" ("non si sa bene la cagione della sua morte") "beyond the fact that such was the pleasure of the prince, who shows us that he can make and unmake men according to their deserts."

The Cronica Civitas Faventiae, the Diariurn Caesenate, and the Cronache Forlivese, all express the people's extreme satisfaction at the deed, and endorse the charges of brutality against the man which are contained in Cesare's letter.

CHAPTER XVII
"THE BEAUTIFUL STRATAGEM"

Cesare left Cesena very early on the morning of December 26—the morning of Ramiro's execution—and by the 29th he was at Fano, where he received the envoys who came from Ancona with protestations of loyalty, as well as a messenger from Vitellozzo Vitelli, who brought him news of the surrender of Sinigaglia. The citadel itself was still being held by Andrea Doria—the same who was afterwards to become so famous in Genoa; this, it was stated, was solely because Doria desired to make surrender to the duke himself. The Prefectress, Giovanna da Montefeltre, had already departed from the city, which she ruled as regent for her eleven-year old boy, and had gone by sea to Venice.

The duke returned answer to Vitelli that he would be in Sinigaglia himself upon the morrow, and he invited the condottieri to receive him there, since he was decided to possess himself of the citadel at once, whether Doria chose to surrender it peacefully or not; and that, to provide for emergencies, he would bring his artillery with him. Lastly, Vitelli was bidden to prepare quarters within the new town for the troops that would accompany Cesare. To do this it was necessary to dispose the soldiers of Oliverotto da Fermo in the borgo. These were the only troops with the condottieri in Sinigaglia; the remainder of their forces were quartered in the strongholds of the territory at distances of from five to seven miles of the town.

On the last day of that year 1502 Cesare Borgia appeared before Sinigaglia to receive the homage of those men who had used him so treacherously, and whom—with the exception of Paolo Orsini—he now met face to face for the first time since their rebellion. Here were Francesco Orsini, Duke of Gravina, with Paolo and the latter's son Fabio; here was Oliverotto, the ruffianly Lord of Fermo, who had won his lordship by the cold-blooded murder of his kinsman, and concerning whom a rumour ran in Rome that Cesare had sworn to choke him with his own hands; and here was Vitellozzo Vitelli, the arch-traitor of them all.

Gianpaolo Baglioni was absent through illness—a matter less fatal to him than was their health to those who were present—and the Cardinal and Giulio Orsini were in Rome.

Were these captains mad to suppose that such a man as Cesare Borgia could so forget the wrong they had done him, and forgive them in this easy fashion, exacting no amends? Were they mad to suppose that, after such proofs as they had given him of what manner of faith they kept, he would trust them hereafter with their lives to work further mischief against him? (Well might Macchiavelli have marvelled when he beheld the terms of the treaty the duke had made with them.) Were they mad to imagine that one so crafty as Valentinois would so place himself into their hands—the hands of men who had sworn his ruin and death? Truly, mad they must have been—rendered so by the gods who would destroy them.

The tale of that happening is graphically told by the pen of the admiring Macchiavelli, who names the affair "Il Bellissimo Inganno." That he so named it should suffice us and restrain us from criticisms of our own, accepting that criticism of his. To us, judged from our modern standpoint, the affair of Sinigaglia is the last word in treachery and iscariotism. But you are here concerned with the standpoint of the Cinquecento, and that standpoint Macchiavelli gives you when he describes this business as "the beautiful stratagem." To offer judgment in despite of that is to commit a fatuity, which too often already has been committed.

Here, then, is Macchiavelli's story of the event:

On the morning of December 31 Cesare's army, composed of 10,000 foot and 3,000 horse,(1) was drawn up on the banks of the River Metauro—some five miles from Sinigaglia—in accordance with his orders, awaiting his arrival. He came at daybreak, and immediately ordered forward 200 lances under the command of Don Michele da Corella; he bade the foot to march after these, and himself brought up the rear with the main body of the horse.

1 This is Macchiavelli's report of the forces; but, it appears to be an exaggeration, for, upon leaving Cesena, Cesare does not appear to have commanded more than 10,000 men in all.

In Sinigaglia, as we have seen, the condottieri had only the troops of Oliverotto—1,000 foot and 150 horse—which had been quartered in the borgo, and were now drawn up in the market-place, Oliverotto at their head, to do honour to the duke.

As the horse under Don Michele gained the little river Misa and the bridge that spanned it, almost directly opposite to the gates of Sinigaglia, their captain halted them and drew them up into two files, between which a lane was opened. Through this the foot went forward and straight into the town, and after came Cesare himself, a graceful, youthful figure, resplendent in full armour at the head of his lances. To meet him advanced now the three Orsini and Vitellozzo Vitelli. Macchiavelli tells us of the latter's uneasiness, of his premonitions of evil, and the farewells (all of which Macchiavelli had afterwards heard reported) which he had taken of his family before coming to Sinigaglia. Probably these are no more than the stories that grow up about such men after such an event as that which was about to happen.

The condottieri came unarmed, Vitelli mounted on a mule, wearing a cloak with a green lining. In that group he is the only man deserving of any respect or pity—a victim of his sense of duty to his family, driven to his rebellion and faithlessness to Valentinois by his consuming desire to avenge his brother's death upon the Florentines. The others were poor creatures, incapable even of keeping faith with one another. Paolo Orsini was actually said to be in secret concert with Valentinois since his mission to him at Imola, and to have accepted heavy bribes from him. Oliverotto you have seen at work, making a holocaust of his family and friends under the base spur of his cupidity; whilst of the absent ones, Pandolfo Petrucci alone was a man of any steadfastness and honesty.

The duke's reception of them was invested with that gracious friendliness of which none knew the art better than did he, intent upon showing them that the past was forgiven and their offences against himself forgotten. As they turned and rode with him through the gates of Sinigaglia some of the duke's gentlemen hemmed them about in the preconcerted manner, lest even now they should be taken with alarm. But it was all done unostentatiously and with every show of friendliness, that no suspicions should be aroused.

From the group Cesare had missed Oliverotto, and as they now approached the market-square, where the Tyrant of Fermo sat on his horse at the head of his troops, Cesare made a sign with his eyes to Don Michele, the purport of which was plain to the captain. He rode ahead to suggest to Ohiverotto that this was no time to have his men under arms and out of their lodgings, and to point out to him that, if they were not dismissed they would be in danger of having their quarters snatched from them by the duke's men, from which trouble might arise. To this he added that the duke was expecting his lordship.

Oliverotto, persuaded, gave the order for the dismissal of his troops, and the duke, coming up at that moment, called to him. In response he went to greet him, and fell in thereafter with the others who were riding with Valentinois.

In amiable conversation with them all, and riding between Vitelli and Francesco Orsini, the duke passed from the borgo into the town itself, and so to the palace, where the condottieri disposed to take their leave of him. But Cesare was not for parting with them yet; he bade them in with him, and they perforce must accept his invitation. Besides, his mood was so agreeable that surely there could be nought to fear.

But scarce were they inside when his manner changed of a sudden, and at a sign from him they were instantly overpowered and arrested by those gentlemen of his own who were of the party and who came to it well schooled in what they were to do.

Buonaccorsi compiled his diary carefully from the letters of Macchiavelli to the Ten, in so far as this and other affairs are concerned; and to Buonaccorsi we must now turn for what immediately follows, which is no doubt from Macchiavelli's second letter of December 31, in which the full details of the affair are given. His first letter no more than briefly states the happening; the second unfortunately is missing; so that the above particulars—and some yet to follow—are culled from the relations which he afterwards penned ("Del modo tenuto," etc.), edited, however, by the help of his dispatches at the time in regard to the causes which led to the affair. Between these and the actual relation there are some minor discrepancies. Unquestionably the dispatches are the more reliable, so that, where such discrepancies occur, the version in the dispatches has been preferred.

To turn for a moment to Buonaccorsi, he tells us that, as the Florentine envoy (who was, of course, Macchiavelli) following the Duke of Valentinois entered the town later, after the arrest of the condottieri, and found all uproar and confusion, he repaired straight to the palace to ascertain the truth. As he approached he met the duke, riding out in full armour to quell the rioting and restrain his men, who were by now all out of hand and pillaging the city. Cesare, perceiving the secretary, reined in and called him.

"This," he said, "is what I wanted to tell Monsignor di Volterra [Soderini] when he came to Urbino, but I could not entrust him with the secret. Now that my opportunity has come, I have known very well how to make use of it, and I have done a great service to your masters."

And with that Cesare left him, and, calling his captains about him, rode down into the town to put an end to the horrors that were being perpetrated there.

Immediately upon the arrest of the condottieri Cesare had issued orders to attack the soldiers of Vitelli and Orsini, and to dislodge them from the castles of the territory where they were quartered, and similarly to dislodge Oliverotto's men and drive them out of Sinigaglia. This had been swiftly accomplished. But the duke's men were not disposed to leave matters at that. Excited by the taste of battle that had been theirs, they returned to wreak their fury upon the town, and were proceeding to put it to sack, directing particular attention to the wealthy quarter occupied by the Venetian merchants, which is said to have been plundered by them to the extent of some 20,000 ducats. They would have made an end of Sinigaglia but for the sudden appearance amongst them of the duke himself. He rode through the streets, angrily ordering the pillage to cease; and, to show how much he was in earnest, with his own hands he cut down some who were insolent or slow to obey him; thus, before dusk, he had restored order and quiet.

As for the condottieri, Vitelli and Oliverotto were dealt with that very night. There is a story that Oliverotto, seeing that all was lost, drew a dagger and would have put it through his heart to save himself from dying at the hands of the hangman. If it is true, then that was his last show of spirit. He turned craven at the end, and protested tearfully to his judges—for a trial was given them—that the fault of all the wrong wrought against the duke lay with his brother-in-law, Vitellozzo. More wonderful was it that the grim Vitelli's courage also should break down at the end, and that he should beg that the Pope be implored to grant him a plenary indulgence and that his answer be awaited.

But at dawn—the night having been consumed in their trial—they were placed back to back, and so strangled, and their bodies were taken to the church of the Misericordia Hospital.

The Orsini were not dealt with just yet. They were kept prisoners, and Valentinois would go no further until he should have heard from Rome that Giulio Orsini and the powerful cardinal were also under arrest. To put to death at present the men in his power might be to alarm and so lose the others. They are right who say that his craft was devilish; but what else was to be expected of the times?

On the morrow—January 1, 1503—the duke issued dispatches to the Powers of Italy giving his account of the deed. It set forth that the Orsini and their confederates, notwithstanding the pardon accorded them for their first betrayal and revolt, upon learning of the departure of the French lances—and concluding that the duke was thereby weakened, and left with only a few followers of no account—had plotted a fresh and still greater treachery.

Under pretence of assisting him in the taking of Sinigaglia, whither it was known that he was going, they had assembled there in their full strength, but displaying only one-third of it, and concealing the remainder in the castles of the surrounding country. They had then agreed with the castellan of Sinigaglia, that on that night they should attack him on every side of the new town, which, being small, could contain, as they knew, but few of his people. This treachery coming to his knowledge, he had been able to forestall it, and, entering Sinigaglia with all his troops, he had seized the traitors and taken the forces of Oliverotto by surprise. He concluded by exhorting all to render thanks unto God that an end was set to the many calamities suffered in Italy in consequence of those malignant ones.(1)

1 See this letter in the documents appended to Alvisi's Cesare Borgia, document 76.

For once Cesare Borgia is heard giving his own side of an affair. But are the particulars of his version true? Who shall say positively? His statement is not by any means contrary to the known facts, although it sets upon them an explanation rather different to that afforded us by Macchiavelli. But it is to be remembered that, after all, Macchiavelli had to fall back upon the inferences which he drew from what he beheld, and that there is no scrap of evidence directly to refute any one of Cesare's statements. There is even confirmation of the statement that the condottieri conceived that he was weakened by the departure of the French lances and left with only a few followers of no account. For Macchiavelli himself dwells upon the artifice with which Cesare broke up his forces and disposed of them in comparatively small numbers here and there to the end that his full strength should remain concealed; and he admires the strategy of that proceeding.

Certainly the duke's narrative tends to increase his justification for acting as he did. But at best it can only increase it, for the actual justification was always there, and by the light of his epoch it is difficult to see how he should be blamed. These men had openly sworn to have his life, and from what has been seen of them there is little reason to suppose they would not have kept their word had they but been given the opportunity.

In connection with Cesare's version, it is well to go back for a moment to the execution of Ramiro de Lorqua, and to recall the alleged secret motives that led to it. Macchiavelli himself was not satisfied that all was disclosed, and that the governor's harshness and dishonesty had been the sole causes of the justice done upon him. "The reason of his death is not properly known," wrote the Florentine secretary. Another envoy of that day would have filled his dispatches with the rumours that were current, with the matters that were being whispered at street corners. But Macchiavelli's habit was to disregard rumours as a rule, knowing their danger—a circumstance which renders his evidence the most valuable which we possess.

It is perhaps permissible to ask: What dark secrets had the torture of the cord drawn from Messer Ramiro? Had these informed the duke of the true state of affairs at Sinigaglia, and had the knowledge brought him straight from Cesena to deal with the matter?

There is justification for these questions, inasmuch as on January 4 the Pope related to Giustiniani—for which see his dispatches—that Ramiro de Lorqua, being sentenced to death, stated that he desired to inform the duke of certain matters, and informed him that he had concerted with the Orsini to give the latter the territory of Cesena; but that, as this could not now be done, in consequence of Cesare's treaty with the condottieri, Vitelli had arranged to kill the duke, in which design he had the concurrence of Oliverotto. They had planned that a crossbow-man should shoot the duke as he rode into Sinigaglia, in consequence of which the duke took great care of himself and never put off his armour until the affair was over. Vitellozzo, the Pope said, had confessed before he died that all that Ramiro had told the duke was true, and at the Consistory of January 6, when the Sacred College begged for the release of the old Cardinal Orsini—who had been taken with the Archbishop of Florence, Giacomo di Santacroce, and Gianbattista da Virginio—the Pope answered by informing the cardinals of this plot against the duke's life.

These statements by Cesare and his father are perfectly consistent with each other and with the events. Yet, for want of independent confirmation, they are not to be insisted upon as affording the true version—as, of course, the Pope may have urged what he did as a pretext to justify what was yet to follow.

It is readily conceivable that Ramiro, under torture, or in the hope perhaps of saving his life, may have betrayed the alleged plot to murder Cesare. And it is perfectly consistent with Cesare's character and with his age that he should have entered into a bargain to learn what Ramiro might have to disclose, and then have repudiated it and given him to the executioner. If Cesare, under such circumstances as these, had learnt what was contemplated, he would very naturally have kept silent on the score of it until he had dealt with the condottieri. To do otherwise might be to forewarn them. He was, as Macchiavelli says, a secret man, and the more dangerous for his closeness, since he never let it be known what he intended until he had executed his designs.

Guicciardini, of course, has called the Sinigaglia affair a villainy ("scelleragine") whilst Fabio Orsini and a nephew of Vitelli's who escaped from Sinigaglia and arrived two days later at Perugia, sought to engage sympathy by means of an extraordinary tale, so alien to all the facts—apart from their obvious reasons to lie and provoke resentment against Cesare— as not to be worth citing.

CHAPTER XVIII
THE ZENITH

Andrea Doria did not remain to make formal surrender of the citadel of Sinigaglia to the duke—for which purpose, be it borne in mind, had Cesare been invited, indirectly, to come to Sinigaglia. He fled during the night that saw Vitelli and Oliverotto writhing their last in the strangler's hands. And his flight adds colour to the versions of the affair that were afforded the world by Cesare and his father. Andrea Doria, waiting to surrender his trust, had nothing to fear from the duke, no reason to do anything but remain. Andrea Doria, intriguing against the duke's life with the condottieri, finding them seized by the duke, and inferring that all was discovered, had every reason to fly.

The citadel made surrender on that New Year's morning, when Cesare summoned it to do so, whilst the troops of the Orsini and Vitelli lodged in the castles of the territory, being taken unawares, were speedily disposed of. So, there being nothing more left to do in Sinigaglia, Cesare once more marshalled his men and set out for Città di Castello—the tyranny of the Vitelli, which he found undefended and of which he took possession in the name of the Church. Thence he rushed on towards Perugia, for he had word that Guidobaldo of Urbino, Fabio Orsini, Annibale and Venanzio Varano, and Vitelli's nephew were assembled there under the wing of Gianpaolo Baglioni, who, with a considerable condotta at his back, was making big talk of resisting the Duke of Romagna and Valentinois. In this, Gianpaolo persevered most bravely until he had news that the duke was as near as Gualdo, when precipitately he fled—leaving his guests to shift for themselves. He had remembered, perhaps, at the last moment how narrow an escape he had had of it at Sinigaglia, and he repaired to Siena to join Pandolfo Petrucci, who had been equally fortunate in that connection.

To meet the advancing and irresistible duke came ambassadors from Perugia with smooth words of welcome, the offer of the city, and their thanks for his having delivered them of the tyrants that oppressed them; and there is not the slightest cause to suppose that this was mere sycophancy, for a more bloody, murderous crew than these Baglioni—whose feuds not only with the rival family of the Oddi, but among their very selves, had more than once embrued the walls of that city in the hills—it would be difficult to find in Italy, or anywhere in Europe. The history of the Baglioni is one record of slaughter. Under their rule in Perugia human blood seems commonly to have flowed anywhere more freely than in human veins. It is no matter for wonder that the people sent their ambassador to thank Cesare for having delivered them from the yoke that had oppressed them.

Perugia having rendered him her oath of fealty, the duke left her his secretary, Agabito Gherardi, as his commissioner, whilst sending Vincenzo Calmeta to Fermo—Oliverotto's tyranny—another State which was very fervent in the thanks it expressed for this deliverance.

Scarcely was Cesare gone from Perugia when into the hands of his people fell the person of the Lady Panthasilea Baglioni d'Alviano—the wife of the famous Venetian condottiero Bartolomeo d'Alviano—and they, aware of the feelings prevailing between their lord and the Government of Venice, bethought them that here was a valuable hostage. So they shut her up in the Castle of Todi, together with her children and the women who had been with her when she was taken.

As in the case of Dorotea Caracciolo, the rumour is instantly put about that it was Cesare who had seized her, that he had taken her to his camp, and that this poor woman had fallen a prey to that lustful monster. So—and in some such words—ran the story, and such a hold did it take upon folks' credulity that we see Piero di Bibiena before the Council of Ten, laying a more or less formal charge against the duke in rather broader terms than are here set down. So much, few of those who have repeated his story omit to tell you. But for some reason, not obviously apparent, they do not think it worth while to add that the Doge himself—better informed, it is clear, for he speaks with finality in the matter—reproved him by denying the rumour and definitely stating that it was not true, as you may read in the Diary of Marino Sanuto. That same diary shows you the husband—a person of great consequence in Venice—before the Council, clamouring for the enlargement of his lady; yet never once does he mention the name of Valentinois. The Council of Ten sends an envoy to wait upon the Pope; and the Pope expresses his profound regret and his esteem for Alviano, and informs the envoy that he is writing to Valentinois to demand her instant release—in fact, shows the envoy the letter.

To that same letter the duke replied on January 29 that he had known nothing of the matter until this communication reached him; that he has since ascertained that the lady was indeed captured and that she has since been detained in the Castle of Todi with all the consideration due to her rank; and that, immediately upon ascertaining this he had commanded that she should be set at liberty, which was done.

And so the Lady Panthasilea returned unharmed to her husband.

In Assisi Cesare received the Florentine ambassador Salviati, who came to congratulate the duke upon the affair of Sinigaglia and to replace Macchiavelli—the latter having been ordered home again. Congratulations indeed were addressed to him by all those Powers that had received his official intimation of the event. Amongst these were the felicitations of the beautiful and accomplished Isabella d'Este, Marchioness of Gonzaga— whose relations with him were ever of the friendliest, even when Faenza by its bravery evoked her pity—and with these she sent him, for the coming carnival, a present of a hundred masks of rare variety and singular beauty, because she opined that "after the fatigues he had suffered in these glorious enterprises, he would desire to contrive for some recreation."

Here in Assisi, too, he received the Siennese envoys who came to wait upon him, and he demanded that, out of respect for the King of France, they should drive out Pandolfo Petrucci from Siena. For, to use his own words, "having deprived his enemies of their weapons, he would now deprive them of their brain," by which he paid Petrucci the compliment of accounting him the "brain" of all that had been attempted against him. To show the Siennese how much he was in earnest, he leaves all baggage and stores at Assisi, and, unhampered, makes one of his sudden swoops towards Siena, pausing on January 13 at Castel della Pieve to publish, at last, his treaty with Bentivogli. The latter being now sincere, no doubt out of fear of the consequences of further insincerity, at once sends Cesare 30 lances and 100 arbalisters under the command of Antonio della Volta.

It was there in Assisi, on the morning of striking his camp again, that Cesare completed the work that had been begun at Sinigaglia by having Paolo Orsini and the Duke of Gravina strangled. There was no cause to delay the matter longer. He had word from Rome of the capture of Cardinal Orsini, of Gianbattista da Virginio, of Giacomo di Santacroce, and Rinaldo Orsini, Archbishop of Florence.

On January 27, Pandolfo Petrucci being still in Siena, and Cesare's patience exhausted, he issued an ultimatum from his camp at Sartiano in which he declared that if, within twenty-four hours, Petrucci had not been expelled from the city, he would loose his soldiers upon Siena to devastate the territory, and would treat every inhabitant "as a Pandolfo and an enemy."

Siena judged it well to bow before that threatening command, and Cesare, seeing himself obeyed, was free to depart to Rome, whither the

Pope had recalled him and where work awaited him. He was required to make an end of the resistance of the barons, a task which had been entrusted to his brother Giuffredo, but which the latter had been unable to carry out.

In this matter Cesare and his father are said to have violently disagreed, and it is reported that high words flew between them; for Cesare—who looked ahead and had his own future to consider, which should extend beyond the lifetime of Alexander VI—would not move against Silvio Savelli in Palombara, nor Gian Giordano in Bracciano, alleging, as his reason for the latter forbearance, that Gian Giordano, being a knight of St. Michael like himself, he was inhibited by the terms of that knighthood from levying war upon him. To that he adhered, whilst disposing, however, to lay siege to Ceri, where Giulio and Giovanni Orsini had taken refuge.

In the meantime, the Cardinal Gianbattista Orsini had breathed his last in the Castle of Sant' Angelo.

Soderini had written ironically to Florence on February 15: "Cardinal Orsini, in prison, shows signs of frenzy. I leave your Sublimities to conclude, in your wisdom, the judgment that is formed of such an illness."

It was not, however, until a week later—on February 22—that he succumbed, when the cry of "Poison!" grew so loud and general that the Pope ordered the cardinal's body to be carried on a bier with the face exposed, that all the world might see its calm and the absence of such stains as were believed usually to accompany venenation.

Nevertheless, the opinion spread that he had been poisoned—and the poisoning of Cardinal Orsini has been included in the long list of the Crimes of the Borgias with which we have been entertained. That the rumour should have spread is not in the least wonderful, considering in what bad odour were the Orsini at the Vatican just then, and—be it remembered— what provocation they had given. Although Valentinois dubbed Pandolfo Petrucci the "brain" of the conspiracy against him, the real guiding spirit, there can be little doubt, was this Cardinal Orsini, in whose stronghold at Magione the diet had met to plot Valentinois's ruin—the ruin of the Gonfalonier of the Church, and the fresh alienation from the Holy See of the tyrannies which it claimed for its own, and which at great cost had been recovered to it.

Against the Pope, considered as a temporal ruler, that was treason in the highest degree, and punishable by death; and, assuming that Alexander did cause the death of Cardinal Orsini, the only just censure that could fall upon him for the deed concerns the means employed. Yet even against that it might be urged that thus was the dignity of the purple saved the dishonouring touch of the hangman's hands.

Some six weeks later—on April 10—died Giovanni Michieli, Cardinal of Sant' Angelo, and Giustiniani, the Venetian ambassador, wrote to his Government that the cardinal had been ill for only two days, and that his illness had been attended by violent sickness. This—and the reticence of it—was no doubt intended to arouse the suspicion that the cardinal had been poisoned. Giustiniani adds that Michieli's house was stripped that very night by the Pope, who profited thereby to the extent of some 150,000 ducats, besides plate and other valuables; and this was intended to show an indecent eagerness on the Pope's part to possess himself of that which by the cardinal's death he inherited, whereas, in truth, the measure would be one of wise precaution against the customary danger of pillage by the mob.

But in March of the year 1504, under the pontificate of Julius II (Cardinal Giuliano della Rovere) a subdeacon, named Asquino de Colloredo, was arrested for defaming the dead cardinal ("interfector bone memorie Cardinalis S. Angeli").(1) What other suspicions were entertained against him, what other revelations it was hoped to extract from him, cannot be said; but Asquino was put to the question, to the usual accompaniment of the torture of the cord, and under this he confessed that he had poisoned Cardinal Michieli, constrained to it by Pope Alexander VI and the Duke of Valentinois, against his will and without reward ("verumtamen non voluisse et pecunias non habuisse").

1 Burchard's Diarium, March 6, 1504.

Now if Asquino defamed the memory of Cardinal Michieli it seems to follow naturally that he had hated the cardinal; and, if we know that he hated him, we need not marvel that, out of that hatred, he poisoned him. But something must have been suspected as a motive for his arrest in addition to the slanders he was uttering, otherwise how came the questions put to him to be directed so as to wring from him the confession that he had poisoned the cardinal? If you choose to believe his further statement that he was constrained to it by Pope Alexander and the Duke of Valentinois, you are, of course, at liberty to do so. But you will do well first to determine precisely what degree of credit such a man might be worth when seeking to extenuate a fault admitted under pressure of the torture—and offering the extenuation likeliest to gain him the favour of the della Rovere Pope, whose life's task—as we shall see—was the defamation of the hated Borgias. You will also do well closely to examine the last part of his confession—that he was constrained to it "against his will and without reward." Would the deed have been so very much against the will of one who went about publishing his hatred of the dead cardinal by the slanders he emitted?

Upon such evidence as that the accusation of the Pope's murder of Cardinal Michieli has been definitely established—and it must be admitted that it is, if anything, rather more evidence than is usually forthcoming of the vampirism and atrocities alleged against him.

Giustiniani, writing to his Government in the spring of 1503, informs the Council of Ten that it is the Pope's way to fatten his cardinals before disposing of them—that is to say, enriching them before poisoning them, that he may inherit their possessions. It was a wild and sweeping statement, dictated by political animus, and it has since grown to proportions more monstrous than the original. You may read usque ad nauseam of the Pope and Cesare's constant practice of poisoning cardinals who had grown rich, for the purpose of seizing their possessions, and you are very naturally filled with horror at so much and such abominable turpitude. In this matter, assertion—coupled with whorling periods of vituperation—have ever been considered by the accusers all that was necessary to establish the accusations. It has never, for instance, been considered necessary to cite the names of the cardinals composing that regiment of victims. That, of course, would be to challenge easy refutation of the wholesale charge; and refutation is not desired by those who prefer the sensational manner.

The omission may, in part at least, be repaired by giving a list of the cardinals who died during the eleven years of the pontificate of Alexander VI. Those deaths, in eleven years, number twenty-one—representing, incidentally, a percentage that compares favourably with any other eleven years of any other pontificate or pontificates. They are:

Ardicino della Porta . . In 1493, at Rome

Giovanni de'Conti. . . In 1493, at Rome

Domenico della Rovere . . In 1494, at Rome

Gonzalo de Mendoza. . . In 1495, in Spain

Louis André d'Epinay . . In 1495, in France

Gian Giacomo Sclafetano. . In 1496, at Rome

Bernardino di Lunati . . In 1497, at Rome

Paolo Fregosi. . . . In 1498, at Rome

Gianbattista Savelli . . In 1498, at Rome

Giovanni della Grolaye . . In 1499, at Rome

Giovanni Borgia . . . In 1500, at Fossombrone

Bartolomeo Martini. . . In 1500, at Rome

John Morton. . . . In 1500, in England

Battista Zeno. . . . In 1501, at Rome

Juan Lopez . . . . In 1501, at Rome

Gianbattista Ferrari . . In 1502, at Rome

Hurtado de Mendoza. . . In 1502, in Spain

Gianbattista Orsini. . . In 1503, at Rome

Giovanni Michieli. . . In 1503, at Rome

Giovanni Borgia (Seniore). . In 1503, at Rome

Federico Casimir . . . In 1503, in Poland

Now, search as you will, not only such contemporary records as diaries, chronicles, and dispatches from ambassadors in Rome during that period of eleven years but also subsequent writings compiled from them, and you shall find no breath of scandal attaching to the death of seventeen of those cardinals, no suggestion that they died other than natural deaths.

Four remain: Cardinals Giovanni Borgia (Giuniore), Gianbattista Ferrari (Cardinal of Modena), Gianbattista Orsini, and Giovanni Michieli, all of whom the Pope and Cesare have, more or less persistently, been accused of poisoning.

Giovanni Borgia's death at Fossombrone has been dealt with at length in its proper place, and it has been shown how utterly malicious and groundless was the accusation.

Giovanni Michieli's is the case that has just been reviewed, and touching which you may form your own conclusions.

Gianbattista Orsini's also has been examined. It rests upon rumour; but even if that rumour be true, it is unfair to consider the deed in any but the light of a political execution.

There remains the case of the Cardinal of Modena, a man who had amassed enormous wealth in the most questionable manner, and who was universally execrated. The epigrams upon his death, in the form of epitaphs, dealt most terribly with "his ignominious memory"—as Burchard has it. Of these the Master of Ceremonies collected upwards of a score, which he gives in his Diarium. Let one suffice here as a fair example of the rest, the one that has it that the earth has the cardinal's body, the bull (i.e. the Borgia) his wealth, and hell his soul.

> "Hac Janus Baptista jacet Ferrarius urna, Terra habuit corpus,
> Bos bona, Styx animam."

The only absolutely contemporary suggestion of his having been poisoned emanated from the pen of that same Giustiniani. He wrote to the Venetian Senate to announce the cardinal's death on July 20. In his letter he relates how his benefices were immediately distributed, and how the lion's share fell to the cardinal's secretary, Sebastiano Pinzone, and that it was said ("é fama") that this man had received them as the price of blood ("in premium sanguinis"), "since it is held, from many evident signs, that the cardinal died from poison" ("ex veneno").

Already on the 11th he had written: "The Cardinal of Modena lies ill, with little hope of recovery. Poison is suspected" ("si dubita di veleno").

That was penned on the eighth day of the cardinal's sickness, for he was taken ill on the 3rd—as Burchard shows. Burchard, further, lays before us the whole course of the illness; tells us how, from the beginning, the cardinal refused to be bled or to take medicine of any kind, tells us explicitly and positively that the cardinal was suffering from a certain fever—so prevalent and deadly in Rome during the months of July and August; he informs us that, on the 11th (the day on which Giustiniani wrote the above-cited dispatch), the fever abated, to return on the 16th. He was attended (Burchard continues) by many able physicians, who strove to induce him to take their medicines; but he refused persistently until the following day, when he accepted a small proportion of the doses proposed. On July 20—after an illness of seventeen days—he finally expired.

Those entries in the diary of the Master of Ceremonies constitute an incontrovertible document, an irrefutable testimony against the charges of poisoning when taken in conjunction with the evidence of fact afforded by the length of the illness.

It is true that, under date of November 20, 1504 (under the pontificate of Julius II), there is the following entry:

"Sentence was pronounced in the 'Ruota' against Sebastiano Pinzone, apostolic scribe, contumaciously absent, and he was deprived of all benefices and offices in that he had caused the death of the Cardinal of Modena, his patron, who had raised him from the dust."

But not even that can shake the conviction that must leap to every honest mind from following the entries in the diary contemporary with the cardinal's decease. They are too circumstantial and conclusive to be overthrown by this recorded sentence of the Ruota two years later against a man who was not even present to defend himself. Besides, it is necessary to discriminate. Burchard is not stating opinions of his own when he writes "in that he caused the death of the Cardinal of Modena," etc.; he is simply— and obviously—recording the finding of the Tribunal of the Ruota, without comment of his own. Lastly, it is as well to observe that in that verdict against Pinzone—of doubtful justice as it is—there is no mention made of the Borgias.

The proceedings instituted against Sebastiano Pinzone were of a piece with those instituted against Asquino de Colloredo and others yet to be considered; they were set on foot by Giuliano della Rovere—that implacable enemy of the House of Borgia—when he became Pope, for the purpose of heaping ignominy upon the family of his predecessor. But that shall be further dealt with presently.

Another instance of the unceasing growth of Borgia history is afforded in connection with this Sebastiano Pinzone by Dr. Jacob Burckhardt (in Der Cultur der Renaissance in Italien) who, in the course of the usual sweeping diatribe against Cesare, mentions "Michele da Corella, his strangler, and Sebastiano Pinzone, his poisoner." It is an amazing statement; for, whilst obviously leaning upon Giustiniani's dispatch for the presumption that Pinzone was a poisoner at all, he ignores the statement contained in it that Pinzone was the secretary and favourite of Cardinal Ferrari, nor troubles to ascertain that the man was never in Cesare Borgia's service at all, nor is ever once mentioned anywhere as connected in any capacity whatever with the duke. Dr. Burckhardt felt, no doubt, the necessity of linking Pinzone to the Borgias, that the alleged guilt of the former may recoil upon the latter, and so he accomplished it in this facile and irresponsible manner.

Now, notwithstanding the full and circumstantial evidence afforded by Burchard's Diarium of the Cardinal of Modena's death of a tertian fever, the German scholar Gregorovius does not hesitate to write of this cardinal's death: "It is certain that it was due to their [the Borgias'] infallible white powders."

Oh the art of writing history in sweeping statements to support a preconceived point of view! Oh that white powder of the Borgias!

Giovio tells us all about it. Cantarella, he calls it—Cantharides. Why Cantarella? Possibly because it is a pleasing, mellifluous word that will help a sentence hang together smoothly; possibly because the notorious aphrodisiac properties of that drug suggested it to Giovio as just the poison to be kept handy by folk addicted to the pursuits which he and others attribute to the Borgias. Can you surmise any better reason? For observe that Giovio describes the Cantarella for you—a blunder of his which gives the lie to his statement. "A white powder of a faint and not unpleasing savour," says he; and that, as you know, is nothing like cantharides, which is green, intensely acrid, and burning. Yet who cares for such discrepancies? Who will ever question anything that is uttered against a Borgia? "Cantarella—a white powder of a faint and not unpleasing savour," answers excellently the steady purpose of supporting a defamation and pandering to the tastes of those who like sensations in their reading—and so, from pen to pen, from book to book it leaps, as unchallenged as it is impossible.

Whilst Cesare's troops were engaged in laying siege to Ceri, and, by engines contrived by Leonardo da Vinci, pressing the defenders so sorely that at the end of a month's resistance they surrendered with safe-conduct, the inimical and ever-jealous Venetians in the north were stirring up what trouble they could. Chafing under the restraint of France, they but sought a pretext that should justify them in the eyes of Louis for making war upon Cesare, and when presently envoys came to lay before the Pope the grievance of the Republic at the pillage by Borgian soldiery of the Venetian traders in Sinigaglia, Cesare had no delusions concerning their disposition towards himself.

Growing uneasy lest they should make this a reason for assailing his frontiers, he sent orders north recommending vigilance and instructing his officers to deal severely with all enemies of his State, whilst he proceeded to complete the provisions for the government of the Romagna. To replace the Governor-General he appointed four seneschals: Cristoforo della Torre for Forli, Faenza and Imola; Hieronimo Bonadies for Cesena, Rimini, and Pesaro; Andrea Cossa for Fano, Sinigaglia, Fossombrone, and Pergola; and Pedro Ramires for the duchy of Urbino. This last was to find a deal of work for his hands; for Urbino was not yet submissive, Majolo and S. Leo still holding for Guidobaldo.

Ramires began by reducing Majolo, and then proceeded to lay siege to S. Leo. But the Castellan—one Lattanzio—encouraged by the assurances given him that the Venetians would render Guidobaldo assistance to reconquer his dominions, resisted stubbornly, and was not brought to surrender until the end of June, after having held the castle for six months.

If Venice was jealous and hostile in the north, Florence was scarcely less so in mid-Italy—though perhaps with rather more justification, for Cesare's growing power and boundless ambition kept the latter Republic in perpetual fear of being absorbed into his dominions—into that kingdom which it was his ultimate aim to found. There can be little doubt that Francesco da Narni, who appeared in Tuscany early in the March of that year, coming from the French Court for the purpose of arranging a league of Florence, Bologna, Siena, and Lucca—the four States more or less under French protection—

had been besought by Florence, to the obvious end that these four States, united, might inter-defend themselves against Valentinois. And Florence even went so far as to avail herself of this to the extent of restoring Pandolfo Petrucci to the lordship of Siena—preferring even this avowed enemy to the fearful Valentinois. Thus came about Petrucci's restoration towards the end of March, despite the fact that the Siennese were divided on the subject of his return.

With the single exception of Camerino, where disturbances still continued, all was quiet in the States of the Church by that summer of 1503.

This desirable state of things had been achieved by Cesare's wise and liberal government, which also sufficed to ensure its continuance.

He had successfully combated the threatened famine by importing grain from Sicily. To Sinigaglia—his latest conquest—he had accorded, as to the other subjected States, the privilege of appointing her own native officials, with, of course, the exception of the Podestà (who never could be a native of any place where he dispensed justice) and the Castellan. In Cesena a liberal justice was measured out by the Tribunal of the Ruota, which Cesare had instituted there, equipping it with the best jurisconsults of the Romagna.

In Rome he proceeded to a military organization on a new basis, and with a thoroughness never before seen in Italy—or elsewhere, for that matter— but which was thereafter the example all sought to copy. We have seen him issuing an edict that every house in the Romagna should furnish him one man-at-arms to serve him when necessary. The men so levied were under obligation to repair to the market-place of their native town when summoned thither by the ringing of the bells, and it was estimated that this method of conscription would yield him six or seven thousand men, who could be mobilized in a couple of days. He increased the number of arquebusiers, appreciating the power and value of a weapon which—although invented nearly a century earlier—was still regarded with suspicion. He was also the inventor of the military uniform, putting his soldiers into a livery of his own, and causing his men-at-arms to wear over their armour a smock, quartered red and yellow with the name CESARE lettered on the breast and back, whilst the gentlemen of his guard wore surcoats of his colours in gold brocade and crimson velvet.

He continued to levy troops and to arm them, and it is scarcely over-stating the case to say that hardly a tyrant of the Romagna would have dared to do so much for fear of the weapons being turned against himself. Cesare knew no such fear. He enjoyed a loyalty from the people he had subjected which was almost unprecedented in Italy. The very officers he placed in command of the troops of his levying were, for the most part, natives of the Romagna. Is there no inference concerning him to be drawn from that!

For every man in his service Cesare ordered a back-and-breast and headpiece of steel, and the armourers' shops of Brescia rang busily that summer with the clang of metal upon metal, as that defensive armour for Cesare's troops was being forged. At the same time the foundries were turning out fresh cannon in that season which saw Cesare at the very height and zenith of his power, although he himself may not have accounted that, as yet, he was further than at the beginning.

But the catastrophe that was to hurl him irretrievably from the eminence to which in three short years he had climbed was approaching with stealthy, relentless foot, and was even now upon him.

BOOK IV
THE BULL CADENT

"Cesar Borgia che era della gente Per armi e per virtú tenuto un sole, Mancar dovendo andó dove andar sole Phebo, verso la sera, al Occidente.

"Girolamo Casio—Epitaffi."

CHAPTER I
THE DEATH OF ALEXANDER VI

Unfortunate Naples was a battle-field once more. France and Spain were engaged there in a war whose details belong elsewhere.

To the aid of France, which was hard beset and with whose arms things were going none too well, Cesare was summoned to fulfil the obligations under which he was placed by virtue of his treaty with King Louis.

Rumours were rife that he was negotiating secretly with Gonzalo de Cordoba, the Great Captain, and the truth of whether or not he was guilty of so base a treachery has never been discovered. These rumours had been abroad since May, and, if not arising out of, they were certainly stimulated by, an edict published by Valentinois concerning the papal chamberlain, Francesco Troche. In this edict Cesare enjoined all subjects of the Holy See to arrest, wherever found, this man who had fled from Rome, and whose flight "was concerned with something against the honour of the King of France."

Francesco Troche had been Alexander's confidential chamberlain and secretary; he had been a diligent servant of the House of Borgia, and when in France had acted as a spy for Valentinois, keeping the duke supplied with valuable information at a critical time, as we have seen.

Villari says of him that he was "one of the Borgias' most trusted assassins." That he has never been so much as alleged to have murdered anyone does not signify. He was a servant—a trusted servant—of the Borgias; therefore the title of "assassin" is, ipso facto, to be bestowed upon him.

The flight of a man holding such an intimate position as Troche's was naturally a subject of much speculation and gossip, but a matter upon which there was no knowledge. Valentinois was ever secret. In common with his father—though hardly in so marked a degree, and if we except the case of the scurrilous Letter to Silvio Savelli—he showed a contemptuous indifference to public opinion on the whole which is invested almost with a certain greatness. At least it is rarely other than with greatness that we find such an indifference associated. It was not for him to take the world into his confidence in matters with which the world was not concerned. Let the scandalmongers draw what inferences they pleased. It was a lofty and dignified procedure, but one that was fraught with peril; and the Borgias have never ceased to pay the price of that excessive dignity of reserve. For tongues must be wagging, and, where knowledge is lacking, speculation will soon usurp its place, and presently be invested with all the authority of "fact."

Out of surmises touching that matter "which concerned the honour of the King of France" grew presently—and contradictorily—the rumour that Troche was gone to betray to France Valentinois's intention of going over to the Spanish side. A motive was certainly required to account for Troche's action; but the invention of motives does not appear ever to have troubled the Cinquecentist.

It was now said that Troche was enraged at having been omitted from the list of cardinals to be created at the forthcoming Consistory. It is all mystery, even to the end he made; for, whereas some said that, after being seized on board a ship that was bound for Corsica, Troche in his despair threw himself overboard and was drowned, others reported that he was brought back to Rome and strangled in a prison in Trastevere.

The following questions crave answer:

If it was Troche's design to betray such a treachery of the Borgias against France, what was he doing on board a vessel bound for Corsica a fortnight after his flight from Rome? Would not his proper goal have been the French camp in Naples, which he could have reached in a quarter of that time, and where not only could he have vented his desire for vengeance by betraying Alexander and Valentinois, but he could further have found complete protection from pursuit?

It is idle and unprofitable to dwell further upon the end of Francesco Troche. The matter is a complete mystery, and whilst theory is very well as theory, it is dangerous to cause it to fill the place of fact.

Troche was drowned or was strangled as a consequence of his having fled out of motives that were "against the honour of the King of France." And straightway the rumour spread of Valentinois's intended treachery, and the rumour was kept alive and swelled by Venice and Florence in pursuit of their never-ceasing policy of discrediting Cesare with King Louis, to the end that they might encompass his expedient ruin.

The lie was given to them to no small extent by the Pope, when, in the Consistory of July 28, he announced Cesare's departure to join the French army in Naples with five hundred horse and two thousand foot assembled for the purpose.

For this Cesare made now his preparations, and on the eve of departure he went with his father—on the evening of August 5—to sup at the villa of Cardinal Adriano Corneto, outside Rome.

Once before we have seen him supping at a villa of the Suburra on the eve of setting out for Naples, and we know the tragedy that followed—a tragedy which he has been accused of having brought about. Here again, in a villa of the Suburra, at a supper on the eve of setting out for Naples, Death was the unseen guest.

They stayed late at the vineyard of Cardinal Corneto, enjoying the treacherous cool of the evening, breathing the death that was omnipresent in Rome that summer, the pestilential fever which had smitten Cardinal Giovanni Borgia (Seniore) on the 1st of that month, and of which men were dying every day in the most alarming numbers.

On the morning of Saturday 12, Burchard tells us, the Pope felt ill, and that evening he was taken with fever. On the 15th Burchard records that he was bled, thirteen ounces of blood being taken from him. It relieved him somewhat, and, seeking distraction, he bade some of the cardinals to come and sit by his bed and play at cards.

Meanwhile, Cesare was also stricken, and in him the fever raged so fierce and violently that he had himself immersed to the neck in a huge jar of ice-cold water—a drastic treatment in consequence of which he came to shed all the skin from his body.

On the 17th the Pope was much worse, and on the 18th, the end being at hand, he was confessed by the Bishop of Culm, who administered Extreme Unction, and that evening he died.

That, beyond all manner of question, is the true story of the passing of Alexander VI, as revealed by the Diarium of Burchard, by the testimony of the physician who attended him, and by the dispatches of the Venetian, Ferrarese, and Florentine ambassadors. At this time of day it is accepted by all serious historians, compelled to it by the burden of evidence.

The ambassador of Ferrara had written to Duke Ercole, on August 14, that it was no wonder the Pope and the duke were ill, as nearly everybody in Rome was ill as a consequence of the bad air ("Per la mala condictione de aere").

Cardinal Soderini was also stricken with the fever, whilst Corneto was taken ill on the day after that supper-party, and, like Cesare, is said to have shed all the skin of his body before he recovered.

Even Villari and Gregorovius, so unrestrained when writing of the Borgias, discard the extraordinary and utterly unwarranted stories of Guicciardini, Giovio, and Bembo, which will presently be considered. Gregorovius does this with a reluctance that is almost amusing, and with many a fond, regretful, backward glance—so very apparent in his manner— at the tale of villainy as told by Guicciardini and the others, which the German scholar would have adopted but that he dared not for his credit's sake. This is not stated on mere assumption. It is obvious to any one who reads Gregorovius's histories.

Burchard tells us—as certainly matter for comment—that, during his last illness, Alexander never once asked for Cesare nor ever once mentioned the name of Lucrezia. So far as Cesare is concerned, the Pope knew, no doubt, that he was ill and bedridden, for all that the gravity of the duke's condition would, probably, have been concealed from him. That he should not have mentioned Lucrezia—nor, we suppose, Giuffredo—is remarkable. Did he, with the hand of Death already upon him, reproach himself with this paternity which, however usual and commonplace in priests of all degrees, was none the less a scandal, and the more scandalous in a measure as the rank of the offender was higher? It may well be that in those last days that sinful, worldly old man bethought him of the true scope and meaning of Christ's Vicarship, which he had so wantonly abused and dishonoured, and considered that to that Judge before whom he was summoned to appear the sins of his predecessors would be no justification or mitigation of his own. It may well be that, grown introspective upon his bed of death, he tardily sought to thrust from his mind the worldly things that had so absorbed it until the spiritual were forgotten, and had given rise to all the scandal concerning him that was spread through Christendom, to the shame and dishonour of the Church whose champion he should have been.

Thus may it have come to pass that he summoned none of his children in his last hours, nor suffered their names to cross his lips.

When the news of his father's death was brought to Cesare, the duke, all fever-racked as he was, more dead than living, considered his position and issued his orders to Michele da Corella, that most faithful of all his captains, who so richly shared with Cesare the execration of the latter's enemies.

Of tears for his father there is no record, just as at no time are we allowed to see that stern spirit giving way to any emotion, conceiving any affection, or working ever for the good of any but himself. Besides, in such an hour as this, the consciousness of the danger in which he stood by virtue of the Pope's death and his own most inopportune sickness, which disabled him from taking action to make his future secure, must have concerned him to the exclusion of all else.

Meanwhile, however, Rome was quiet, held so in the iron grip of Michele da Corella and the ducal troops. The Pope's death was being kept secret for the moment, and was not announced to the people until nightfall, by when Corella had carried out his master's orders, including the seizure of the Pope's treasure. And Burchard tells us how some of Valentinois's men entered the Vatican—all the gates of which were held by the ducal troops—and, seizing Cardinal Casanova, they demanded, with a dagger at his throat and a threat to fling his corpse from the windows if he refused them, the Pope's keys. These the cardinal surrendered, and Corella possessed himself of plate and jewels to the value of some 200,000 ducats, besides two caskets containing about 100,000 ducats in gold. Thereafter the servants of the palace completed the pillage by ransacking the wardrobes and taking all they could find, so that nothing was left in the papal apartments but the chairs, a few cushions, and the tapestries of the walls.

All his life Alexander had been the victim of the most ribald calumnies. Stories had ever sprung up and thriven, like ill weeds, about his name and reputation. His sins, great and scandalous in themselves, were swelled by popular rumour, under the spur of malice, to monstrous and incredible proportions. As they had exaggerated and lied about the manner of his life, so—with a consistency worthy of better scope—they exaggerated and lied about the manner of his death, and, the age being a credulous one, the stories were such that writers of more modern and less credulous times dare not insist upon them, lest they should discredit—as they do—what else has been alleged against him.

Thus when, in his last delirium, the Pope uttered some such words as: "I am coming; I am coming. It is just. But wait a little," and when those words were repeated, it was straightway asserted that the Devil was the being he thus addressed in that supreme hour. The story grew in detail; that is inevitable with such matter. He had bargained with the devil, it was said, for a pontificate of twelve years, and, the time being completed, the devil was come for him. And presently, we even have a description of Messer the Devil as he appeared on that occasion—in the shape of a baboon. The Marquis Gonzaga of Mantua, in all seriousness, writes to relate this. The chronicler Sanuto, receiving the now popularly current story from another source, in all seriousness gives it place in his Diarii, thus:

"The devil was seen to leap out of the room in the shape of a baboon. And a cardinal ran to seize him, and, having caught him, would have presented him to the Pope; but the Pope said, 'Let him go, let him go. It is the devil,' and that night he fell ill and died."(1)

1 "Il diavolo sarebbe saltato fuori della camera in forma di babuino, et un cardinale corso per piarlo, e preso volendolo presentar al papa, il papa disse lasolo, lasolo ché ii diavolo. E poi la notte si amaló e morite." —Marino Sanuto, Diarii.

That story, transcending the things which this more practical age considers possible, is universally rejected; but it is of vast importance to the historical student; for it is to be borne in mind that it finds a place in the pages of those same Diarii upon the authority of which are accepted many defamatory stories without regard to their extreme improbability so long as they are within the bounds of bare possibility.

After Alexander was dead it was said that water boiled in his mouth, and that steam issued from it as he lay in St. Peter's, and much else of the same sort, which the known laws of physiology compel so many of us very reluctantly to account exaggerations. But, again, remember that the source of these stories was the same as the source of many other exaggerations not at issue with physiological laws.

The circumstances of Alexander's funeral are in the highest degree scandalous, and reflect the greatest discredit upon his age.

On the morrow, as the clergy were chanting the Libera me, Domine in St. Peter's, where the body was exposed on a catafalque in full pontificals, a riot occurred, set on foot by the soldiers present for reasons which Burchard—who records the event—does not make clear.

The clerics fled for shelter to the sacristy, the chants were cut short, and the Pope's body almost entirely abandoned.

But the most scandalous happening occurred twenty-four hours later. The Pope's remains were removed to the Chapel of Santa Maria delle Febbre by six bearers who laughed and jested at the expense of the poor corpse, which was in case to provoke the coarse mirth of the lower classes of an age which, setting no value upon human life, knew no respect for death. By virtue of the malady that had killed him, of his plethoric habit of body, and of the sweltering August heat, the corpse was decomposing rapidly, so that the face had become almost black and assumed an aspect grotesquely horrible, fully described by Burchard:

"Factus est sicut pannus vel morus nigerrimus, livoris totus plenus, nasus plenus, os amplissimum, lingua duplex in ore, que labia tota implebat, os apertum et adeo horribile quod nemo viderit unquam vel esse tale dixerit."

Two carpenters waited in the chapel with the coffin which they had brought; but, either through carelessness it had been made too narrow and too short, or else the body, owing to its swollen condition, did not readily fit into this receptable; whereupon, removing the mitre, for which there was no room, they replaced it by a piece of old carpet, and set themselves to force and pound the corpse into the coffin. And this was done "without candle or any light being burned in honour of the dead, and without the presence of any priest or other person to care for the Pope's remains." No explanation of this is forthcoming; it was probably due to the panic earlier occasioned the clergy by the ducal men-at-arms.

The story that he had been poisoned was already spreading like a conflagration through Rome, arising out of the appearance of the body, which was such as was popularly associated with venenation.

But a Borgia in the rôle of a victim was altogether too unusual to be acceptable, and too much opposed to the taste to which the public had been educated; so the story must be edited and modified until suitable for popular consumption. The supper-party at Cardinal Corneto's villa was remembered, and upon that a tale was founded, and trimmed by degrees into plausible shape.

Alexander had intended to poison Corneto—so ran this tale—that he might possess himself of the cardinal's vast riches; in the main a well-worn story by now. To this end Cesare had bribed a butler to pour wine for the cardinal from a flask which he entrusted to him. Exit Cesare. Exit presently the butler, carelessly leaving the poisoned wine upon a buffet. (The drama, you will observe, is perfectly mechanical, full of author's interventions, and elementary in its "preparations"). Enter the Pope. He thirsts, and calls for wine. A servant hastens; takes up, of course, the poisoned flask in ignorance of its true quality, and pours for his Beatitude. Whilst the Pope drinks re-enters Cesare, also athirst, and, seating himself, he joins the Pope in the poisoned wine, all unsuspicious and having taken no precautions to mark the flask. Poetic justice is done, and down comes the curtain upon that preposterous tragi-farce.

Such is the story which Guicciardini and Giovio and a host of other more or less eminent historians have had the audacity to lay before their readers as being the true circumstances of the death of Alexander VI.

It is a noteworthy matter that in all that concerns the history of the House of Borgia, and more particularly those incidents in it that are wrapped in mystery, circumstantial elucidation has a habit of proceeding from the same quarters.

You will remember, for instance, that the Venetian Paolo Capello (though not in Rome at the time) was one of those who was best informed in the matter of the murder of the Duke of Gandia. And it was Capello again who was possessed of the complete details of the scarcely less mysterious business of Alfonso of Aragon. Another who on the subject of the murder of Gandia "had no doubts"—as he himself expressed it—was Pietro Martire d'Anghiera, in Spain at the time, whence he wrote to inform Italy of the true circumstances of a case that had happened in Italy.

It is again Pietro Martire d'Anghiera who, on November 10, 1503, writes from Burgos in Spain to inform Rome of the true facts of Alexander's death—for it is in that letter of his that the tale of the flask of wine, as here set down, finds place for the first time.

It is unprofitable to pursue the matter further, since at this time of day even the most reluctant to reject anything that tells against a Borgia have been compelled to admit that the burden of evidence is altogether too overwhelming in this instance, and that it is proved to the hilt that Alexander died of the tertian fever then ravaging Rome.

And just as the Pope's death was the subject of the wildest fictions which have survived until very recent days, so too, was Cesare's recovery.

Again, it was the same Pietro Martire d'Anghiera who from Burgos wrote to inform Rome of what was taking place in the privacy of the Duke of Valentinois's apartments in the Vatican. Under his facile and magic pen, the jar of ice-cold water into which Cesare was believed to have been plunged was transmuted into a mule which was ripped open that the fever-stricken Cesare might be packed into the pulsating entrails, there to sweat the fever out of him.

But so poor and sexless a beast as this seeming in the popular mind inadequate to a man of Cesare's mettle, it presently improved upon and converted it into a bull—so much more appropriate, too, as being the emblem of his house.

Nor does it seem that even then the story has gone far enough. Facilis inventis addere. There comes a French writer with an essay on the Borgias, than which—submitted as sober fact—nothing more amazingly lurid has been written. In this, with a suggestive cleverness entirely Gallic, he causes us to gather an impression of Cesare in the intestinal sudatorium of that eventrated bull, as of one who is at once the hierophant and devotee of a monstrous, foul, and unclean rite of some unspeakable religion—a rite by comparison with which the Black Mass of the Abbé Gribourg becomes a sweet and wholesome thing.

But hear the man himself:

"Cet homme de meurtres et d'inceste, incarné dans l'animal des hécatombes et des bestialités antiques en évoque les monstrueuses images. Je crois entendre le taureau de Phalaris et le taureau de Pasiphaë répondre, de loin, par d'effrayants mugissements, aux cris humains de ce bucentaure."

That is the top note on this subject. Hereafter all must pale to anticlimax.

CHAPTER II
PIUS III

The fever that racked Cesare Borgia's body in those days can have been as nothing to the fever that racked his mind, the despairing rage that must have whelmed his soul to see the unexpected—the one contingency against which he had not provided—cutting the very ground from underneath his feet.

As he afterwards expressed himself to Macchiavelli, and as Macchiavelli has left on record, Cesare had thought of everything, had provided for everything that might happen on his father's death, save that in such a season—when more than ever he should have need for all his strength of body and of mind—he should, himself, be lying at the point of death.

Scarce was Alexander's body cold than the duke's enemies began to lift their heads. Already by the 20th of that month—two days after the Pope had breathed his last—the Orsini were in arms and had led a rising, in retort to which Michele da Corella fired their palace on Montegiordano.

Venice and Florence bethought them that the protection of France had been expressly for the Church and not for Cesare personally. So the Venetians at once supplied Guidobaldo da Montefeltre with troops wherewith to reconquer his dominions, and by the 24th he was master of S. Leo. In the city of Urbino itself Ramires, the governor, held out as long as possible, then beat a retreat to Cesena, whilst Valentinois's partisans in Urbino were mercilessly slaughtered and their houses pillaged.

Florence supported the Baglioni in the conquest of Magione from the Borgias, and they aided Giacopo d'Appiano to repossess himself of Piombino, which had so gladly seen him depart out of it eighteen months ago.

From Magione, Gianpaolo Baglioni marches his Florentine troops to Camerino to aid the only remaining Varano to regain the tyranny of his fathers. The Vitelli are back in Città di Castello, carrying a golden calf in triumph through the streets; and so by the end of August, within less than a fortnight, all the appendages of the Romagna are lost to Cesare, whilst at

Cesare's very gates the Orsini men-at-arms are clamouring with insistent menace.

The Duke's best friend, in that crisis, was his secretary Agabito Gherardi. For it is eminently probable—as Alvisi opines—that it was Gherardi who urged his master to make an alliance with the Colonna, Gherardi himself being related to that powerful family. The alliance of these old enemies—Colonna and Borgia—was in their common interests, that they might stand against their common enemy, Orsini—the old friends of the Borgias.

On August 22 Prospero Colonna came to Rome, and terms were made and cemented, in the usual manner, by a betrothal—that of the little Rodrigo—(Lucrezia's child)—to a daughter of the House of Colonna. On the same day the Sacred College confirmed Cesare in his office of Captain-General and Gonfalonier of the Church, pending the election of a new Pope.

Meanwhile, sick almost to the point of death, and scarce able to stir hand or foot, so weak in body had he been left by the heroic treatment to which he had submitted, Cesare continued mentally a miracle of energy and self-possession. He issued orders for the fortifying of the Vatican, and summoned from Romagna 200 horse and 1,000 foot to his aid in Rome, bidding Remolino, who brought these troops, to quarter himself at Orvieto, and there await his further orders.

Considering that the Colonna were fighting in Naples under the banner of Gonzalo de Cordoba, it was naturally enough supposed, from Cesare's alliance with the former, that this time he was resolved to go over to the side of Spain. Of this, M. de Trans came to protest to Valentinois on behalf of Louis XII, to be answered by the duke's assurances that the alliance into which he had entered was strictly confined to the Colonna, that it entailed no treaty with Spain; nor had he entered into any; that his loyalty to the King of France continued unimpaired, and that he was ready to support King Louis with the entire forces he disposed of, whenever his Majesty should desire him so to do. In reply, he was assured by the French ambassador and Cardinal Sanseverino of the continued protection of Louis, and that France would aid him to maintain his dominions in Italy and reconquer any that might have seceded; and of this declaration copies were sent to Florence, Venice, and Bologna on September 1, as a warning to those Powers not to engage in anything to the hurt of Valentinois.

Thus sped the time of the novendiali—the nine days' obsequies of the dead Pope—which were commenced on September 4.

As during the conclave that was immediately to follow it was against the law for armed men to be in Rome, Cesare was desired by the Sacred

College to withdraw his troops. He did so on September 2, and himself went with them.

Cardinal Sanseverino and the French ambassador escorted him out of Rome and saw him take the road to Nepi—a weak, fever-ravaged, emaciated man, borne in a litter by a dozen of his halberdiers, his youth, his beauty, his matchless strength of body all sapped from him by the insidious disease which had but grudgingly spared his very life.

At Nepi he was awaited by his brother Giuffredo, who had preceded him thither from Rome. A shadowy personage this Giuffredo, whose unimportant personality is tantalizingly elusive in the pages where mention is made of him. His incontinent wife, Doña Sancia, had gone to Naples under the escort of Prospero Colonna, having left the Castle of Sant' Angelo where for some time she had been confined by order of her father-in-law, the Pope, on account of the disorders of her frivolous life.

And now the advices of the fresh treaty between Cesare Borgia and the King of France were producing their effect upon Venice and Florence, who were given additional pause by the fierce jealousy of each other, which was second only to their jealousy of the duke.

From Venice—with or without the sanction of his Government—Bartolomeo d'Alviano had ridden south into the Romagna with his condotta immediately upon receiving news of the death of Alexander, and, finding Pandolfaccio Malatesta at Ravenna, he proceeded to accompany him back to that Rimini which the tyrant had sold to Cesare. Rimini, however, refused to receive him back, and showed fight to the forces under d'Alviano. So that, for the moment, nothing was accomplished. Whereupon the Republic, which at first had raised a feeble, make-believe protest at the action of her condottiero, now deemed it as well to find a pretext for supporting him. So Venice alleged that a courier of hers had been stripped of a letter, and, with such an overwhelming cause as that for hostilities, dispatched reinforcements to d'Alviano to the end that he might restore Pandolfaccio to a dominion in which he was abhorred. Further, d'Alviano was thereafter to proceed to do the like office for Giovanni Sforza, who already had taken ship for Pesaro, and who was restored to his lordship on September 3.

Thence, carrying the war into the Romagna itself, d'Alviano marched upon Cesena. But the Romagna was staunch and loyal to her duke. The governor had shut himself up in Cesena with what troops he could muster, including a thousand veterans under the valiant Dionigio di Naldo, and there, standing firm and resolute, he awaited the onslaught of the Venetians.

D'Alviano advanced rapidly and cruelly, a devastator laying waste the country in his passage, until to check him came suddenly the Borgia troops, which had ventured upon a sally. The Venetians were routed and put to flight.

On September 16 the restored tyrants of Rimini, Pesaro, Castello, Perugia, Camerino, Urbino, and Sinigaglia entered into and signed at Perugia a league, whose chiefs were Bartolomeo d'Alviano and Gianpaolo Baglioni, for their common protection.

Florence was invited to join the allies. Intimidated, however, by France, not only did the Signory refuse to be included, but—in her usual manner—actually went so far as to advise Cesare Borgia of that refusal and to offer him her services and help.

On the same date the Sacred College assembled in Rome, at the Mass of the Holy Spirit, to beseech the grace of inspiration in the election of the new Pontiff. The part usually played by the divine afflatus in these matters was so fully understood and appreciated that the Venetian ambassador received instructions from the Republic(1) to order the Venetian cardinals to vote for Giuliano della Rovere, whilst the King of France sent a letter—in his own hand—to the Sacred College desiring it to elect his friend the Cardinal d'Amboise, and Spain, at the same time, sought to influence the election of Carvajal.

1 See Sanuto's Diarrii.

The chances of the last-named do not appear ever to have amounted to very much. The three best supported candidates were della Rovere, d'Amboise, and Ascanio Sforza—who made his reappearance in Rome, released from his French prison at last, in time to attend this Conclave.

None of these three factions was strong enough to ensure the election of its own candidate, but any two were strong enough to prevent the election of the candidate of the third. Wherefore it happened that, as a result of so much jealousy and competition, recourse was had to temporizing by electing the oldest and feeblest cardinal in the College. Thus there should presently be another election, and meantime the candidates would improve the time by making their arrangements and canvassing their supporters so as to control the votes of the College at that future Conclave. Therefore Francesco Piccolomini, Cardinal of Siena (nephew of Pius II), a feeble octogenarian, tormented by an ulcer, which, in conjunction with an incompetent physician, was to cut his life even shorter than they hoped, was placed upon the throne of St. Peter, and assumed with the Pontificate the name of Pius III.

The new Pope was entirely favourable to Cesare Borgia, and confirmed him in all his offices, signifying his displeasure to Venice at her attempt upon the Romagna, and issuing briefs to the allied tyrants commanding them to desist from their opposition to the will of the Holy See.

Cesare returned to Rome, still weak on his legs and ghastly to behold, and on October 6 he received in St. Peter's his confirmation as Captain-General and Gonfalonier of the Church.

The Venetians had meanwhile been checked by a letter from Louis from lending further assistance to the allies. The latter, however, continued their hostilities in spite of that. They had captured Sinigaglia, and now they made an attempt on Fano and Fermo, but were repulsed in both places by Cesare's loyal subjects. At the same time the Ordelaffi—who in the old days had been deposed from the Tyranny of Forli to make room for the Riarii—deemed the opportunity a good one to attempt to regain their lordship; but their attempt, too, was frustrated.

Cesare sat impotent in Rome, no doubt vexed by his own inaction. He cannot have lacked the will to go to the Romagna to support the subjects who showed him such loyalty; but he lacked the means. Owing to the French and Spanish dispute in Naples, his army had practically melted away. The terms of his treaty with Louis compelled him to send the bulk of it to the camp at Garigliano to support the French, who were in trouble. The force that Remolino had quartered at Orvieto to await the duke's orders he had been unable to retain there. Growing uneasy at their position, and finding it impossible either to advance or to retreat, being threatened on the one side by the Baglioni and on the other by the Orsini, these troops had steadily deserted; whilst most of Cesare's Spanish captains and their followers had gone to the aid of their compatriots under Gonzalo de Cordoba in response to that captain's summons of every Spaniard in the peninsula.

Thus did it come about that Cesare had no force to afford his Romagna subjects. His commissioners in the north did what was possible to repair the damage effected by the allies, and they sent Dionigio di Naldo with six hundred of his foot, and, further, a condotta of two hundred horse, against Rimini. This was captured by them in one day and almost without resistance, Pandolfaccio flying for his life to Pesaro.

Next the allies, by attempting to avenge the rout they had suffered at Cesena, afforded the ducal troops an opportunity of scoring another victory. They prepared a second attack against Cesare's capital, and with an army of considerable strength they advanced to the very walls of the stronghold, laying the aqueduct in ruins and dismantling what other buildings they found in their way. But in Cesena the gallant Pedro Ramires lay in wait for them. Issuing to meet them, he not only put them to flight and drove them for shelter into the fortress of Montebello, but laid siege to them there and broke them utterly, with a loss, as was reputed, of some three hundred men in slain alone.

The news of this came to cheer Valentinois, who, moreover, had now the Pope and France to depend upon. Further, and in view of that same protection, the Orsini were already treating with him for a reconciliation, despite the fact that the Orsini blood was scarce dry upon his hands. But he had a resolute, sly, and desperate enemy in Venice, and on October 10 there arrived in Rome Bartolomeo d'Alviano and Gianpaolo Baglioni, who repaired to the Venetian ambassador and informed him that they were come in quest of the person of Valentinois, intending his death.

To achieve their ends they united themselves to the Orsini, who were now in arms in Rome, their attempted reconciliation with Cesare having ·aborted. Valentinois's peril became imminent, and from the Vatican he withdrew for shelter to the Castle of Sant' Angelo, going by way of the underground passage built by his father.

Thence he summoned Michele da Corella, who was at Rocca Soriana with his foot, and Taddeo della Volpe (a valiant captain and a great fighter, who had already lost an eye in Cesare's service) and Baldassare Scipione, who were in the Neapolitan territory with their men-at-arms. He was gathering his sinews for a spring, when suddenly the entire face of affairs was altered and all plans were checked by the death of Pius III on October 18, after a reign of twenty-six days.

Once more there was an end to Cesare's credit. No man might say what the future held in store. Giustiniani, indeed, wrote to his Government that Cesare was about to withdraw to France, and that he had besought a safe-conduct of the Orsini—which report is as true as many another communication from the same Venetian pen, ever ready to write what it hoped might be true; and it is flatly contradicted by the better-informed Macchiavelli, who was writing at the same time:

"The duke is in Sant' Angelo, and is more hopeful than ever of accomplishing great things, presupposing a Pope according to the wishes of his friends."

But the Romagna was stirred once more to the turbulence from which it had scarcely settled. Forli and Rimini were lost almost at once, the Ordelaffi succeeding in capturing the former in this their second attempt, whilst Pandolfaccio once more sat in his palace at Rimini, having cut his way to it through a sturdy resistance. Against Imola Bentivogli dispatched a force of two thousand foot; but this was beaten off.

The authority of France appeared to have lost its weight, and in vain did Cardinal d'Amboise thunder threats in the name of his friend King Louis, and send envoys to Florence, Venice, Bologna, and Urbino, to complain of the injuries that were being done to the Duke of Valentinois.

CHAPTER III
JULIUS II

Giuliano della Rovere, Cardinal of S. Pietro in Vincoli, had much in his character that was reminiscent of his terrible uncle, Sixtus IV. Like that uncle of his, he had many failings highly unbecoming any Christian—laic or ecclesiastic—which no one has attempted to screen; and, incidentally, he cultivated morality in his private life and observed his priestly vows of chastity as little as did any other churchman of his day. For you may see him, through the eyes of Paride de Grassi,(1) unable one Good Friday to remove his shoes for the adoration of the cross in consequence of his foot's affliction—ex morbo gallico. But with one great and splendid virtue was he endowed in the eyes of the enemies of the House of Borgia—contemporary, and subsequent down to our times—a most profound, unchristian, and mordacious hatred of all Borgias.

1 Burchard's successor in the office of Master of Ceremonies.

Roderigo Borgia had defeated him in the Conclave of 1492, and for twelve years had kept him out of the coveted pontificate. You have seen how he found expression for his furious jealousy at his rival's success. You have seen him endeavouring to his utmost to accomplish the deposition of the Borgia Pope, wielding to that end the lever of simony and seeking a fulcrum for it, first in the King of France and later in Ferdinand and Isabella; but failing hopelessly in both instances. You have seen him, when he realized the failure of an attempt which had made Rome too dangerous for him and compelled him to remain in exile, suddenly veering round to fawn and flatter and win the friendship of one whom his enmity could not touch.

This man who, as Julius II, was presently to succeed Pius III, has been accounted a shining light of virtue amid the dark turpitude of the Church in the Renaissance. An ignis fatuus, perhaps; a Jack-o'-lanthorn begotten of putrescence. Surely no more than that.

Dr. Jacob Burckhardt, in that able work of his to which reference already has been made, follows the well-worn path of unrestrained invective against the Borgias, giving to the usual empty assertions the place which should be assigned to evidence and argument. Like his predecessors along that path, he causes Giuliano della Rovere to shine heroically by contrast—a foil to throw into greater relief the blackness of Alexander. But he carries assertion rather further than do others when he says of Cardinal della Rovere that "He ascended the steps of St. Peter's Chair without simony and amid general applause, and with him ceased, at all events, the undisguised traffic in the highest offices of the Church."

Other writers in plenty have suggested this, but none has quite so plainly and resoundingly thrown down the gauntlet, which we will make bold to lift.

That Dr. Burckhardt wrote in other than good faith is not to be imputed. It must therefore follow that an entry in the Diarium of the Caerimoniarius under date of October 29, 1503, escaped him utterly in the course of his researches. For the Diarium informs us that on that day, in the Apostolic Palace, Giuliano della Rovere, Cardinal of S. Pietro in Vincoli, concluded the terms of an agreement with the Duke of Valentinois and the latter's following of Spanish cardinals, by which he undertook that, in consideration of his receiving the votes of these Spanish cardinals and being elected Pope, he would confirm Cesare in his office of Gonfalonier and Captain-General, and would preserve him in the dominion of the Romagna. And, in consideration of that undertaking, the Spanish cardinals, on their side, promised to give him their suffrages.

Here are the precise words in which Burchard records the transaction:

"Eadem die, 29 Octobris, Rmus. D. S. Petri ad Vincula venit in palatio apostolico cum duce Valentino et cardinalibus suis Hispanis et concluserunt capitula eorum per que, inter alia, cardinalis S. Petri ad Vincula, postquam esset papa, crearet confalonierium Ecclesiae generalem ducem ac ei faveret et in statibus suis (relinqueret) et vice versa dux pape; et promiserunt omnes cardinalis Hispani dare votum pro Cardinali S. Petri ad Vincula ad papatum."

If that does not entail simony and sacrilege, then such things do not exist at all. More, you shall hunt in vain for any accusation so authoritative, formal and complete, regarding the simony practised by Alexander VI on his election. And this same Julius, moreover, was the Pope who later was to launch his famous Bull de Simoniaca Electione, to add another stain to the besmirched escutcheon of the Borgia Pontiff.

His conciliation of Cesare and his obtaining, thus, the support of the Spanish cardinals, who, being Alexander's creatures, were now Cesare's very faithful servants, ensured the election of della Rovere; for, whilst those cardinals' votes did not suffice to place him in St. Peter's Chair, they would abundantly have sufficed to have kept him out of it had Cesare so desired them.

In coming to terms with Cardinal della Rovere, Cesare made the first great mistake of his career, took the first step towards ruin. He should have known better than to have trusted such a man. He should have remembered the ancient bitter rancour; should have recognized, in the amity of later times, the amity of the self-seeker, and mistrusted it. But della Rovere had acquired a reputation for honesty and for being a man of his word. How far he deserved it you may judge from what is presently to follow. He had acquired it, however, and Cesare, to his undoing, attached faith to that reputation. He may, to some extent, have counted upon the fact that, of Cardinal della Rovere's bastard children, only a daughter—Felice della Rovere—survived. Raffaele, the last of his bastard boys, had died a year ago. Thus, Cesare may have concluded that the cardinal having no sons whose fortunes he must advance, would lack temptation to break faith with him.

From all this it resulted that, at the Conclave of November 1, Giuliano della Rovere was elected Pope, and took the name of Julius II; whilst Valentinois, confident now that his future was assured, left the Castle of Sant' Angelo to take up his residence at the Vatican, in the Belvedere, with forty gentlemen constituting his suite.

On November 3 Julius II issued briefs to the Romagna, ordering obedience to Cesare, with whom he was now in daily and friendliest intercourse.

In the Romagna, meanwhile, the disturbances had not only continued, but they had taken a fresh turn. Venice, having reseated Malatesta on the throne, now vented at last the covetousness she had ever, herself, manifested of that dominion, and sent a force to drive him out again and conquer Rimini for the Republic.

Florence, in a spasm of jealous anger at this, inquired was the Pope to become the chaplain of Venice, and dispatched Macchiavelli to bear the tale of these doings to Julius.

Under so much perpetual strife the strength of the Romagna was gradually crumbling, and Cesare, angry with Florence for never going beyond lip-service, expressed that anger to Macchiavelli, informing the ambassador that the Signory could have saved the Romagna for him with a hundred men-at-arms.

The duke sent for Giustiniani, the ambassador of Venice, who, however, excused himself and did not go. This within a week of the new Pope's election, showing already how men discerned what was in store for Valentinois. Giustiniani wrote to his Government that he had not gone lest his going should give the duke importance in the eyes of others.(1) The pettiness and meanness of the man, revealed in that dispatch, will enable you to attach to Giustiniani the label that belongs to him.

1 "Per non dar materia ad altri che fazino un po di lui mazor estimazion di quel che fanno quando lo vedessero in parte alcuna favorito." — Giustiniani, Dispatch of November 6, 1503.

To cheer Valentinois in those days of depression came news that his subjects of Imola had successfully resisted an attack on the part of the Venetians. So stimulated was he that he prepared at once to go, himself, into the Romagna, and obtained from the Pope, from d'Amboise, and from Soderini, letters to Florence desiring the Signory to afford him safe-conduct through Tuscany for himself and his army.

The Pope expressed himself, in his letter, that he would count such safe-conduct as a great favour to himself, and urged the granting of it out of his "love for Cesare," owing to the latter's "great virtues and shining merits."(2) Yet on the morrow of dispatching that brief, this man, who was accounted honest, straightforward, and imbued with a love of truth, informed Giustiniani—or else Giustiniani lied in his dispatches—that he understood that the Venetians were assailing the Romagna, not out of enmity to the Church, but to punish the demerits of Cesare, and he made it plain to Giustiniani that, if he complained of the conduct of the Venetians, it was on his own behalf and not on Cesare's, as his aim was to preserve the Romagna, not for the duke, but for the Church.

2 "In quo nobis rem gratissimam facietis ducis enim ipsum propter ejus insignes virtutes et praeclara merita praecipuo affectur et caritate praecipua complectimur." — Archivio di Stato, Firenze. (See Alvisi, Doct. 96.)

With the aim we have no quarrel. It was laudable enough in a Pontiff. But it foreshadows Cesare's ruin, in spite of the love-protesting letter to Florence, in spite of the bargain struck by virtue of which Julius had obtained the pontificate. Whether the Pope went further in his treachery, whether, having dispatched that brief to Florence, he sent other communications to the Signory, is not ascertainable; but the suspicion of some such secret action is inspired by what ensued.

On November 13 Cesare was ready to leave Rome; but no safe-conduct had arrived. Out of all patience at this, he begged the Pope that the captain of the pontifical navy should prepare him five galleons at Ostia, by which he could take his foot to Genoa, and thence proceed into Romagna by way of Ferrara.

Macchiavelli, at the same time, was frenziedly importuning Florence to grant the duke the desired safe-conduct lest in despair Cesare should make a treaty with Venice—"or with the devil"—and should go to Pisa, employing all his money, strength, and influence to vent his wrath upon the Signory. But the Signory knew more, perhaps, than did Macchiavelli, for no attention was paid to his urgent advice.

On the 19th Cesare left Rome to set out for Genoa by way of Ostia, and his departure threw Giustiniani into alarm—fearing that the duke would now escape.

But there was no occasion for his fears. On the very day of Cesare's departure Julius sent fresh briefs to the Romagna, different indeed from those of November 3. In these he now expressed his disapproval of Alexander's having conferred the vicarship of the Romagna upon Cesare Borgia, and he exhorted all to range themselves under the banner of the Church, under whose protection he intended to keep them.

Events followed quickly upon that. Two days later news reached the Pope that the Venetians had captured Faenza, whereupon he sent a messenger after Valentinois to suggest to the latter that he should surrender Forli and the other fiefs into pontifical hands. With this Cesare refused to comply, and, as a result, he was detained by the captain of the navy, in obedience to the instructions from Julius. At the same time the Pope broke the last link of the treaty with Cesare by appointing a new Governor of Romagna in the person of Giovanni Sacchi, Bishop of Ragusa. He commanded the latter to take possession of the Romagna in the name of the Church, and he issued another brief—the third within three weeks—demanding the State's obedience to the new governor.

On November 26, Remolino, who had been at Ostia with Cesar; came to Rome, and, throwing himself at the feet of the Pontiff, begged for mercy for his lord, whom he now accounted lost. He promised Julius that Cesare should give him the countersigns of the strongholds, together with security for their surrender. This being all that the Pope could desire, he issued orders that Cesare be brought back to Rome, and in Consistory advised the Sacred College—by way, no doubt, of exculpating himself to men who knew that he was refusing to pay the price at which he had bought the Papacy—that the Venetians in the Romagna were not moving against the Church, but against Cesare himself—wherefore he had demanded of Cesare the surrender of the towns he held, that thus there might be an end to the war.

It was specious—which is the best that can be said for it.

As for putting an end to the war, the papal brief was far indeed from achieving any such thing, as was instantly plain from the reception it met with in the Romagna, which persisted in its loyalty to Cesare in despite of the very Pope himself. When that brief was read in Cesena a wild tumult ensued, and the people ran through the streets clamouring angrily for their duke.

It was very plain what short work would have been made of such men as the Ordelaffi and the Malatesta had Cesare gone north. But Cesare was fast at the Vatican, treated by the Pope with all outward friendliness and consideration, but virtually a prisoner none the less. Julius continued to press for the surrender of the Romagna strongholds, which Remolino had promised in his master's name; but Cesare persisted obstinately to refuse, until the news reached him that Michele da Corella and della Volpe, who had gone north with seven hundred horse to support his Romagnuoli, had been cut to pieces in Tuscany by the army of Gianpaolo Baglioni.

Cesare bore his burning grievance to the Pope. The Pope sympathized with him most deeply; then went to write a letter to the Florentines to thank them for what had befallen and to beg them to send him Michele da Corella under a strong escort—that redoubtable captain having been taken prisoner together with della Volpe.

Corella was known to be fully in the duke's confidence, and there were rumours that he was accused of many things perpetrated on the duke's behalf. Julius, bent now on Cesare's ruin, desired to possess himself of this man in the hope of being able to put him upon his trial under charges which should reflect discredit upon Cesare.

At last the duke realized that he was betrayed, and that all was lost, and so he submitted to the inevitable, and gave the Pope the countersigns he craved. With these Julius at once dispatched an envoy into the Romagna, and, knowing the temper of Cesare's captains, he insisted that this envoy should be accompanied by Piero d'Orvieto, as Cesare's own commissioner, to demand that surrender.

But the intrepid Pedro Ramires, who held Cesena, knowing the true facts of the case, and conceiving how his duke had been constrained, instead of making ready to yield, proceeded further to fortify for resistance. When the commissioners appeared before his gates he ordered the admission of Piero d'Orvieto. That done, he declared that he desired to see his duke at liberty before he would surrender the citadel which he held for him, and, taking d'Orvieto, he hanged him from the battlements as a traitor and a bad servant who did a thing which the duke, had he been at liberty, would never have had him do.

Moncalieri, the papal envoy, returned to Rome with the news, and this so inflamed the Pope that the Cardinals Lodovico Borgia and Francesco Remolino, together with other Borgia partisans, instantly fled from Rome, where they no longer accounted themselves safe, and sought refuge with Gonzalo de Cordoba in the Spanish camp at Naples, imploring his protection at the same time for Cesare.

The Pope's anger first vented itself in the confiscation of the Duke of Valentinois's property wherever possible, to satisfy the claims of the Riarii (the Pope's nephews) who demanded an indemnity of 50,000 ducats, of Guidobaldo, who demanded 200,000 ducats, and of the Florentine Republic, which claimed the same. The duke's ruin was by now—within six weeks of the election of Julius II—an accomplished fact; and many were those who chose to fall with him rather than abandon him in his extremity. They afford a spectacle of honour and loyalty that was exceedingly rare in the Italy of the Renaissance; clinging to their duke, even when the last ray of hope was quenched, they lightened for him the tedium of those last days at the Vatican during which he was no better than a prisoner of state.

Suddenly came news of Gonzalo de Cordoba's splendid victory at Garigliano—a victory which definitely broke the French and gave the throne of Naples to Spain. Naturally this set Spanish influence once more, and mightily, in the ascendant, and the Spanish cardinals, together with the ambassador of Spain, came to exert with the Pope an influence suddenly grown weighty.

As a consequence, Cesare, escorted by Carvajal, Cardinal of Santa Croce, was permitted to depart to Ostia, whence he was to take ship for France. Leastways, such was the understanding upon which he left the Vatican. But the Pope was not minded, even now, to part with him so easily, and his instructions to Carvajal were that at Ostia he should await further orders before sailing.

But on December 26, news reaching the Spanish cardinal that the Romagna fortresses—persuaded that Cesare had been liberated—had finally surrendered, Carvajal took it upon himself to allow Cesare to depart, upon receiving from him a written undertaking never to bear arms against Pope Julius II.

So the Duke of Valentinois at last regained his freedom. Whether, in repairing straight to Naples, as he did, he put a preconceived plan into execution, or whether, even now, he mistrusted his enlargement, and thought thus to make himself secure, cannot be ascertained. But straight to

Gonzalo de Cordoba's Spanish camp he went, equipped with a safe-conduct from the Great Captain, obtained for Cesare by Cardinal Remolino.

There he found a court of friends already awaiting him, among whom were his brother Giuffredo and the Cardinal Lodovico Borgia, and he received from Gonzalo a very cordial welcome.

Spain was considering the invasion of Tuscany with the ultimate object of assailing Milan and driving the French out of the peninsula altogether. Piero de'Medici—killed at Garigliano—had no doubt been serving Spain with some such end in view as the conquest of Florence, and, though Piero was dead, there was no reason why the plan should be abandoned; rather, all the more reason to carry it forward, since now Spain would more directly profit by it. Bartolomeo d'Alviano was to have commanded the army destined for that campaign; but Cesare, by virtue of his friends and influence in Pisa, Siena, and Piombino, was so preferable a captain for such an expedition that Gonzalo gave him charge of it within a few days of his arrival at the Spanish camp.

To Cesare this would have been the thin end of a mighty edge. Here was a chance to begin all over again, and, beginning thus, backed by Spanish arms, there was no saying how far he might have gone. Meanwhile, what a beginning! To avenge himself thus upon that Florentine Republic which, under the protection of France, had dared at every turn to flout him and had been the instrument of his ultimate ruin! Sweet to him would have been the poetic justice he would have administered—as sweet to him as it would have been terrible to Florence, upon which he would have descended like another scourge of God.

Briskly and with high-running hopes he set about his preparations during that spring of 1504 what time the Pope's Holiness in Rome was seeking to justify his treachery by heaping odium upon the Borgias. Thus he thought to show that if he had broken faith, he had broken faith with knaves deserving none. It was in pursuit of this that Michele da Corella was now pressed with questions, which, however, yielded nothing, and that Asquino de Colloredo (the sometime servant of Cardinal Michaeli) was tortured into confessing that he had poisoned his master at the instigation of Alexander and Cesare—as has been seen—which confession Pope Julius was very quick to publish.

But in Naples, it may well be that Cesare cared nought for these matters, busy and hopeful as he was just then. He dispatched Baldassare da Scipione to Rome to enlist what lances he could find, and Scipione put it about that his lord would soon be returning to his own and giving his enemies something to think about.

And then, suddenly, out of clearest heavens, fell a thunderbolt to shiver this last hope.

On the night of May 26, as Cesare was leaving Gonzalo's quarters, where he had supped, an officer stepped forward to demand his sword. He was under arrest.

Julius II had out-manoeuvred him. He had written to Spain setting forth what was his agreement with Valentinois in the matter of the Romagna—the original agreement which was the price of the Pontificate, had, of course, been conveniently effaced from the pontifical memory. He addressed passionate complaints to Ferdinand and Isabella that Gonzalo de Cordoba and Cardinal Carvajal between them were affording Valentinois the means to break that agreement, and to undertake matters that were hostile to the Holy See. And Ferdinand and Isabella had put it upon Gonzalo de Cordoba, that most honourable and gallant captain, to do this thing in gross violation of his safe-conduct and plighted word to Valentinois. It was a deed under the shame of which the Great Captain confessedly laboured to the end of his days, as his memory has laboured under it ever since. For great captains are not afforded the immunity enjoyed by priests and popes jointly with other wearers of the petticoat from the consequences of falsehood and violated trust.

Fierce and bitter were Valentinois's reproaches of the Great Captain for this treachery—as fierce and bitter as they were unavailing. On August 20, 1504, Cesare Borgia took ship for Spain—a prisoner bound for a Spanish dungeon. Thus, at the early age of twenty-nine, he passed from Italy and the deeds that well might have filled a lifetime.

Conspicuous amid those he left behind him who remained loyal to their duke was Baldassare Scipione, who published throughout Christendom a cartel, wherein he challenged to trial by combat any Spaniard who dared deny that the Duke of Valentinois had been detained a prisoner in Naples in spite of the safe-conduct granted him in the name of Ferdinand and Isabella, "with great shame and infamy to their crown."(1)

1 *Quoted by Alvisi, on the authority of a letter of Luigi da Porto, March 16, 1510, in Lettere Storiche.*

This challenge was never taken up.

Amongst other loyal ones was that fine soldier of fortune, Taddeo della Volpe, who, in his Florentine prison, refused all offers to enter the service of the Signory until he had learnt that his lord was gone from Italy.

Fracassa and Mirafuente had held Forli until they received guarantees for Cesare's safety (after he had left Ostia to repair to the Spanish camp).

They then rode out, with the honours of war, lance on thigh. Dionigio di Naldo, that hardy captain of foot, entered the service of Venice; but to the end he wore the device of his dear lord, and imposed the same upon all who served under his banner.

Don Michele da Corella was liberated by Julius II after an interrogatory which can have revealed nothing defamatory to Cesare or his father; as it is unthinkable that a Pope who did all that man could do to ruin the House of Borgia and to befoul its memory, should have preserved silence touching any such revelations as were hoped for when Corella was put to torture. That most faithful of all Cesare's officers—and sharer of the odium that has been heaped upon Cesare's name—entered the service of the Signory of Florence.

CHAPTER IV
ATROPOS

Vain were the exertions put forth by the Spanish cardinals to obtain Cesare's enlargement, and vainer still the efforts of his sister Lucrezia, who wrote letter after letter to Francesco Gonzaga of Mantua—now Gonfalonier of the Church, and a man of influence at the Vatican—imploring him to use his interest with the Pope to the same end.

Julius II remained unmoved, fearing the power of Cesare Borgia, and resolved that he should trouble Italy no more. On the score of that, no blame attaches to the Pope. The States which Borgia had conquered in the name of the Church should remain adherent to the Church. Upon that Julius was resolved, and the resolve was highly laudable. He would have no duke who controlled such a following as did Cesare, using those States as stepping-stones to greater dominions in which, no doubt, he would later have absorbed them, alienating them, so, from the Holy See.

In all this Julius II was most fully justified. The odious matter in his conduct, however, is the abominable treachery it entailed, following as it did upon the undertaking by virtue of which he gained the tiara.

For some months after his arrival in Spain, Cesare was confined in the prison of Chinchilla, whence—as a result, it is said, of an attempt on his part to throw the governor bodily over the battlements—he was removed to the fortress of Medina del Campo, and kept well guarded by orders of the Pope.

Rumours that he had been liberated by the King of Spain overran the Romagna more than once, and set the country in a ferment, even reaching the Vatican and shaking the stout-hearted Julius into alarm.

One chance of regaining his ancient might, and wreaking a sweet and terrific vengeance upon his betrayers came very close to him, but passed him by. This chance occurred in 1505, when—Queen Isabella being dead—King Ferdinand discovered that Gonzalo de Cordoba was playing him false in Naples. The Spanish king conceived a plan—according to the chronicles of Zurita—to employ Cesare as a flail for the punishment of the Great Captain. He proposed to liberate the duke, set him at the head of an army, and loose him upon Naples, trusting to the formidable alliance of Cesare's military talents with his hatred of Gonzalo—who had betrayed him—to work the will of his Catholic Majesty.

Unfortunately for Cesare, there were difficulties. Ferdinand's power was no longer absolute in Castille now that Isabella was dead. He sought to overcome these difficulties; but the process was a slow one, and in the course of it, spurred also by increased proofs of his lieutenant's perfidy, Ferdinand lost patience, and determined—the case having grown urgent—to go to Naples in person to deal with Gonzalo.

Plainly, Cesare's good fortune, which once had been proverbial, had now utterly deserted him.

He had received news of what was afoot, and his hopes had run high once more, only to suffer cruel frustration when he learnt that Ferdinand had sailed, himself, for Naples. In his despair the duke roused himself to a last effort to win his freedom.

His treatment in prison was fairly liberal, such as is usually measured out to state prisoners of consideration. He was allowed his own chaplain and several attendants, and, whilst closely guarded and confined to the Homenaje Tower of the fortress, yet he was not oppressively restrained. He was accorded certain privileges and liberties; he enjoyed the faculty of corresponding with the outer world, and even of receiving visits. Amongst his visitors was the Count of Benavente—a powerful lord of the neighbourhood, who, coming under the spell of Cesare's fascination, became so attached to him, and so resolved to do his will and effect his liberation, that—says Zurita—he was prepared even to go the length of accomplishing it by force of arms should no other way present itself.(1)

1 Sanuto confirms Zurita, in the main, by letters received by the Venetian Senate.

Another way, however, did present itself, and Benavente and the duke hatched a plot of evasion in which they had the collaboration of the chaplain and a servant of the governor's, named Garcia.

One September night a cord was let down from the crenels of the tower, and by this the duke was to descend from his window to the castle ditch, where Benavente's men awaited him. Garcia was to go with him since, naturally, it would not be safe for the servants to remain behind, and Garcia now let himself down that rope, hand over hand, from the terrible height of the duke's window. It was only when he had reached the end of it that he discovered that the rope was not long enough, and that below him there was still a chasm that might well have appalled even desperate men.

To return was impossible. The duke above was growing impatient. Garcia loosed his hold, and dropped the remainder of the distance, breaking both his legs in the fall. Groaning, he lay there in the ditch, whilst hand over hand now came the agile, athletic duke, unconscious of his predecessor's fate, and of what awaited him at the end. He reached it, and was dangling there, perhaps undecided whether or not to take that daring leap, when suddenly his doubts were resolved for him. His evasion was already discovered. The castle was in alarm, and some one above him cut the rope and precipitated him into the ditch.

Benavente's men—we do not know how many of them were at hand— ran to him instantly. They found him seriously injured, and that he, too, had broken bones is beyond doubt. They lifted him up, and bore him with all speed to the horses. They contrived, somehow, to mount him upon one, and, holding him in the saddle, they rode off as fast as was possible under the circumstances. There was no time to go back for the unfortunate Garcia. The castle was all astir by now to stop the fugitives, and to have returned would have been to suffer capture themselves as well as the duke, without availing the servant.

So poor Garcia was left to his fate. He was found by the governor where he had fallen, and he was immediately put to death.

If the people of Medina organized a pursuit it availed them nothing, for Cesare was carried safely to Benavente's stronghold at Villalon.

There he lay for some five or six weeks to recover from the hurts he had taken in escaping, and to allow his hands—the bones of which were broken—to become whole again. At last, being in the main recovered, though with hands still bandaged, he set out with two attendants and made for Santander. Thence they took ship to Castro Urdiales, Cesare aiming now at reaching the kingdom of Navarre and the protection of his brother-in-law the king.

At the inn at Santander, where, weary and famished, they sat down to dine after one of the grooms had made arrangements for a boat, they had a near escape of capture. The alcalde, hearing of the presence of these strangers, and his suspicions being aroused by the recklessly high price they had agreed to pay the owner of the vessel which they had engaged, came to examine them. But they had a tale ready that they were wheat-merchants in great haste to reach Bernico, that a cargo of wheat awaited them there, and that they would suffer great loss by delay. The tale was smooth enough to satisfy the alcalde, and they were allowed to depart. They reached Castro Urdiales safely, but were delayed there for two days, owing to the total lack of horses; and they were forced, in the end, to proceed upon mules obtained from a neighbouring convent. On these they rode to Durango, where they procured two fresh mules and a horse, and so, after further similar vicissitudes, they arrived at Pampeluna on December 3, 1506, and Cesare startled the Court of his brother-in-law, King Jean of Navarre, by suddenly appearing in it—"like the devil."

The news of his evasion had already spread to Italy and set it in a ferment, inspiring actual fear at the Vatican. The Romagna was encouraged by it to break out into open and armed insurrection against the harsh rule of Julius II—who seems to have been rendered positively vindictive towards the Romagnuoli by their fidelity to Valentinois. Thus had the Romagna fallen again into the old state of insufferable oppression from which Cesare had once delivered it. The hopes of the Romagnuoli rose in a measure, as the alarm spread among the enemies of Cesare—for Florence and Venice shared now the anxiety of the Vatican. Zurita, commenting upon this state of things, pays Cesare the following compliment, which the facts confirm as just:

"The duke was such that his very presence was enough to set all Italy agog; and he was greatly beloved, not only by men of war, but also by many people of Tuscany and of the States of the Church."

Cesare's wife—Charlotte d'Albret—whom he had not seen since that September of 1499, was at Bourges at the Court of her friend, the saintly, repudiated first wife of Louis XII. It is to be supposed that she would be advised of her husband's presence at her brother's Court; but there is no information on this score, nor do we know that they ever met.

Within four days of reaching Pampeluna Cesare dispatched his secretary Federico into Italy to bear the news of his escape to his sister Lucrezia at Ferrara, and a letter to Francesco Gonzaga, of Mantua, which was little more than one of introduction, the more important matters to be conveyed to Gonzaga going, no doubt, by word of mouth. Federico was arrested at Bologna by order of Julius II, after he had discharged his mission.

France was now Cesare's only hope, and he wrote to Louis begging his royal leave to come to take his rank as a prince of that country, and to serve her.

You may justly have opined, long since, that the story here set down is one never-ending record of treacheries and betrayals. But you will find little to surpass the one to come. The behaviour of Louis at this juncture is contemptible beyond words, obeying as it does the maxim of that age, which had it that no inconvenient engagement should be observed if there was opportunity for breaking it.

Following this detestable maxim, Louis XII had actually gone the length of never paying to Charlotte d'Albret the dot of 100,000 livres Tournois, to which he had engaged himself by written contract. When Cesare, in prison at Medina and in straits for money, had solicited payment through his brother-in-law of Navarre, his claim had been contemptuously disregarded.

But there was worse to follow. Louis now answered Cesare's request for leave to come to France by a letter (quoted in full by M. Yriarte from the Archives des Basses Pyrénées) in which his Very Christian Majesty announces that the duchy of Valentinois and the County of Dyois have been restored to the crown of France, as also the lordship of Issoudun. And then follows the pretext, of whose basely paltry quality you shall judge for yourselves. It runs:

"After the decease of the late Pope Alexander, when our people and our army were seeking the recovery of the kingdom of Naples, he [Cesare] went over to the side of our enemies, serving, favouring, and assisting them at arms and otherwise against ourselves and our said people and army, which resulted to us in great and irrecoverable loss."

The climax is in the deliberate falsehood contained in the closing words. Poor Cesare, who had served France at her call—in spite of what was rumoured of his intentions—as long as he had a man-at-arms to follow him, had gone to Naples only in the hour of his extreme need. True, he had gone to offer himself to Spain as a condottiero when naught else was left to him; but he took no army with him—he went alone, a servant, not an ally, as that false letter pretends. He had never come to draw his sword against France, and certainly no loss had been suffered by France in consequence of any action of his. Louis's army was definitely routed at Garigliano, with Cesare's troops fighting in its ranks.

But Pope Alexander was dead; Cesare's might in in Italy was dissipated; his credit gone. There lay no profit for Louis in keeping faith with him; there lay some profit in breaking it. Alas, that a king should stain his honour with base and vulgar lies to minister to his cupidity, and that he should set them down above his seal and signature to shame him through centuries still in the womb of Time!

Cesare Borgia, landless, without right to any title, he that had held so many, betrayed and abandoned on every side, had now nothing to offer in the world's market but his stout sword and his glad courage. These went to the first bidder for them, who happened to be his brother-in-law King Jean.

Navarre at the time was being snarled and quarrelled over by France and Spain, both menacing its independence, each pretending to claims upon it which do not, in themselves, concern us.

In addition, the country itself was torn by two factions—the Beaumontes and the Agramontes—and it was entrusted to Cesare to restore Navarre to peace and unity at home before proceeding—with the aid upon which he depended from the Emperor Maximilian—to deal with the enemies beyond her frontiers.

The Castle of Viana was being held by Louis de Beaumont—chief of the faction that bore his name—and refused to surrender to the king. To reduce it and compel Beaumont to obedience went Cesare as Captain-General of Navarre, early in February of 1507. He commanded a considerable force, some 10,000 strong, and with this and his cannon he laid siege to the citadel.

The natural strength of the place was such as might have defied any attempt to reduce it by force; but victuals were running low, and there was every likelihood of its being speedily starved into surrender. To frustrate this, Beaumont conceived the daring plan of attempting to send in supplies from Mendavia. The attempt being made secretly, by night and under a strong escort, was entirely successful; but, in retreating, the Beaumontese were surprised in the dawn of that February morning by a troop of reinforcements coming to Cesare's camp. These, at sight of the rebels, immediately gave the alarm.

The most hopeless confusion ensued in the town, where it was at once imagined that a surprise attack was being made upon the Royalists, and that they had to do with the entire rebel army.

Cesare, being aroused by the din and the blare of trumpets calling men to arms, sprang for his weapons, armed himself in haste, flung himself on a horse, and, without pausing so much as to issue a command to his waiting men-at-arms, rode headlong down the street to the Puerta del Sol. Under the archway of the gate his horse stumbled and came down with him. With an oath, Cesare wrenched the animal to its feet again, gave it the spur, and was away at a mad, furious gallop in pursuit of the retreating Beaumont rearguard.

The citizens, crowding to the walls of Viana, watched that last reckless ride of his with amazed, uncomprehending eyes. The peeping sun caught his glittering armour as he sped, so that of a sudden he must have seemed to them a thing of fire—meteoric, as had been his whole life's trajectory which was now swiftly dipping to its nadir.

Whether he was frenzied with the lust of battle, riding in the reckless manner that was his wont, confident that his men followed, yet too self-centred to ascertain, or whether—as seems more likely—it was simply that his horse had bolted with him, will never be known until all things are known.

Suddenly he was upon the rearguard of the fleeing rebels. His sword flashed up and down; again and again they may have caught the gleam of it from Viana's walls, as he smote the foe. Irresistible as a thunderbolt, he clove himself a way through those Beaumontese. He was alone once more, a flying, dazzling figure of light, away beyond that rearguard which he left scathed and disordered by his furious passage. Still his mad career continued, and he bore down upon the main body of the escort.

Beaumont sat his horse to watch, in such amazement as you may conceive, the wild approach of this unknown rider.

Seeing him unsupported, some of the count's men detached themselves to return and meet this single foe and oblige him with the death he so obviously appeared to seek.

They hedged him about—we do not know their number—and, engaging him, they drew him from the road and down into the hollow space of a ravine.

And so, in the thirty-second year of his age, and in all the glory of his matchless strength, his soul possessed of the lust of combat, sword in hand, warding off the attack that rains upon him, and dealing death about him, he meets his end. From the walls of Viana his resplendent armour renders him still discernible, until, like a sun to its setting, he passes below the rim of that ravine, and is lost to the watcher's view.

Death awaited him amid the shadows of that hollow place.

Unhorsed by now, he fought with no concern for the odds against him, and did sore execution upon his assailants, ere a sword could find an opening in his guard to combine with a gap in his armour and so drive home. That blade had found, maybe, his lungs. Still he swung his sword, swaying now upon his loosening knees. His mouth was full of blood. It was growing dark. His hands began to fail him. He reeled like a drunkard, sapped of strength, and then the end came quickly. Blows unwarded showered upon him now.

He crashed down in all the glory of his rich armour, which those brigand-soldiers already coveted. And thus he died—mercifully, maybe happily, for he had no time in which to taste the bitterness of death—that awful draught which he had forced upon so many.

Within a few moments of his falling, this man who had been a living force, whose word had carried law from the Campagna to the Bolognese, was so much naked, blood-smeared carrion—for those human vultures stripped him to the skin; his very shirt must they have. And there, a stark, livid corpse, of no more account than any dog that died last Saturday, they left Cesare Borgia of France, Duke of Romagna and Valentinois, Prince of Andria, and Lord of a dozen Tyrannies.

The body was found there anon by those who so tardily rode after their leader, and his dismayed troopers bore those poor remains to Viana. The king, arriving there that very day, horror-stricken at the news and sight that awaited him, ordered Cesare a magnificent funeral, and so he was laid to rest before the High Altar of Sainte Marie de Viane.

To rest? May the soul of him rest at least, for men—Christian men—have refused to vouchsafe that privilege to his poor ashes.

Nearly two hundred years later—at the close of the seventeenth century, a priest of God and a bishop, one who preached a gospel of love and mercy so infinite that he dared believe by its lights no man to have been damned, came to disturb the dust of Cesare Borgia. This Bishop of Calahorra—lineal descendant in soul of that Pharisee who exalted himself in God's House, thrilled with titillations of delicious horror at the desecrating presence of the base publican—had his pietist's eyes offended by the slab that marked Cesare Borgia's resting-place.(1)

1 It bore the following legend:

AQUI YACE EN POCA TIERRA

AL QUE TODO LE TEMIA

EL QUE LA PAZ Y LA GUERRA

EN LA SUA MANO TENIA.

OH TU QUE VAS A BUSCAR

COSAS DIGNAS DE LOAR

SI TU LOAS LO MAS DIGNO

AQUI PARE TU CAMINO

NO CURES DE MAS ANDAR.

which, more or less literally may be Englished as follows: "Here in a little earth, lies one whom all did fear; one whose hands dispensed both peace and war. Oh, you that go in search of things deserving praise, if you would praise the worthiest, then let your journey end here, nor trouble to go farther."

The pious, Christian bishop had read of this man—perhaps that life of him published by the apostate Gregorio Leti under the pen-name of

Tommaso Tommasi, which had lately seen the light—and he ordered the tomb's removal from that holy place. And thus it befell that the ashes of Cesare Borgia were scattered and lost.

Charlotte d'Albret was bereft of her one friend, Queen Jeanne, in that same year of Cesare's death. The Duchess of Valentinois withdrew to La MotteFeuilly, and for the seven years remaining of her life was never seen other than in mourning; her very house was equipped with sombre, funereal furniture, and so maintained until her end, which supports the view that she had conceived affection and respect for the husband of whom she had seen so little.

On March 14, 1514, that poor lady passed from a life which appears to have offered her few joys.

Louise de Valentinois—a handsome damsel of the age of fourteen—remained for three years under the tutelage of the Duchess of Angoulême—the mother of King Francis I—to whom Charlotte d'Albret had entrusted her child. Louise married, at the age of seventeen, Louis de la Trémouille, Prince de Talmont and Vicomte de Thouars, known as the Knight Sans Peur et Sans Reproche. She maintained some correspondence with her aunt, Lucrezia Borgia, whom she had never seen, and ever signed herself "Louise de Valentinois." At the age of thirty—Trémouille having been killed at Pavia—she married, in second nuptials, Philippe de Bourbon-Busset.

Lucrezia died in 1519, one year after her mother, Vanozza de'Catanei, with whom she corresponded to the end.

REQUIESCANT!